Talent Development in School

Talent Development in School

An Educator's Guide to Implementing a Culturally Responsive Talent Identification and Development Program

EDITED BY
JULIE DINGLE SWANSON, ED.D.,
AND META VAN SICKLE, PH.D.

PRUFROCK PRESS INC.
WACO, TEXAS

Library of Congress Cataloging-in-Publication Data

Names: Dingle Swanson, Julie, 1954- editor. | Van Sickle, Meta L., 1956- editor.
Title: Talent development in school : an educator's guide to implementing a culturally responsive talent identification and development program / Edited by Julie Dingle Swanson, Ed.D., and Meta Van Sickle, Ph.D.
Description: Waco, TX : Prufrock Press Inc., [2021] | Includes bibliographical references. | Summary: ""Talent Development in School" helps educators utilize research-based curriculum and strategies to implement talent development in the classroom"-- Provided by publisher.
Identifiers: LCCN 2021001319 (print) | LCCN 2021001320 (ebook) | ISBN 9781646321223 (paperback) | ISBN 9781646321230 (ebook) | ISBN 9781646321247 (epub)
Subjects: LCSH: Gifted children--Education. | Curriculum planning. | Culturally relevant pedagogy. | Teachers of gifted children. | Educational equalization.
Classification: LCC LC3993 .T35 2021 (print) | LCC LC3993 (ebook) | DDC 371.95--dc23
LC record available at https://lccn.loc.gov/2021001319
LC ebook record available at https://lccn.loc.gov/2021001320

Edited by Katy McDowall

Cover design by Allegra Denbo and layout design by Shelby Charette

ISBN-13: 978-1-64632-122-3

Printed in the United States of America.

Prufrock Press Inc.
P.O. Box 8813
Waco, TX 76714-8813
Phone: (800) 998-2208
Fax: (800) 240-0333
https://www.prufrock.com

Table of Contents

Acknowledgements

We dedicate this book to Dodie Marshall, Lara Russell, and Lindsey Anderson. We recognize and give sincere and heartfelt thanks to Dodie, Lara, and Lindsey for their individual and collective commitment, effort, creativity, and expertise that allowed teachers to see their students' talents during the transformation of schools. Their significant contributions made this transition possible.

We are equally grateful to the teachers and principals who participated in the work of transforming schools into Talent Development Academies where students' and teachers' talents are recognized and nurtured.

Finally, we acknowledge that this work was funded by the Jacob K. Javits Gifted and Talented Education Program, Grant Award #S206A140029.

Foreword

Talent development, a conceptual and programmatic approach to education of high-ability children, has gained increasing attention and adherents in the last 10 years. Although the keystone of traditional gifted education is possession of a top-percentile IQ, general academic "smarts," or intellectual giftedness, talent development concerns itself with enhancing abilities in specific domains, such as mathematics, music, chess, or creative writing. The desired outcome of talent development is the production of creative ideas or performances.

Talent development is a promising direction for a field under constant critical observation. It's easier to explain to the public, for example, the need for a program to develop student talent in mathematics or writing than one designed for high-IQ children. With traditional gifted education as currently practiced, new participants have difficulty entering after early grades because IQ is assumed to be identifiable and stable by age 8. In contrast, talent development acknowledges that different talent domains can start at different ages. Although math talent may be identified as early as kindergarten, other subjects or domains that require more insight into human behavior, like history, civics, and leadership, leave open the possibility of finding older students with gifts in those domains. Clearly, the number of gifted children and youth who can be served is greater when looking to develop excellence in individual subjects or domains.

Author and scholar Julie Dingle Swanson and the other researchers and practitioners in this publication integrate contributions from the Talent Development Megamodel (Subotnik et al., 2011, 2018, 2019), as well as from Bloom (1985) and Gagné (2013), to practical talent development application. As early as 1981, Bloom and his colleague Sosniak argued that talent development, even in academic subjects, cannot be conducted exclusively in school. Swanson's Talent Development Instructional Model (TDIM), for example, promotes coordinating with clubs, summer and weekend programs, as well as secondary and tertiary education to reinforce and support the persistence of students on their talent path. Experienced educators and researchers know that out-of-school institutions are in the position of providing increased opportunities for young people to meet peers and get mentoring in addition to advanced content and skills.

I especially enjoyed reading about authors' ideas for implementing initial stages of the talent development process. Their suggestions are based on what's known in the literature about successful implementation of new interventions. The level of detail offered provides a sense of safety for what the authors call "puddle jumpers," or teachers and coordinators who influence their colleagues to give ideas a try. They also encourage talent development educators to coopt relevant components of existing school interventions that share similar goals. In my view, these two approaches exemplify innovative and effective strategies that readers can count on. Finally, the central focus on psychosocial skill development, another distinguishing feature of talent development, is deeply embedded in the program applications found in this volume.

Two features make this book especially valuable. One is that it is born from relationships forged between university researchers and practitioners in the field. Such partnerships ensure that evidence-based strategies are assessed and applied by expert instructors. The second is the book's focus on underserved communities in gifted education. The approaches found on these pages provide a pathway to making our field not only excellent but truly equitable.

Paula Olszewski-Kubilius, Frank Worrell, and I, authors of the Talent Development Megamodel, are honored to have the model serve as a founding conceptual framework for the chapters in this book. It is most exciting to engage with these innovative and original applications by people whom we so admire.

—Rena F. Subotnik
Director, Center for Psychology in Schools and Education
American Psychological Association

References

Bloom, B. S. (Ed.). (1985). *Developing talent in young people*. Ballantine Books.

Bloom, B. S., & Sosniak, L. A. (1981). Talent development vs. schooling. *Educational Leadership, 39*, 86–94.

Gagné, F. (2013). The DMGT 2.0: From gifted inputs to talented outputs. In C. M. Callahan & H. L. Hertberg-Davis (Eds.), *Fundamentals of gifted education: Considering multiple perspectives* (pp. 56–68). Routledge.

Subotnik, R. F., Olszewski-Kubilius, P., & Worrell, F. C. (2011). Rethinking giftedness and gifted education: A proposed direction forward based on psychological science. *Psychological Science in the Public Interest, 12*(1), 3–54. https://doi.org/10.1177/1529100611418056

Subotnik, R. F., Olszewski-Kubilius, P., & Worrell, F. C. (2018). The talent development framework: Overview of components and implications for policy and practice. In P. Olszewski-Kubilius, R. F. Subotnik, & F. C. Worrell (Eds.), *Talent development as a framework for gifted education: Implications for best practices and applications in schools* (pp. 7–24). Prufrock Press.

Subotnik, R. F., Olszewski-Kubilius, P., & Worrell, F. C. (2019). High performance: The central psychological mechanism for talent development. In R. F. Subotnik, P. Olszewski-Kubilius, & F. C. Worrell (Eds.), *The psychology of high performance: Developing human potential into domain-specific talent* (pp. 7–20). American Psychological Association.

Introduction

Julie Dingle Swanson

This edited book provides a review of talent development practices and where talent development fits within the current context of gifted education. Based on work done over 5 years, the authors propose an instructional model for talent development centered on teacher learning and its impact on culturally, ethnically, and linguistically diverse learners. The book draws on what has been learned about how to open access and opportunity to bright students who are underrepresented in gifted programs by extending talent development services to many students and their teachers. The book chapters are authored and coauthored by higher education faculty partners and teachers in the field who have worked directly with talent development for one or more years.

How does one "do" talent development? This book is focused on practitioners and teacher education faculty who seek to deepen their knowledge and understanding of talent development. Grounded in research and evidence-based practice, the book offers practical ideas of how to apply a talent development philosophy in your classroom, school, or district. Teachers share their lesson adaptations and student learning and engagement results through examples and stories.

This book has five sections with differing emphases. The first section explores the question, "What is talent development?" In the opening chapter, Swanson describes concepts and theories that help practitioners understand what talent development is and how gifted education easily fits within a talent development framework. Examples of research and application of talent development illustrate varied ways in which educators have implemented a talent development approach. In Chapter 2, Stambaugh and Fecht describe teaching using a talent development lens. Their in-depth discussion of curriculum is applicable to many academic domains and offers practical strategies to incorporate into daily teaching practice, ways to infuse those strategies into curriculum, and guidelines for using that curriculum as a platform for spotting and growing student abilities. The first section of the book concludes with Chapter 3, which details an instructional model for implementing talent development in your school. Swanson describes guiding principles and essential instructional pillars for schools using a talent development model. How those pillars grow from the Talent Development Megamodel (Subotnik et al., 2018) is explicated.

How is talent development applied instructionally through content? What are results of the application of high-end, evidence-based curriculum, strategies, and thinking models with all students? The second section examines approaches in the specific academic domains, with teachers from schools using a talent development model sharing "how-to" details. The authors show ways in which they draw upon existing curriculum and strategies to grow students' potential in language arts, mathematics, and science. Blake explains instructional strategies she implemented in high-end language arts curriculum with her students with examples of thinking models and students' responses to illustrate the intersection with talent development. Zacherl describes how a specialized math curriculum using a conceptual and relevant inquiry approach engages and grows mathematical thinkers. She explains specific evidence-based practices that develop mathematical thinking in students. Van Sickle describes her experiences in teaching with rigorous science units and how use of the practices of the discipline reveals emerging talent in scientific problem finding and solving. She shows how science is a unique domain for talent spotting and culturally responsive practice. This section offers insight into ways in which teachers have used powerful and advanced curriculum in language arts, mathematics, and science for talent development.

What is the role of culturally responsive practices in talent spotting and development? In other words, how does a school develop teacher talent scouts through emphasis and understanding of culturally responsive practices? The third section explicates the role of culturally responsive teachers in seeing and growing talent in their students. Lichtenstein opens this section with examination of the teacher's role and how their beliefs, values, and cultural awareness powerfully influences their students' success. She provides a strong and practical foundation of culturally responsive practice, linking it to the Talent Development Megamodel so that the connections are clearly evident. This section concludes with Tartt and Van Sickle sharing the teacher's perspective of putting a talent development philosophy into practice through cultural awareness and responsiveness. Examples demonstrate how open, self-aware teachers using keen eyes and ears in combination with powerful and interesting curriculum are able to see students' strengths and build upon those strengths.

Why are the psychology of learning and noncognitive influences key to talent development? The book's fourth section explains the significance of neuroscience and psychological influences on talent development and their role in promoting a key to development—student engagement in learning. Gutshall and Adams describe basics teachers need to better understand their students' learning, cognition, and motivation. They share important, powerful content used in growing teacher understanding of the psychology of learning. Lee's chapter covers feedback, its connection to student learning and motivation, and its connection to talent development. Lee shares how students learn to use feedback in constructive and growth-oriented ways. To conclude this section, Ross relates classroom experiences as an early childhood teacher where she translated her neuroscience understandings into learning experiences for her students, increasing their motivation and grit to face challenges and "grow their brains."

How do you use talent development as a lever for student learning? The final section addresses how to build and assess the Talent Development Instructional Model in a school or district. Adams and Brock describe the significance of relevant and authentic teacher learning as a consideration for schools moving toward a talent development philosophy. They illustrate how one might assess the impact of teacher learning through a case study of teachers in schools using the Talent Development Instructional Model. Swanson concludes the book by revisiting how to get started and the recurring themes from the book (e.g., teachers as key, the significance of leadership and buy-in, and what schools and districts implementing the Talent Development Instructional Model should expect).

In closing, the goal is to share our journey in growing teachers and schools using a talent development model in the hope that what we have learned enables you to create your version of a talent-focused school and district.

Reference

Subotnik, R. F., Olszewski-Kubilius, P., & Worrell, F. C. (2018). The talent development framework: Overview of components and implications for policy and practice. In P. Olszewski-Kubilius, R. F. Subotnik, & F. C. Worrell (Eds.), *Talent development as a framework for gifted education: Implications for best practices and applications in schools* (pp. 7–24). Prufrock Press.

Part I

What Is Talent Development?

1

An Introduction to Talent Development in Schools

Theories and Applications

Julie Dingle Swanson

What is talent development? Why is talent development important? How can educators be purposeful in infusing talent development into the daily work of schools? What can be done to support teachers and principals in learning more about spotting and growing the potential in all students? In a time when social justice and culturally responsive practice are viewed as cornerstones of equitable access to high-quality education for all, talent development offers a guiding conceptual framework to strengthen equitable practice. Talent development as a framework guides creation of schools where all students' strengths are the starting point for learning. This introduction provides an overview of the concept of talent development, building understanding of what it is, how it looks in practice, and what its power is. A brief review of experts' perspectives on talent development grounds the practitioner in what is known about talent development. In order to offer guidance for schools seeking to adopt a talent development model and philosophy, this chapter offers an exploration of what talent development is, why talent development is essential in opening up access and opportunity to many students, and key theories and concepts that inform school-based practice in implementation of talent development.

As a long-time gifted educator, "Rethinking Giftedness and Gifted Education" (Subotnik et al., 2011) caused a shift in my thinking about talent development. I became aware of the need for a multipronged approach to search for and grow talent, moving beyond a singular focus on who is labeled as gifted. I understood the need for a broader view, encompassing curriculum and instruction as a tool to spot emergent and domain-specific talent, addressing psychosocial issues that support and hinder student learning, and using culturally responsive practice to create learning environments that recognize, nurture, and support talent. Often, gifted education services are limited to those students already performing at high levels relative to their same-age peers. Talent development viewed as an umbrella over gifted programs is a philosophical orientation that encourages the search for strengths, abilities, and potential in all students.

Educators can learn to approach their work with a talent spotting orientation and work systematically to support the development of student potential into high performance. Specifically, Subotnik et al. (2011) recognized stages in talent development and noted that the stages are best addressed through a systemwide approach with varied services and programs. They advocated for early enrichment for all students, followed by acceleration opportunities for above-grade-level students and, later, as appropriate, individualized student opportunities to pursue unique strengths, passions, and interests. The Talent Development Megamodel (Subotnik et al., 2011, 2018, 2019) lays out the talent development stages as emergent potential to growing competence to expertise, with some individuals progressing into high accomplishment and/or eminence. In the model, educators and parents of talented children and youth show purposeful and deliberate attention to and cultivation of both domain-specific cognitive abilities (e.g., mathematical or scientific aptitudes) as well as psychosocial attributes (e.g., persistence, collegiality) of the individual. Further, Subotnik et al. (2011) noted that the individual has a shared responsibility in the development of their potential in that opportunities must be taken.

Definition and Concept: What If?

What if looking for student ability that is above average, that stands out, and that is different was as common as looking for what students are *not* able to do? What if educators first looked for where students were strong and had skills and knowledge, instead of searching, testing, assessing, drilling, and remediating weaknesses? What if the starting point for learning was where a student's strengths lie? Teachers could move students quickly through what they already know, focus on new learning, and use interests, passions, and areas of strength to design instruction. Looking for what students can do well is the opposite of common classroom practice.

Noticing strengths and building on strengths are often used in gifted education, so the reader may assume that talent development is only for gifted and talented students and their teachers. Although most would agree that not everyone is gifted, most everyone has a talent, strength, high ability in, or passion about or interest in something. Talent development is working to build and grow the abilities and strengths that students have. Talent development is a way to take students' passions and interests, their potential to excel, and provide learning experiences that grow that potential into performance. A way to reimagine gifted education as talent-oriented education might be:

> Rather than seeing "The Gifted Program" as a one-time assessment or class in a single room, it would be beneficial to reconceive gifted education as a diverse continuum of services, including early enrichment for *all* students, so talent and abilities can emerge and be noticed. Equally important are acceleration opportunities for students who are functioning above grade-level in particular areas, as well as individualized opportunities for students to pursue their unique strengths and interests. In other words, we need different kinds of programs for students who have different kinds of talents and who are at different stages of developing those talents. (Northwestern University Center for Talent Development, 2015, para. 4)

There is much to take from this quote. First, what if educators started early with rich and interesting experiences for all children? What if exposure and enrichment to people, places, things, events, and more was the basis for learning about the world? What if enrichment was used early and with all students to find their interests and passions, and what if those interests and passions were the starting point for learning? How would that rich learning environment look? This type of approach is seen in the Schoolwide Enrichment Model (Renzulli, 1977; Renzulli & Reis, 2010), in early childhood developmentally appropriate practice (e.g., Bredekamp & Copple, 2009), and in Montessori programs (e.g., Harris, 2007). Emerging talent is more easily seen in rich and stimulating environments where hard-to-see potential in students becomes visible. In classrooms and other environments using enrichment, talents emerge and are spotted by teachers and parents. Students who are "at-potential" (Coleman et al., 2007) have opportunities to grow knowledge, skills, and abilities embedded in those emergent talents in schools and classrooms that provide opportunities and experiences to promote growth. Growth leads to the emergence of domain-specific interests and abilities, so planning for and allowing students to move through learning in an accelerated way is a key to continued engagement on the part of the young person. Simply stated, talent development is growing strengths, interests, and passions into knowledge, skills, and abilities, leading to exceptional performance.

Talent and Giftedness

In a qualitative study on 120 talented individuals in diverse fields, including arts, athletics, and academics, Bloom (1985a) drew several generalizations about talent development from the cases. One area of particular interest was what researchers inferred about early learning of highly talented individuals studied. In many of the cases, researchers found that parents were child-oriented, meaning that they supported their child's interests with time and resources. Hard work and effort were the norm in the families studied, and early teachers were also encouraging and supportive of these individuals. Initial learning was progressive, based on practice, and was fun and interesting to the youngster. Teachers liked the children and rewarded and encouraged them, making "the initial learning very pleasant and rewarding" (Bloom, 1985b, p. 514). Motivation grew from teacher praise of the student's progress and growth and the student's desire to do well. For example, "For most mathematicians, the joy of discovering a new way of solving a problem was more important than a high test score" (Bloom, 1985b, p. 515). Sosniak (1985), who studied concert pianists and sculptors, found that the "early years of learning were playful and filled with immediate rewards. 'Tinkering around' at the piano, 'tapping out melodies' was 'fun.' Musical activities were games that could be played over and over again" (p. 411). Bloom's (1985a) seminal study described common factors across different domains that influence talent development at different stages, from early development to development of expertise and high accomplishment in a field.

Gagné (2018) made a distinction between the concepts of giftedness and talent development in his Differentiated Model of Giftedness and Talent (DMGT). He asserted that giftedness is high, outstanding, and natural ability in a domain, with the individual in the top 10% when compared to same-age peers. In the DMGT, although giftedness is a natural ability, talent develops over a lifetime. In a talented individual, knowledge and skills called competencies are systematically developed over time, and the individual's talent in at least one field of human activity falls in the top 10% of other individuals in that field. According to Gagné (2018), "From these two definitions we can extract a simple definition for the talent development process: *talent development corresponds to the progressive transformation of gifts into talents*" (p. 57). Gagné saw giftedness, talent, and the talent development process as the basis of the DMGT. Rounding out his developmental theory are intrapersonal catalysts and environmental catalysts that either support or hinder talent development in an individual. Interpersonal catalysts include everything from physical (e.g., appearance, disabilities, health) and mental traits (e.g., temperament, personality, resilience), to goal-management processes that include, for example, self-awareness of strengths and weaknesses, motivation and drive to pursue passions and interests, and volition to persist in the face of obstacles. Environmental catalysts include talent development influences of family, community, peers, time and place, mentors, teachers, and schooling (Gagné, 2018).

Tannenbaum (1997) is included in this discussion on talent development, as he described giftedness in terms of performance and/or production that is extraordinary and stands out from that of peers. He observed that there is no guarantee that early precocity translates to extraordinary performance or production. He stated:

> Keeping in mind that developed talent exists only in adults, a proposed definition of giftedness in children is that it denotes their potential for becoming critically acclaimed performers or exemplary producers of ideas in spheres of activity that enhance the moral, physical, emotional, social, intellectual, or aesthetic life of humanity. (p. 27)

For Tannenbaum, talent development for children and youth with potential is essential for an individual's performance and/or production to rise to the level of extraordinary, standing apart from that of the individual's peers.

Components of the Talent Development Megamodel

The chapter opened with an introduction to Subotnik et al.'s (2011, 2018, 2019) Talent Development Megamodel. As this model undergirds many of the ideas and experiences reported in this book, further discussion follows. Subotnik et al. (2018) viewed their model as a program model with seven components to guide practitioners interested in a talent-focused program in their school and/or district. First, student abilities are specific and malleable. Domain-specific ability (instead of general cognitive ability) means that specific talent is visible in the student, for example, as precocity in math, high verbal ability, or an ability to build and create. Specific talent in a specific domain is more easily understood than general high ability. It is more inclusive and allows for a better fit between students and the program. In other words, the educational focus is clear: Grow the domain-specific ability. Subotnik et al. (2018) asserted that, rather than general intellectual ability, looking for specific strengths is a first step on the path to growing and developing that ability into talent. Malleability is key in this component; malleability simply means that ability can be shaped and can be easily influenced. A growth orientation toward learning and challenge is of particular importance in growing domain-specific abilities. When students have a growth orientation to learning, they believe that challenge is essential in learning, that effort, working hard, and persisting to meet challenges supports their learning (Dweck, 2006/2016). When an individual has a fixed orientation toward learning, the individual believes that one either has "it" (with "it" being talent, skills, knowledge, ability, etc.) or not, and if effort has to be exerted to get "it," then the individual believes they are not talented.

Further, domains have differing trajectories. How and when talents in differing domains emerge vary. For example, math ability develops differently than athletic ability. In sports such as gymnastics, talent requires early and intense instruction. In highly talented gymnasts, careers end at an early age. In music, violin can be learned and practiced early, while other musical instruments may require physical development that occurs later (e.g., wind instruments). Academic areas, too, have differing trajectories, so awareness of how and when talents may emerge is crucial. Linked to differing trajectories and especially critical for students from low-income households is the idea that students must have opportunities to learn, be exposed to excellence and interesting challenges in domains, and have opportunities to practice and develop skills and competencies. No one develops skills and competencies that grow into extraordinary talent without extensive opportunities to learn, be coached, practice, fail, and grow. The need for opportunity ties back to malleability and a growth orientation as necessary for talent development. Opportunities for growth are found in school with teachers, coaches, mentors, and peers, as well as in outside-of-school activities, summer programs, and community activities.

It is not enough for opportunities to be open to all students; those opportunities must be able to be taken. This component of the megamodel underlines the importance of the individual's interests, confidence, and willingness to engage. Subotnik et al. (2018) saw the importance of the individual's mental skills and social skills as key in growing and developing expertise. For example, an individual must learn how to persist and develop the willingness to put in the effort and practice. An individual must learn how to accept and use feedback and criticism to improve. In order to achieve at high levels, an individual must learn how to use failure and rejection for growth. Social skills are important, too. How an individual interacts with others, humility and grace, as well as assertiveness are important in high levels of success and achievement. These components are highly related and demonstrate that long-range thinking and planning is absolutely essential in talent development. Subotnik et al. (2019) stated:

> Talent development is a process that consists of opportunities offered within and outside of educational institutions, including psychosocial skill development that moves individuals forward on trajectories from potential to competence, to expertise to eminence. Talent trajectories are domain specific and based on the principle that talent is malleable and not fixed. In other words, although individuals may be born with different levels of ability in various domains, abilities are not inherent and permanent characteristics of a person. (p. 12)

Opportunities that are developmental must be available for one's potential to be nurtured, supported, and grow into talent. A range of opportunities and support include, for example, development of persistence, a growth orientation toward learning, and a passion for rigor and challenge.

Why Talent Development?

In this book, the authors advocate for the more comprehensive approach of talent development reflected in Subotnik et al.'s (2018) megamodel for two reasons. First, there is a lack of consensus in the field of gifted education around underlying concepts of the nature of giftedness and talent, how those concepts should be operationalized in schools, programs, and classrooms, and what the goals of gifted programming should be for students who need specialized education. This lack of consensus and clarity around the purpose of gifted education undermines the opportunities and support for specialized education for many students with high abilities, resulting in untapped and underdeveloped potential. Secondly, gifted education as a field continues to struggle with systematically providing services inclusive of diverse, high-ability students with both potential and performance. This results in persistent inequity and blocked access to opportunity for many students.

These issues embedded within gifted education have been understood for some time now. In the early 1990s, O'Connell-Ross (1993) raised awareness when she reported:

> The United States is squandering one of its most precious resources: the gifts, talents, and high interests of many of its students. In a broad range of intellectual and artistic endeavors, these youngsters are not challenged to do their best work. This problem is especially severe among economically disadvantaged and minority students, who have access to fewer advanced educational opportunities and whose talents often go unnoticed. (p. 1)

O'Connell-Ross continued:

> The talents of disadvantaged and minority children have been especially neglected. Almost one in four American children lives in poverty, representing an enormous pool of untapped talent. Yet most programs for these children focus on solving the problems they bring to school, rather than on challenging them to develop their strengths. (p. 5)

Is it possible that in the nearly 3 decades since this report was published that little has changed? How much untapped and lost potential has been caused by this neglect? How much has been done to address issues raised?

More recently, Olszewski-Kubilius and Clarenbach (2012) discussed promising students from low-income backgrounds and their chronic low achievement, unequivocally stating that expectations of more than proficiency from these students are required. The authors recommended a perspective focused on students' strengths as essential. Olszewski-Kubilius and Clarenbach provided examples of programs with a record of success in talent development and built a persuasive case, as they offered evidence of the impact of poverty on student achievement:

> National Assessment of Educational Progress exams remain shamefully low. For example, between 1998 and 2007, 1.7% or fewer of free and reduced lunch program-eligible students scored at the advanced level on the eighth-grade math exam compared to between 6% and 10% of non-eligible students. Since 1998, 1% or fewer of 4th-, 8th-, and 12th grade free or reduced lunch students, compared to between 5% and 6% of non-eligible students scored at the advanced level on the civics exam. (p. 4)

To unlock untapped student talent, more opportunities in and access to curriculum that is rigorous and advanced, before- and afterschool programs that offer supplemental programs, and services that support and enhance student learning are imperative. Further, Olszewski-Kubilius and Clarenbach (2012) advocated for an early focus on emergent talent, enrichment, and achievement. They suggested that educators "identify successful program models and interventions that work with low-income, high-ability students from different geographical, cultural, and racial backgrounds" (p. 3) and use those programs to address the talent development of underserved students.

Other sources document inequities found in education and, specifically, in gifted education. In a study through the Children's Defense Fund (2020), data from 2018 showed that:

- More than 1 in 6 children under 6 were poor and almost half of them lived in extreme poverty.
- Nearly 1 in 3 Black (30.1 percent) and American Indian/Alaska Native children (29.1 percent) and nearly 1 in 4 Hispanic children (23.7 percent) were poor compared with 1 in 11 white children (8.9 percent). (p. 12)

Further, the Children's Defense Fund (2020) provided evidence that:

> Poor children are more likely to have poor academic achievement, drop out of high school and later become unemployed, experience economic hardship and be involved in the criminal justice system. Children who experience poverty are also more likely to be poor at age 30 than children who never experience poverty. (p. 12)

According to the data reported, schools and student achievement "have slipped backwards into patterns of deep racial and socioeconomic segregation" (Children's Defense Fund, 2020, p. 24). These data alone paint a grim picture of the effects of poverty on the life options for many children.

Further, in a national survey (Kurtz et al., 2019) conducted on gifted education programming, selected results on equity and access reflect the disconnect between respondents' view that almost all gifted students are being served, while most surveyed reported underrepresentation of linguistically and culturally diverse learners in gifted programs. The survey results stated:

> Most educators say their district's screening process identifies all or almost all of the students who should be in the gifted education program. However, a majority of educators also say that black, Hispanic, Native American, low-income, and emerging bilingual students are under-represented in their districts' gifted programs. Despite this widespread perception of under-representation, fewer than 1 in 3 educators say their district has made a big effort in the past five years to address this issue. (p. 4)

Finally, excellence gaps studies (e.g., Plucker et al., 2013, 2015) show gaps between the achievement of White students and that of students of color. These varied sources offer evidence that there continues to be much untapped potential in students. Talent development is a way to reconceptualize how to recognize and nurture this potential.

Lohman (2005) argued that a student's domain-specific aptitudes that are beyond grade-level peers help educators to see which students are already exhibiting high performance and accomplishment. Highly accomplished students have access to advanced classes and gifted programs. Lohman asserted that high-performing students are easier to see than students belonging to what he called the high-potential group. He described high-potential students as those who "do not currently display academic excellence in the target academic domain, but are likely to do so if they are willing to put forth the effort required to achieve excellence and are given the proper educational assistance" (p. 334). He further noted that some students "who do not display high accomplishment might currently do so if they had the opportunities to develop these skills. Put differently, high-potential students display the aptitude to develop high levels of accomplishment offered by a particular class of instructional treatments" (p. 334). Lohman made the important point that the goal of using aptitude measures is not to celebrate a student's high ability or potential; rather the goal is to provide learning that grows students into "excellent engineers, scientists, writers, and so forth" (p. 336).

Talent development is particularly important for students from low-income backgrounds and those who are underrepresented in gifted programs whose abilities and aptitudes may not be at the level of high accomplishment *yet*. High potential does not translate into high accomplishment without the opportunity to develop and grow skills and abilities. Opportunities to develop potential can be found in educational settings where students' talent is recognized, valued, and developed. The use of specialized, high-level, engaging curriculum (Stambaugh, 2018) can tap into students' passions and interests. Afterschool programs, clubs, and teams bring together students for enrichment, exposure, and advanced learning through interest-based activities (Horn, 2018). Horn (2018) asserted that:

> A focus on talent development recognizes that each student has a profile of strengths and abilities within and across specific domains. Talent development requires opportunities for talent to emerge, as well as an educational setting in which talent is recognized and nurtured over time. (p. 129)

Why does talent development make sense with regard to clarifying the purpose of gifted education? Why does talent development make sense in practice with regard to underrepresentation? Talent development creates stronger understanding and support for gifted and talented education programming by offering clear direction for teachers and schools as to their role in promoting growth and learning in high-ability students, both those who are performing and those who are at potential. It specifies opportunities needed to provide pathways for bright students to grow into successful and productive individuals who use their talents. It promotes building on students' strengths, passions, and interests to engage them in learning and growth.

Talent Development in Practice

This section explores ways that talent development has been put into practice in schools and districts, including a description of specific, evidence-based and domain-based projects that have used curriculum as a platform for student talent development and provided a talent development approach to learning. These school- and district-based talent development programs include STEM

Starters + (Robinson et al., 2018), the Young Scholars Program (Horn, 2018), and Project SPARK (Little et al., 2018).

STEM Starters + (Robinson et al., 2018) targets young children in low-income schools and shows how early introduction of novel and interesting curriculum uncovers talent in students. Robinson et al. used engineering curriculum with young students from low-income households as a platform for talent spotting and development. They used this novel curriculum, asserting that:

> the conditions of poverty where young children learn early that they must "make-do" and solve problems of everyday challenges such as broken household items, dilapidated or missing school backpacks, or a lack of traditional toys may allow children of poverty to develop early "talents for tinkering"—the very talents and habits of mind that adult engineers put to use in practice of their profession and that prompt teachers to spot these talents in context with everyday objects. (Brophy & Mann, 2008, as cited in Robinson et al., 2018, p. 131)

The curriculum in STEM Starters + included an acoustical engineering unit and a biographical unit based on Jane Goodall's life. The engineering curriculum came from the Engineering is Elementary curriculum series, which was developed by the Museum of Science, Boston, and covers a range of engineering specialties. The biography study was developed at the Jodie Mahony Center for Gifted Education at the University of Arkansas at Little Rock. These units were purposefully chosen as novel and accelerated; engineering is typically studied in college, not first grade, and biography study is a way for students to understand how eminent individuals meet and overcome obstacles in their chosen fields. In their study of more than 1,300 first-grade students, the researchers found that the intervention group students experiencing the innovative engineering curriculum resulted in an effect size of 0.66 in the engineering knowledge domain (Robinson et al., 2018). Equally significant, researchers found that many teachers in the study nominated students from underrepresented groups (i.e., low-income households and ethnically or culturally diverse) for gifted program services. In other words, teachers were able to "talent spot" (Robinson, 2017) students as they engaged in innovative, hands-on engineering curriculum (Robinson et al., 2018). This project and research exemplify how use of an interesting and novel curriculum with students exposes abilities not previously visible, allows teachers to see talent as it emerges, and impacts student learning in a new domain.

A second example is Young Scholars, a comprehensive, district-based program developed for finding and developing potential in students from underserved populations (Horn, 2015, 2018). In her work, Horn (2018) noted that she decided to expand her district's gifted education purpose more broadly as "a talent development framework designed to elicit, identify, and nurture gifts and talents as they emerge" (p. 148). In developing the framework, Young Scholars became part of a continuum of how the district served gifted students. The way the program worked was that, first, teachers were trained to spot student potential. These specially trained "talent spotters" observed students as classroom teachers used advanced and challenging curriculum with all students in the regular classroom. In these observations, the talent spotting teachers identified students at potential. Once identified, these students were called Young Scholars and opportunities for developing domain-specific abilities were opened to them through special classes and summer enrichment opportunities. The opportunity and access enabled the students' potential to grow into performance and ability.

Goals of the Young Scholars model were "to identify gifted potential in children from diverse . . . backgrounds as early as possible, and to nurture, guide, and support the development of their exceptional potential so [that] students will discover their talents and be prepared for increasingly higher levels of challenge as they advance" (Horn, 2018, p. 133). During both in-school and summer school programs, Young Scholars engaged in problem-based, culturally responsive, authentic learning designed to challenge them to think in more complex ways, to find and solve problems, and to communicate and collaborate with others. Longitudinal studies of Young Scholars provided evidence that these students increasingly took advanced coursework and participated in enrichment opportunities. The district has tracked more than 12,000 Young Scholars in grades K–12 and found the following:

> Of the 6,763 Young Scholars in grades K–8, 44% received differentiated instruction at a higher level provided by the classroom teacher (Level II). 23% received part-time direct services provided by the gifted and talented resource teacher (Level III), and 33% are in a full-time gifted and talented center program with highly challenging curricula (Level IV). (Horn, 2018, pp. 145–146)

The Jacob K. Javits Gifted and Talented Education Program has provided a wealth of knowledge on how to support teachers in their work with culturally, linguistically, and ethnically diverse (CLED) gifted learners. Project SPARK (Little et al., 2018), a scale-up project based on the Young Scholars model, worked with teachers to educate them on how to better recognize potential in young students from low-income backgrounds. Teachers then referred students at potential to participate in a summer math enrichment program using Project M^2 (Gavin et al., 2011), and the summer program exposed students to more advanced mathematics content. Results from the first year of intervention showed that students who participated in the summer program made larger gains from spring to fall than students who did not participate in the summer program. This study offers additional evidence that students from low-income backgrounds made gains from their participation in out-of-school programs, providing evidence that more time, enrichment, and exposure in a domain-specific area grows skills and abilities. Other research results for talent development in out-of-school activities—either in the summer or before or after school—is positive (e.g., Olszewski-Kubilius & Clarenbach, 2012; Olszewski-Kubilius & Lee, 2008; VanTassel-Baska, 2017). Mentorships, internships, competitions, contests, and service learning (Corwith, 2018) have shown success in providing additional opportunities for developing domain-specific competencies and growing mental and social skills.

I return to the model developed by Subotnik et al. (2011, 2018, 2019) discussed earlier in this chapter to emphasize again that schools using a talent development lens start early with enrichment and exposure for all learners. Exposure and enrichment can be accomplished in school through use of novel and advanced curriculum as a platform for spotting potential. Along with powerful and engaging curriculum that challenges learners, educators must also attend to psychosocial factors and culturally responsive practice. Finally, having a plan for varied and systemwide opportunities to develop potential into talent is key. More specifics about the importance of, as well as how to build higher level support in administration at the school and district levels for, talent development follows in other parts of this book. Creating and sustaining a talent development philosophy that impacts children and youth takes hard work, resources, support, and effort on all levels in a school and a district.

Conclusion

This chapter and the first section of this book ground the reader in what is known about talent development, including theories, definitions, models, application, and research. For the practitioner considering implementing talent development in your school or district, the following guiding points are offered to get you started:

1. Be able to articulate what talent development means, how it is different from gifted education, and what it can do for all students, including those with high ability.
2. Have a clear rationale of the value that a talent development approach in your school or district can offer students.
3. Offer examples of how talent development has been implemented and what the results of these approaches have been with students and teachers.
4. Generate questions of interest and plan for data collection to answer questions. This effort enables you to track your talent development efforts. What are your goals in implementing talent development? What issues are you addressing? How will you measure progress toward those goals and/or issues resolution (i.e., what data do you need to collect to track progress?)?

End-of-Chapter Discussion/ Reflection Questions

1. In your own words, define *talent development.*
2. In what ways are gifted education and talent development similar and different?
3. What are the key components of the Talent Development Megamodel? What does each component look like in practice?
4. Of the examples of talent development applied in schools and student learning found in this chapter, which resonates most with you, and why? Which example might be adapted for use in your current educational setting?
5. For what reasons is talent development important? What value does the talent development approach add in education?

References

Bloom, B. S. (Ed.). (1985a). *Developing talent in young people.* Ballantine Books.

Bloom, B. S. (1985b). Generalizations about talent development. In B. S. Bloom (Ed.), *Developing talent in young people* (pp. 507–549). Ballantine Books.

Bredekamp, S., & Copple, C. (Eds.). (2009). *Developmentally appropriate practice in early childhood* (3rd ed.). National Association for the Education of Young Children.

Brophy, S. P., & Mann, G. (2008, June). *Teachers noticing engineering in everyday objects and processes* [Paper presentation]. Annual Conference of the American Society of Engineering Education, Pittsburg, PA, United States.

Children's Defense Fund. (2020). *The state of America's children 2020*. https://www.childrensdefense.org/the-state-of-americas-children-2020

Coleman, M. R., Coltrane, S. S., Harradine, C., & Timmons, L. A. (2007). Impact of poverty on promising learners, their teachers, and their schools. *Journal of Urban Education: Focus on Enrichment, 6*, 59–67.

Corwith, S. (2018). Programming for talent development outside of school. In P. Olszewski-Kubilius, R. F. Subotnik, & F. C. Worrell (Eds.), *Talent development as a framework for gifted education: Implications for best practices and applications in schools* (pp. 63–94). Prufrock Press.

Dweck, C. S. (2016). *Mindset: The new psychology of success*. Ballantine Books. (Original work published 2006)

Gagné, F. (2018). The DMGT/IMTD: Building talented outputs out of gifted inputs. In C. M. Callahan & H. L. Hertberg-Davis (Eds.), *Fundamentals of gifted education: Considering multiple perspectives* (2nd ed., pp. 55–70). Routledge.

Gavin, M. K., Casa, T. M., Chapin, S. H., & Sheffield, L. J. (2011). *Exploring shape games: Geometry with Imi and Zani*. Kendall Hunt.

Harris, M. A. (2007). Differences in mathematics scores between students who receive traditional Montessori instruction and students who receive music enriched Montessori instruction. *Journal for Learning through the Arts, 3*(1). https://doi.org/10.21977/D93110059

Horn, C. V. (2015). Young Scholars: A talent development model for finding and nurturing potential in underserved populations. *Gifted Child Today, 38*(1), 19–31. https://doi.org/10.1177/1076217514556532

Horn, C. V. (2018). Serving low-income and underrepresented students in a talent development framework. In P. Olszewski-Kubilius, R. F. Subotnik, & F. C. Worrell (Eds.), *Talent development as a framework for gifted education: Implications for best practices and applications in schools* (pp. 129–152). Prufrock Press.

Kurtz, H., Lloyd, S., Harwin, A., Chen, V., & Furuya, Y. (2019). *Gifted education: Results of a national survey*. Editorial Projects in Education. https://www.edweek.org/research-center/gifted-education-results-of-a-national-survey

Little, C. A., Adelson, J. L., Kearney, K. L., Cash, K., & O'Brien, R. L. (2018). Early opportunities to strengthen academic readiness: Effects of summer learning on mathematics achievement. *Gifted Child Quarterly, 62*(1), 83–95. https://doi.org/10.1177/0016986217738052

Lohman, D. F. (2005). An aptitude perspective on talent: Implications for identification of academically gifted minority students. *Journal for the Education of the Gifted, 28*(3–4), 333–360.

Northwestern University Center for Talent Development. (2015, October 5). *Cultivating talent and serving underrepresented gifted students.* https://www.ctd.northwestern.edu/blog/cultivating-talent-serving-underrepresented-gifted-students

O'Connell-Ross, P. (1993). *National excellence: A case for developing America's talent.* Office of Educational Research and Improvement.

Olszewski-Kubilius, P., & Clarenbach, J. (2012). *Unlocking emergent talent: Supporting high achievement of low-income, high-ability students.* National Association for Gifted Children.

Olszewski-Kubilius, P., & Lee, S.-Y. (2008). Specialized programs serving the gifted. In F. A. Karnes & K. P. Stevens (Eds.), *Achieving excellence: Educating the gifted and talented* (pp. 192–208). Pearson.

Plucker, J. A., Giancola, J., Healey, G., Arndt, D., & Wang, C. (2015). *Equal talents, unequal opportunities: A report card on state support for academically talented low-income students.* Jack Kent Cooke Foundation.

Plucker, J. A., Hardesty, J., & Burroughs, N. (2013). *Talent on the sidelines: Excellence gaps and America's persistent talent underclass.* University of Connecticut, Center for Education Policy Analysis.

Renzulli, J. S. (1977). The enrichment triad model: A plan for developing defensible programs for the gifted and talented. *Gifted Child Quarterly, 21*(2), 227–233. https://doi.org/10.1177/001698627702100216

Renzulli, J. S., & Reis, S. (2010). The Schoolwide Enrichment Model: A focus on student strengths and interests. *Gifted Education International, 26*(2–3), 140–156. https://doi.org/10.1177/026142941002600303

Robinson, A. (2017). Conceptual frameworks in gifted education as a foundation for services. In J. L. Roberts, T. F. Inman, & J. H. Robins (Eds.), *Introduction to gifted education* (pp. 5–15). Prufrock Press.

Robinson, A., Adelson, J. L., Kidd, K. A., & Cunningham, C. M. (2018). A talent for tinkering: Developing talents in children from low-income households through engineering curriculum. *Gifted Child Quarterly, 62*(1), 130–144. https://doi.org/10.1177/0016986217738049

Sosniak, L. (1985). Phases of learning. In B. S. Bloom (Ed.), *Developing talent in young people* (pp. 409–438). Ballantine Books.

Stambaugh, T. (2018). Curriculum and instruction within a talent development framework. In P. Olszewski-Kubilius, R. F. Subotnik, & F. C. Worrell (Eds.), *Talent development as a framework for gifted education: Implications for best practices and applications in schools* (pp. 95–128). Prufrock Press.

Subotnik, R. F., Olszewski-Kubilius, P., & Worrell, F. C. (2011). Rethinking giftedness and gifted education: A proposed direction forward based on psychological science. *Psychological Science in the Public Interest, 12*(1), 3–54. https://doi.org/10.1177/1529100611418056

Subotnik, R. F., Olszewski-Kubilius, P., & Worrell, F. C. (2018). The talent development framework: Overview of components and implications for policy and practice. In P. Olszewski-Kubilius, R. F. Subotnik, & F. C. Worrell (Eds.), *Talent development as a framework for gifted education: Implications for best practices and applications in schools* (pp. 7–24). Prufrock Press.

Subotnik, R. F., Olszewski-Kubilius, P., & Worrell, F. C. (2019). High performance: The central psychological mechanism for talent development. In R. F. Subotnik, P. Olszewski-Kubilius, & F. C. Worrell (Eds.), *The psychology of high performance: Developing human potential into domain-specific talent* (pp. 7–20). American Psychological Association.

Tannenbaum, A. J. (1997). The meaning and making of giftedness. In N. Colangelo & G. A. Davis (Eds.), *Handbook of gifted education* (2nd ed., pp. 27–42). Allyn & Bacon.

VanTassel-Baska, J. (2017). Curricular considerations for advanced learners from low-income and minority backgrounds. In J. VanTassel-Baska & C. A. Little (Eds.), *Content-based curriculum for high-ability learners* (3rd ed., pp. 47–62). Prufrock Press.

2

Practical Strategies for Teaching Through a Talent Development Lens[1]

Tamra Stambaugh and Sarah DeLisle Fecht

Examples of talent are all around. An athlete pitches a no-hitter in a crucial playoff game. A skilled guitarist nails the set and establishes a thrilling atmosphere in a sold-out amphitheater of thousands of captivated fans. A chef creates the perfect menu that excites patrons' taste buds and builds acclaim across a city. It is easy to recognize individuals who have a unique talent in an area, and it is important to appreciate the diversity of talent areas. From athletes and musicians to visual artists and composers, to chefs and bakers, to mathematicians and writers, to research scientists and medical professions, talent domains for individuals run the gamut. As educators, we must acknowledge that, just as a young athlete showing an early ability for accuracy in pitching is trained to hone their skills, students showing ability or exhibiting potential in specific academic domains need curriculum opportunities that develop their abilities in content areas of strength and passion. This is where the idea of teaching through a talent development lens is anchored.

---

1 Information in this chapter is adapted with permission from Stambaugh, 2018, 2020a, 2020b.

Research in the field of talent development emphasizes that talent is developed into elite performance, regardless of the area of talent, through a process that takes into account the developmental nature of the specific talent being developed (Subotnik et al., 2011). From this research, educators know that students must not only be exposed to, but also take advantage of "opportunities that develop their abilities and interests before they can embark on curriculum endeavors that move them toward expertise in the area" (Stambaugh, 2020b, p. 149). Therefore, as educators, we can acknowledge that schools and teachers, specifically, play a crucial role in talent development for students who may have a proclivity for a particular academic area or areas (Stambaugh, 2018). This begs the question—how can you begin thinking about teaching through a talent development lens?

Considering this question while also acknowledging the diversity of particular talent domains available to students might initially be quite overwhelming. At first thought, the fear of missing the opportunity to identify each of a student's unique areas of talent and then developing that talent might make the task seem daunting and exhausting. However, it is important to recognize that, although talent development is "individualized and dependent upon a student's ability, acquired knowledge, interest, and performance at a given point in time, a well-designed curriculum can serve as a foundation for the cultivation of [most areas of] talent" (Stambaugh, 2018, p. 95). Therefore, we can rely on curriculum to serve as a catalyst for supporting talent by exposing students to appropriately challenging material. Deliberate use and selection of curriculum and carefully crafted instructional supports expose all students to areas of interest in specific content areas so that students' talents can be realized and, ultimately, nurtured (Stambaugh, 2018, p. 96).

This chapter has been designed to help teachers identify the components of teaching through a talent development lens so that they can select appropriate curriculum or modify curriculum that they are already using, incorporating what is important for developing talent in an area. Educators must be able to justify curricular decisions to administrators and parents, so the chapter begins with a focus on key principles of teaching through a talent development lens (adapted from Stambaugh, 2018), along with evidence surrounding the importance of these principles. This is followed by an overview of how to approach teaching through a talent development framework, embedding practical curriculum examples for this form of teaching. The chapter concludes with additional considerations for successful curriculum design that promotes talent development.

Key Principles for Teaching Through a Talent Development Lens

Talent development should not be considered a program or a service. Rather, teaching through a talent development lens should be considered a philosophy—a way of designing your lessons and classroom structure to invest in human capital and to develop individual strengths. Teachers using a talent development lens to design lessons and curriculum anchor their instructional practices in key principles that relate back to this central goal of investment in their students with a focus on individual strength development. The following sections outline the talent development principles and expand upon how these principles are focused on developing talent and building expertise.

Principle 1: Focus on the Long-Term Outcomes of Expertise and Creative Production

As teachers, instead of asking, "What am I going to teach my students today to meet a specific standard?" we need to be asking, "How can I continue to develop expertise in my students' areas of strength within the subject area I am teaching?" The difference in thinking is critical in shifting our lesson planning paradigm because it is counter to how most teachers learn to plan in teacher education programs. In preservice education programs, future teachers often learn that in lesson planning they should begin with the end in mind. This "end" is often seen as the grade-level standard their lesson or unit is addressing. With this approach to standards-based teaching, teachers determine what students need to know, understand, and be able to do related to a specific content standard before planning activities and selecting resources. This is a great strategy in order to ensure grade-level mastery of content, but it is not sufficient for developing talent and encouraging the development of expertise. Teachers must shift their thinking so that the end goal is not simply the mastery of a standard but rather how to begin thinking like an expert in a content area.

As you ponder how this principle relates to the specific grade or content area that you teach, remember that your goals for the year should go beyond mastery of the end-of-unit standard(s) or grade-level standard(s) and consider the development of future experts and creative producers. In changing your thinking, the curriculum and instructional opportunities you offer your students will reflect this shift. For example, instead of your goal being students' mastery of the ABCs through skills-based assignments, you might focus on your students' understanding of how experts read to gain knowledge and solve problems. You might utilize assignments that involve students applying their ABC knowledge to reading texts and discussing meaning or word choice. In science, instead of your goal being that students list the steps of the scientific process, you might focus on students being able to describe how scientists apply the scientific process to solve problems; then students develop their own study that applies the process. No matter the age of the students you work with, consistently exposing students to a variety of content areas or domains within an area will help all students begin to think like experts. Teaching for talent is about determining where students enter the domain and moving them forward along the continuum toward developing expertise regardless of the current grade-level standards (which many academically advanced students may already know or could quickly master).

Principle 2: Provide Opportunity and Exposure to All Students, Then Adapt Instruction as Needed

Studying eminent individuals has shown that early exposure to a variety of opportunities is critical. Early access is the first step toward development of expertise and creative contribution to a field (Csikszentmihalyi et al., 1993). Teachers who teach through a talent development lens understand that without exposure and opportunity, talents are less likely to be discovered. Therefore, teachers who focus on talent development provide numerous opportunities for students to be exposed to a variety of topics, ideas, thinking skills, and fields. It is part of a general classroom approach. Particularly, teachers should recognize that some students may arrive at their classroom with less prior access. Students from low-income households are among the least likely to receive advanced curriculum (Milner, 2014), which could ultimately block their path toward fulfilling their talents (Cawelti, 2006; Subotnik et al., 2011). Teachers who teach through a talent development lens understand the critical role that exposure and access play in talent acquisition, especially for students who have not had previous opportunity.

Throughout a teaching process focused on opportunity and exposure, teachers skilled in talent development are careful observers. Teachers take note of those students who are interested and show abilities or potential in a given area. Teachers respond to these students' needs and interests by providing more rigorous opportunities and more advanced curriculum opportunities. This approach of exposure and enrichment for all with increasing levels of opportunity for advanced learning, expertise, and creative production is an effective strategy to promote talent development in an area of strength (Renzulli, 1977; Treffinger & Selby, 2009).

Teachers who teach through a development lens understand that exposure is not something reserved for students who have been identified as advanced or who have already shown advanced ability. Exposure to interesting and diverse content is part of a rigorous curriculum for all students. Students' responses through performance and interest, in turn, allow teachers to provide more rigorous opportunities in content domains, if needed. Once students have been exposed to high-level and engaging curricula, teachers have preassessment data from which to support students and provide equitable instruction. When students are provided with equal advanced opportunities, teachers can begin to monitor who shows increased interest, who already knows the content, and who is learning more quickly once exposure occurs.

Principle 3: Integrate the Development of Psychosocial Skills Into the Classroom

Think back to the examples of expertise at the beginning of the chapter. In addition to having content expertise in their specific field, the athlete, musician, and chef all likely have another thing in common that has contributed to their achievements in their respective fields. They all probably have inter- and intrapersonal factors that contribute to their success. Factors such as motivation, productive mindset, psychological strength, and social skills are also collectively known as *psychosocial factors*. They are important skills, outside of having content expertise, for being successful in a field. Research suggests that psychosocial skills are a determining factor in discerning which students rise to elite levels of performance and which do not (Csikszentmihalyi et al., 1993; Duckworth, 2016; Subotnik et al., 2011)—especially when abilities and opportunities are equivalent.

Because of the important role that psychosocial factors play in elite performance, curriculum that develops expertise embeds psychosocial skill development (Subotnik et al., 2011). Curriculum opportunities developed through a talent development lens, therefore, address not only the content knowledge needed to move toward expertise, but also the psychosocial skills necessary for students to succeed as experts. Students need to learn how and when to apply these habits early in their school career.

Note that if students are not given appropriately challenging curriculum and the curriculum is too easy, they will not learn perseverance or how to study. An appropriately challenging curriculum can instill perseverance, encourage a strong work ethic, and enhance self-esteem. Appropriate levels of challenge within the curriculum coupled with long-term projects encourage goal setting and time management. Additionally, exposure to work that is challenging and requires long-term problem solving or multiple trials to arrive at an answer develops perseverance and a strong work ethic when paired with modeling persistence.

Just as students need curriculum that specifically creates opportunities for diverse experiences so that students can identify interests and strengths, students also need experiences through curriculum that explicitly support the development of psychosocial skills within the context of the content. Teachers who understand teaching through a talent development lens understand that psychosocial skills are not automatically developed and should not be assumed just by the nature of providing a rigorous curriculum. The development of psychosocial skills should be an intentional and explicit part of a comprehensive talent development approach. Classroom discussions, reflections, interviews with experts, or biography studies that examine how experts handle failures, successes, motivation, and work-life balance in a field allow students to learn what an expert's life might entail. Examples are provided later in this chapter.

Principle 4: Differentiate Content, Process, Concepts, and Products in a Way That Promotes Expertise and Creative Production

Most people would agree that all students in third grade do not need the exact same level of training or intervention to throw a baseball. Some students already know the techniques of throwing a baseball and are ready for more advanced use of the techniques, while others need to continue working on the fundamentals. This concept of different instruction to move talent forward can be applied to classroom instruction within academic content domains as well. Teachers who develop curriculum through a talent development lens understand that within specific content areas, not all students are ready for the same level of intensity, pacing, or depth as others. This is where differentiation of the content is critical for meeting students' needs and propelling students with unique talents forward in their areas of strength.

Successful differentiation requires teachers to consider how an expert would approach a topic or standard, what processes an expert might use, what products an expert creates, and what concepts, theories, laws, or generalizations an expert might use as a foundation. Therefore, differentiation for advanced students within a talent development model involves appropriately leveled (and likely accelerated) content (e.g., resources, standards, pacing) for a student's readiness level. Such differentiated instruction also incorporates discipline-specific frameworks, models, and discussions that mimic the way experts approach a topic or problem. These frameworks, models, and discussions are used to support the processing of the accelerated content. Furthermore, teachers differentiating within a talent development framework connect concepts, theories, principles, and laws of the discipline to the accelerated content.

In order to gauge if the materials, instruction, and assignments are differentiated to move a student forward within an area where they have shown advanced ability, we recommend using Passow's (1982) "Would, Could, Should" test. Passow asked educators to consider the following three questions when considering appropriateness for developing talent in students ready for more challenge: (1) *Would* all students want to do this? (2) *Could* all students do this? (3) *Should* all students be doing this? (p. 12). If all students would, could, *or* should be able to access the specific lesson or content, then it is likely not differentiated in a way that promotes expertise and creative production in students who are ready for more challenge. We also understand the power of "yet"—noting that all students are on a path toward developing expertise, but not all students are ready for the same material at the same time. Therefore, we have added to Passow's considerations: "at this point in time." Some students can learn something more quickly once exposed, while others are not yet there but are moving along a continuum toward a higher level of understanding and production.

In order to develop experiences that pass the "Would, Could, Should" test, teachers should differentiate the content, processes, products, and concepts within lessons and units. For example, instead of asking students to simply memorize more challenging vocabulary or spelling words, you might connect vocabulary development to the concept of patterns. You might ask students to determine patterns among prefixes, suffixes, or spellings, just as experts connect facts to larger concepts and generalizations or rules, or determine generalizations based on the details and facts provided. Because products should be differentiated as well and designed based on what experts would create, students should be asked to create products that incorporate specific criteria that would be expected within that particular discipline. For example, an expert in writing would not likely create a glitter paper bag character puppet to help them craft a character's backstory; however, an expert in writing might develop a timeline of their character to develop a backstory so that they can justify decisions that the character makes in their present story. Similarly, an engineer might not make a bridge out of gumdrops and toothpicks, but an engineer may make a model to test force and load given a specific set of criteria.

Principle 5: Create Experiences That Support Access and Continued Growth for All Students

Teachers who are skilled in talent development recognize that talent can be acquired at different times and will be different for each person. These teachers understand that developing talent in an area is based on a variety of factors that not only relate to a student's natural ability and talent in the area, but also include a student's level of motivation, prior exposure and experience in the area, and interests (Subotnik et al., 2011). Good teaching considers the student in planning. Teachers and researchers can develop amazing curriculum resources, but if the student is not ready, has already mastered the content, is not interested, or lacks the skills necessary to engage at higher levels, even the best efforts will be less effective. Preassessments using multiple data points, knowing the student and their interests, and consistently allowing for opportunities in the classroom where students are introduced to advanced content and processes of experts in a variety of ways allow teachers to view student strengths and match instruction to individual needs. Additionally, recognition of a student's interests, culture, and context make the curriculum more meaningful and may encourage engagement. Not all students are interested in all areas in which they may perform well. At the same time, students who do not have opportunities for exposure may never uncover new interests. When teaching through a talent development lens, exposure is critical for all students regardless of their original entry point.

Monitoring growth is also critical to teaching through a talent development lens, as teachers can recognize that not all students have had equal levels of exposure previously. Some students will show strong achievement gains after initial exposure to content-specific areas, opportunities to explore high-level curriculum, and explicit training in thinking skills of a discipline (Horn, 2015). Access to high-quality and rigorous curriculum and instruction can be a great equalizer for students who have not had prior access or opportunity. Teachers can support access and encourage continued growth by understanding that when a more robust curriculum is foundational and is taught to all students then student strengths and talents are more likely to emerge. Teachers rooting their instruction in a talent development philosophy understand that they will not know the extent to which students can solve problems or reason through situations if they never give their students the instruction for how to do it and the opportunity to do it. Therefore, teachers have to teach it and look for it if they are to see it.

When students are given curriculum and support that allows their true talents to emerge, teachers can build upon these talents in ways that move students forward in developing content expertise. However, note that some students will need more support and scaffolding for a talent to emerge. In a review of curriculum designed to provide access and opportunity in Title I schools, Stambaugh (2012) found the following components to be common:

- **Conceptual:** Concepts and relevant problems or scenarios specific to the content domain should be infused in the teaching. Conceptual understanding can be promoted in two different ways: (1) emphasis on subject-specific concepts that are explicitly taught, practiced, and applied to real-world scenarios with further application to universal generalizations, and (2) focus on cross-disciplinary concepts (change, systems, conflict, etc.). When focused on cross-disciplinary concepts, students apply a real-world scenario just studied or learned to a generalization associated with a concept. For example, students may look at how systems are interdependent or how change is linked to time with specific content examples.
- **Relevant:** Relevance might be infused into classroom instruction in three different ways: (1) real-world problem-based scenarios, (2) embedded opportunities for students to gain hands-on or created/simulated experiences, and (3) culturally relevant readings and examples. Relevance is context-dependent and allows students to have access and opportunity in the classroom through experiences that may not be afforded in the real world. Relevance also allows for students to see others like themselves and also different perspectives and cultures than their own through readings, studies of individuals, and real-world problems or scenarios to solve as related to the curriculum. For example, students might look at how ecosystems within their backyard impact tourism in their town, or they, as scientists, may study Black inventors in engineering in order to emulate.
- **Modeling and scaffolding:** Scaffolding assumes that higher level thinking skills and content can be attained with some targeted assistance. Rather than focusing solely on lower level skills, teachers can teach higher level skills with scaffolding and with the expectation that given additional supports, structures, and time, students will attain the skills. One must teach what they want to see. Therefore, units focused on talent development begin at a high level and provide needed scaf-

folding, such as graphic organizers and models. Ultimately, teachers need to deliberately think about components of their curriculum that help foster talent within their students and allow students to recognize potential areas of talent in themselves. Curriculum should not be viewed as only a response to talent but rather as an opportunity to find new talent and build upon it.

Students who have fewer opportunities to gain conceptual understanding, see the curriculum as relevant and engaging, or experience higher level thinking and processes are less likely to show habits of experts or develop their talents.

Principle 6: Assess Talent and Progress Toward Content Expertise and Creative Production Through Performance-Based Products

If the goal of teaching through a talent development lens is to prepare students to be experts and creative producers in their field, then students need opportunities along the way for creation, performance, feedback, and success. Therefore, a curriculum focused on talent development includes projects and experiences that allow students to mimic the work of experts or actually design creative products. Instead of asking students to design a glitter poster, make a duct tape purse, create a diorama, or make a mobile, student products are tied specifically to the types of projects experts in a field might be involved in producing. For example, students who are studying engineering content might have a performance-based assignment that involves the creation of scale models, drawings, or replicas, while students in a literary analysis class may be asked to write a critique, editorial, or book review.

Teachers developing performance-based tasks that are linked to the work of experts ask themselves how their classroom curriculum and instruction provide appropriate content in the area to increase the likelihood for success on the task. For example, a scientist might create a model, a simulation, a presentation, a hypothesis, or a paper. Teachers should ask themselves why students wouldn't participate in similar tasks, and what content application would be necessary to complete the task with success. A mathematician might develop a proof to explain a mathematical principle. Why wouldn't students do the same in the classroom? A writer might study a particular time in history and create a storyboard about how the era impacts the characters before establishing the components of the setting and the characters. Why wouldn't students do the same? Authentic products not only are motivating to learners who are interested in becoming experts in an area because they mimic the work of more skilled individuals, but also allow educators to see the extent to which students are able to perform, create, or synthesize ideas in a field. If students do not have the opportunity early on or are not motivated to produce products that show how they are applying their learning and expertise, then it will be harder for them to learn the importance of creative synthesis to gain notice in a field later in their career.

Examples of a Talent Development Curriculum

To review, a talent development curriculum incorporates ways to develop expertise in a content area by providing opportunities for students to think like a scholar in the field, which includes opportunities to develop authentic products in a given domain. Teaching through a talent lens also provides access and opportunities to higher level thinking so that teachers are continually scouting for talent. Additionally, teachers focused on talent acquisition know the importance of developing the psychosocial skills necessary for continued growth. But how does this really look in practice?

Developing Expertise Through Content

One of the main purposes of teaching through a talent development lens is to encourage the development of expertise and high performance or creative productivity in a field over time (Dai & Chen, 2013; Subotnik et al., 2011). If expertise is the goal, it is important to understand how expertise is developed and to teach students how experts think about and process information within a specific content domain of interest. Expertise is developed through exposure to content-specific thinking models important within a subject-specific domain (Bransford et al., 2000). This means that educators need to scaffold habits of experts and continually infuse more complex problems, readings, resources, or dilemmas into the curriculum as students gain more information. Explicitly teaching content-specific thinking models supports the development of expert thinking and content acquisition. Therefore, students not only need to know how to think like an expert in a field, but also need that thinking modeled for them and need opportunities to practice these skills of experts with increasing levels of difficulty. There is research to support the need for overtly teaching thinking skills in context to students, even students who already have fairly well-developed thinking skills (Kettler, 2014; Rogers, 2007; Stambaugh, 2007).

You may also be asking yourself, how do I scaffold habits of experts, teach the thinking habits of experts, and continually infuse more complex problems, particularly in areas that I might not have as much expertise? This is a common question of teachers we work with, so we will now discuss practical ideas and teaching models to support you. One place to start is to understand that expert thinking is supported when questions such as these are considered when planning lessons: "How would a _______ approach this?" "What would they do?" "What processes would they use?" (Stambaugh, 2018).

Additionally, we encourage educators developing lessons to seek out experts and ask about their thinking habits. This is exactly what Stambaugh and Mofield (2021) did when designing curricula and models that support talent development. After researching and conversing with experts in a variety of content domains, the authors created and vetted models to support how experts think. Figures 2.1, 2.2, and 2.3 are examples of a framework for thinking through literary works, science phenomena, and social studies problems, respectively. These frameworks support the processes of thinking like an expert in the particular domain they represent. They all involve a similar process because regardless of the content area, all experts consulted agreed that the items listed individually in each framework are not to be considered as separate or isolated factors. This idea that Stambaugh and Mofield (2021) learned from their conversations with experts supports research showing that experts automatically notice patterns and relationships (Bransford et al., 2000). Within the framework, all components are interrelated and influence the interpretation of a text, event, or phenomenon, depending on the content area. Therefore, the big idea that Stambaugh and Mofield (2021) worked to capture in all of their thinking models is that great thinkers in their respective field do not think about different components of what they are studying in isolation (the text, phenomena, or event); they think about how these components interact. The following are examples that specifically explain how the specific models are taught with a focus on the interactions within each wheel.

The Literary Analysis Wheel. The Literary Analysis Wheel (see Figure 2.1) is divided into sections that show the basic information that students in upper elementary, middle, and high school need to know to analyze text. A wheel for primary students is also available, following the same ideas. When teaching the wheel, students are first taught to identify individual elements (the individual sections in the wheel), such as the setting, conflict, specific literary

Figure 2.1
Literary Analysis Wheel

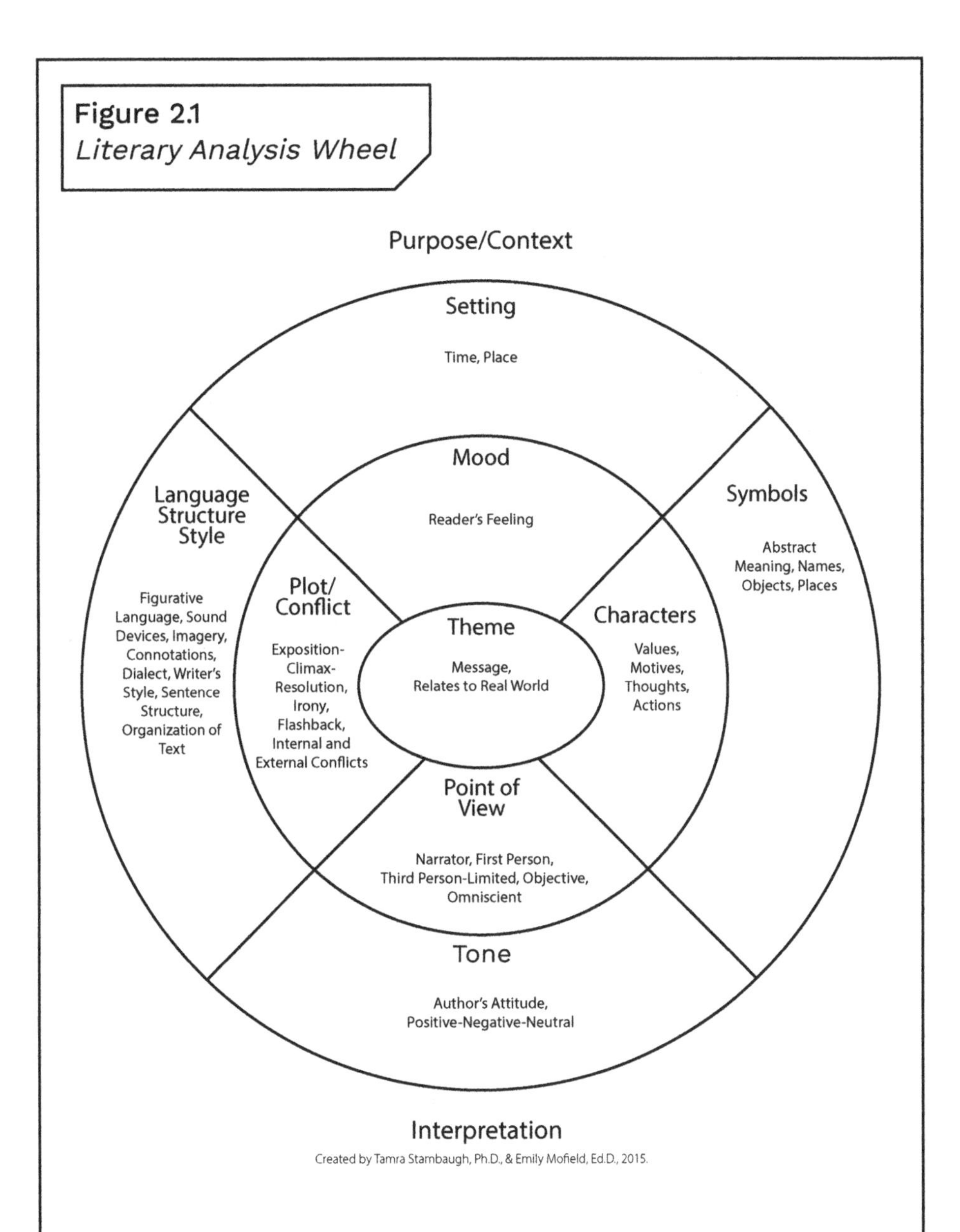

Note. From *Encounters With Archetypes: Integrated ELA Lessons for Gifted and Advanced Learners in Grades 4–5* (p. 233), by T. Stambaugh, E. Mofield, E. Fecht, and K. Knauss, 2019, Prufrock Press. Copyright 2019 by Prufrock Press. Reprinted with permission.

Figure 2.2
Science Analysis Wheel

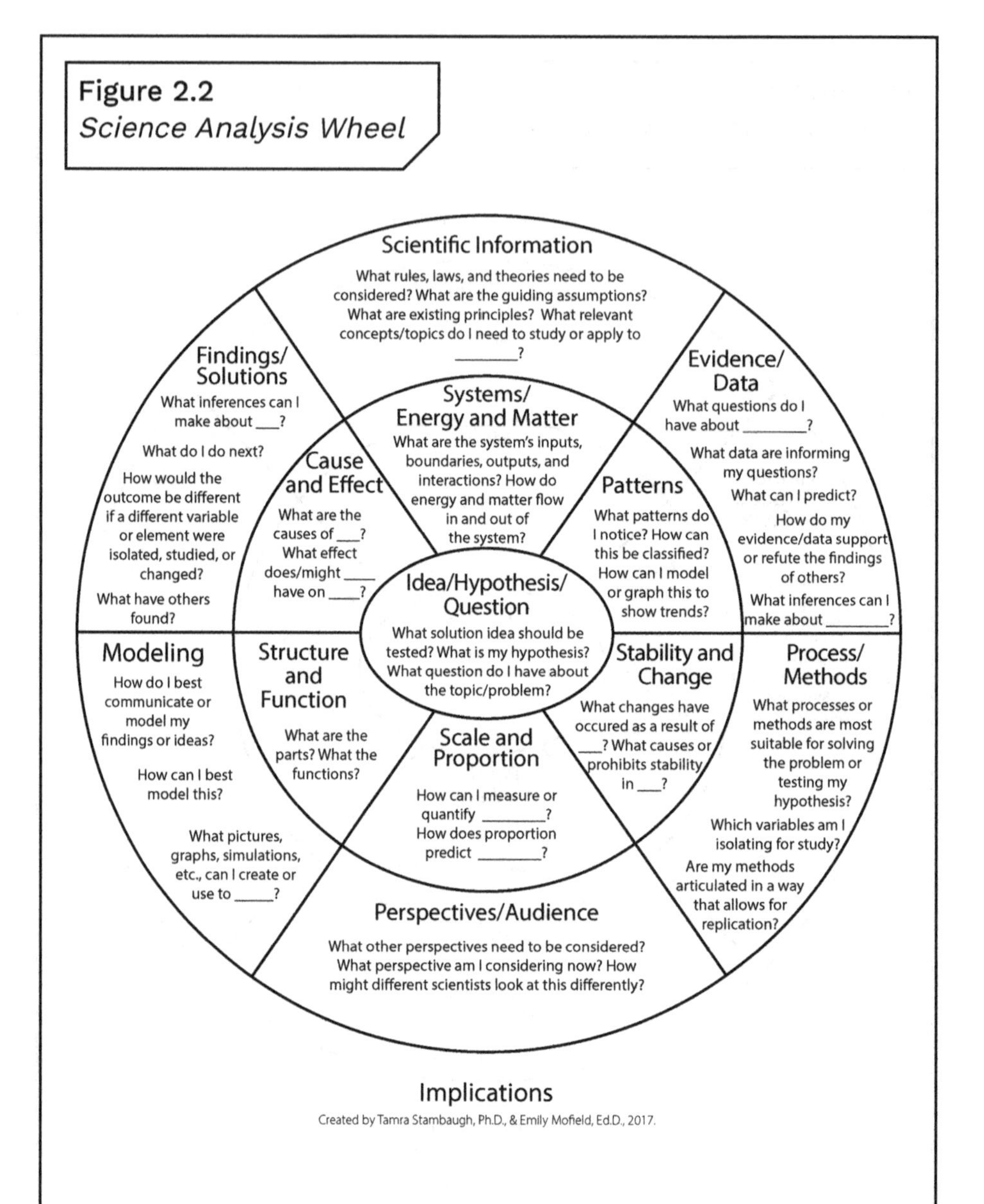

Note. From *Interactions in Ecology and Literature: Integrated Science and ELA Lessons for Gifted and Advanced Learners in Grades 2–3* (p. 233), by T. Stambaugh, E. Fecht, and E. Mofield, 2018, Prufrock Press.

Figure 2.3
Social Studies Connections Wheel

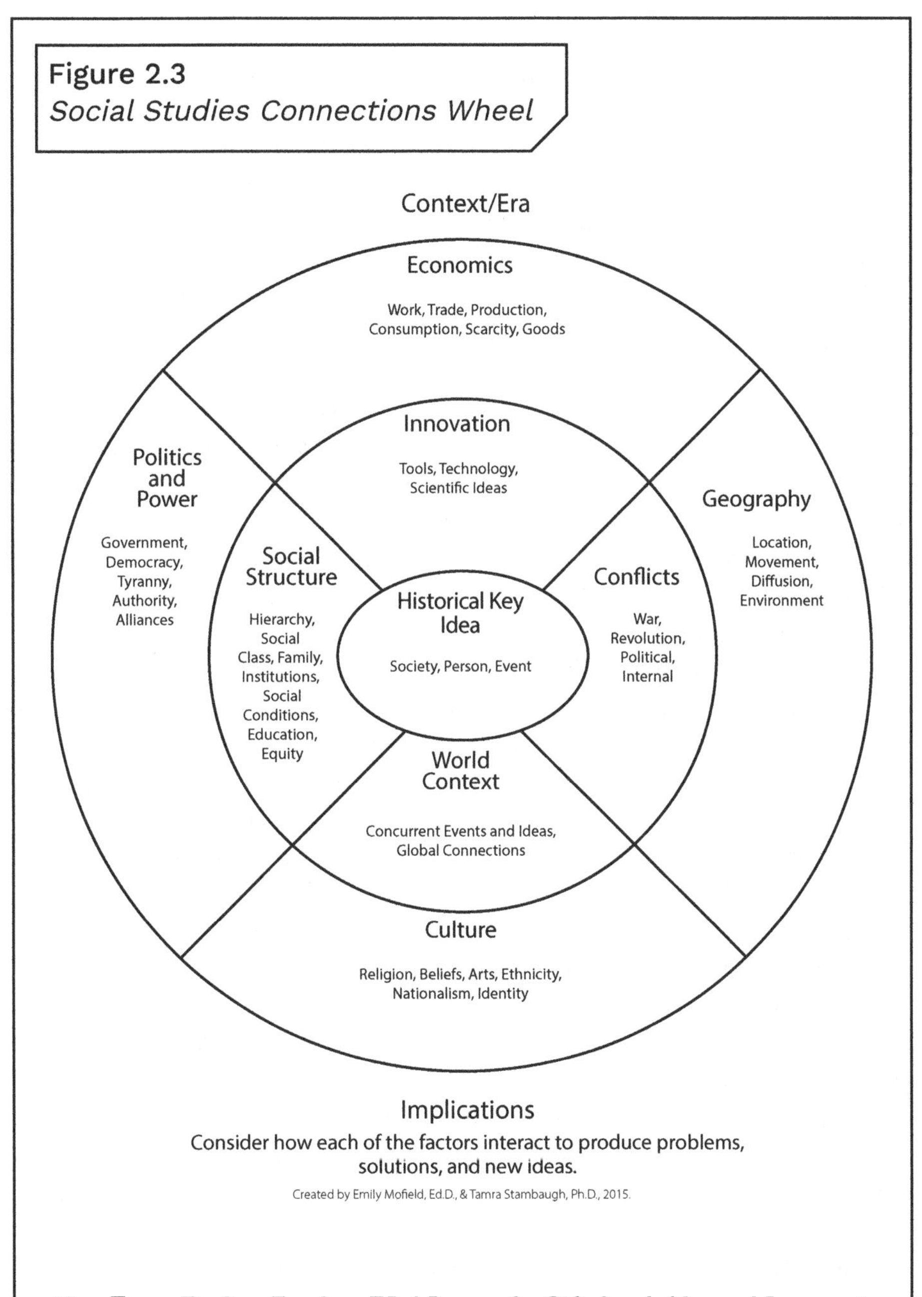

Note. From *Finding Freedom: ELA Lessons for Gifted and Advanced Learners in Grades 6–8* (p. 201), by E. Mofield and T. Stambaugh, 2016, Prufrock Press. Copyright 2016 by Prufrock Press. Reprinted with permission.

techniques (e.g., simile, metaphor, personification), mood, and tone. However, this is not the end goal. Remember, from the principles of teaching through a talent development lens, the end goal is expertise and creative production or output of that expertise. Experts do not just think through literary elements in isolation when they analyze a text. Instead, experts examine how the interactions or development of multiple factors influence each other and lead toward an interpretation or solution. Because experts automatically synthesize information and view relationships among multiple techniques in ways that create meaning, teachers using the wheel work toward developing this process in students. Thus, teachers' model for students how to examine relationships among the different sections of the wheel by combining two or three categories on the wheel and discussing how they interact. For example, the teacher can ask students about Mood + Theme (e.g., "How does the mood of the story impact the theme?"), about Techniques + Conflict/Problem (e.g., "How does the author use simile and metaphor to develop the problem?"), or about Theme + Symbols + Tone + Techniques (e.g., "How is the theme of identity shown through the use of symbolism, imagery, and tone?").

The Science Analysis Wheel. In science, students need to understand how scientists approach a problem or new idea, solve problems, or investigate and test new ideas. Scientists read and gather scientific information. They examine evidence or data. They consider multiple perspectives. They communicate their findings. They look for patterns, consider how their findings impact other systems, or consider how their new ideas or hypotheses may allow for stability or change. Similar to the Literature Analysis Wheel (Figure 2.1), Figure 2.2 shows how a curriculum focused on developing expertise supports expert thinking in science. Scientists do not look at a problem in isolation. When students have an idea or hypothesis (e.g., "Should humans intervene to cull overpopulated animal populations?"), they may create a model of population growth over time (Modeling + Stability and Change) or discuss how culling a population impacts the larger ecosystem and subsystems over time (Methods + Systems + Stability and Change). They may also research what has worked or not worked in the past and how the context of where the problem is focused might impact their solution (Scientific Information + Perspectives).

The Social Studies Analysis Wheel. In social studies (see Figure 2.3), when studying a person or event, the influences of geography, culture, world context, social structure, and economics, for example, all need to be considered as interrelated factors to better understand why the event took place, decisions that were made at the time, or how someone's societal impact was influenced by other factors.

The information concerning content-area wheels is only one example of many that can assist teachers in helping students think like experts. Other models such as the Literature Web from the Center for Gifted Education at William & Mary, the problem-based learning units designed by Shelagh Gallagher, and work by Kathy Gavin and colleagues on Mentoring Mathematical Minds (M^3) also support developing experts by encouraging students to apply content-specific models to their work.

Developing Expertise Through Concepts, Generalizations, Theories, and Laws

Several of the principles outlined earlier touched on the idea that experts make generalizations about a field, set of data, or relationships within content. Generalizations are made by experts because experts are able to think about their field conceptually and connect big ideas together. Generalizations are typically related to overarching concepts; however, the definition of what determines a concept varies. There are discipline-specific concepts (e.g., laws, theories, rules) that have content-specific principles (e.g., Newton's laws), but there are also interdisciplinary concepts (e.g., systems, patterns, change) that have more global generalizations (e.g., change can be positive or negative). An important thing to remember when thinking about developing curriculum that supports conceptual thinking is that both discipline-specific concepts and interdisciplinary concepts are important and can be used to organize and make sense of content.

Content that is focused on a more interdisciplinary concept can be connected to generalizations associated with the concept. If organizing a unit around a more interdisciplinary concept like systems, students would need to understand important generalizations, such as (a) systems are made of subsystems, (b) systems interact, and (c) when elements of a system change, the inputs and outputs change. Focusing on the generalizations for systems across disciplines in your teaching might mean discussing how these generalizations are true in the content students are learning. For example, you might focus on the systems generalization that "when one element of a system changes, the inputs and outputs change" as students discuss how this is true for events during World War II, when balancing a math equation, when conducting a chemical bond experiment, or when analyzing a character's reactions in a story. It is important to mention that defending or creating generalizations by organizing facts requires higher level thinking, especially as compared to linking an idea or fact to a concept without a generalization (Taba, 1967). Instead of universal generalizations, domain-specific concepts (theories, principles, and laws) may also be used. Students can link ideas to scientific principles such as Newton's laws, design and justify formulas or properties in math, or examine literature or history through a specific theoretical lens, concept, or perspective. Ultimately, helping students develop conceptual understandings by seeing key principles, linking content to big concepts and generalizations, and recognizing the application of theories in a discipline are all essential in a curriculum that promotes talent development.

You may have already had experience with conceptual teaching. The Next Generation Science Standards (NGSS Lead States, 2013) recognize the importance of cross-cutting concepts and list several concepts for students to know (as listed on the inner circle of the wheel in Figure 2.2). Similarly, the National Council for Social Studies (NCSS, 2013) organizes its concepts around 10 different themes, such as culture, continuity and change, power, authority, and governance, and emphasizes the importance of interactions among those themes and concepts. Concepts and generalizations, such as systems, cause and effect, change, interactions, and individuality versus conformity, are found in published curriculum units from the Center for Gifted Education at William & Mary and Vanderbilt Programs for Talented Youth. A simple web search for universal themes and generalizations results in lists of concepts and generalizations that are widely agreed upon and widely used.

When thinking about teaching conceptually it is important to acknowledge that experts also understand that multiple concepts may be at play and need to be considered when evaluating a situation. You will need to help students understand this as well. For example, if you were applying the systems idea to ecosystems in science, then you might have students articulate how living and nonliving things interact within an ecosystem and discuss how when one food source changes, the inputs and outputs of the entire ecosystem change. Similarly, in social studies students might examine interactions within political or government systems. Because it is misleading to convey to students that only one concept or generalization applies, other concepts may be examined in relation to previous concepts. For example, within a study of systems students may also examine how systems are affected by power structures or changes over time (two different concepts).

Developing Expertise Through Products of an Expert

Products of experts are expected in a talent development model. Therefore, using such an approach requires teachers to create opportunities for students to be involved in creating authentic products. These products are tied directly to the content and concepts of the field and include specific criteria that are accepted within the field. As previously discussed, in a talent development model, the products students develop focus on authentic issues, problems, and creations that are typical in a given field.

You may wonder how to make sure that your authentic projects are designed in a way that demands students apply the knowledge of the field. This is where specific criteria come into play. Specific criteria are necessary—even for creative production. Criteria also encourage students to dig deeper into a subject area and add more complex relationships or concepts. Criteria should always focus on more than just mechanics (i.e., neatness, spelling). Criteria in a talent development framework support and measure content knowledge and communication, processes, and the synthesis of content learned into key concepts, generalizations, ideas, and solutions. Students are expected to synthesize information, provide evidence, articulate their ideas, or embed multiple concepts into a new theme or idea.

Designing authentic tasks that are challenging and have measurable, specific criteria might be difficult for teachers who are just learning to develop such tasks. One simple way to think about crafting appropriate task demands that have built-in criteria within the product requirement is by using two words—"that" and "and" (Stambaugh, 2013). Using these words helps teachers add parameters to tasks. Having parameters can increase the depth and complexity of a task and encourage more critical thinking related to application of content. The following are examples of how "that" and "and" are used in task development:

- Ask students to create a multimedia presentation about what they have learned about ecosystems, by designing a model *that* shows how living and nonliving things within an ecosystem interact *and how those interactions* bring about change.
- Ask students to create an editorial *that* discusses how the use of symbolism, tone, and literary techniques interact *and* influence the theme of power.
- Study a famous person *that* contributed to your state *and show how the interaction* of geography, world context, and social structure (or

three other areas on the social studies wheel) impacted their life and influence.

These examples illustrate the power of "that" and "and" in supporting the application of content, advanced processes, and concepts into authentic products that still allow for creativity but ultimately encourage deeper thinking.

"That" and "and" is one easy way to add criteria. Teachers can also create their own list of criteria as long as the criteria are considered to be higher level like those that are expected of experts. For example, a set of criteria for writing a narrative story should include more than grammar and page length. Although these are important criteria for budding writers to include, they do not capture structure, character development, or engaging and believable interactions among the character, conflict, plot and setting. Similarly, criteria designed to guide a presentation for a study of a famous person would include more than the logistics, such as when a person was born, when they died, and what they contributed. Instead criteria would include examples of how multiple factors interacted to influence the person's contributions based on the specific time period. In this way students are able to practice thinking like a historian. Of course, quality presentations are also important, and there are visual effects, appropriate grammar, and engagement, but these are separate from the content-specific criteria of the discipline. The point here is that there are content-specific criteria and logistic criteria that work in tandem. Experts create products that are high quality and content rich. Both need to be required.

Embedding Psychosocial Skills

As discussed in the principles section of this chapter, psychosocial skills can and should be taught to support talent development. These skills are intentionally and explicitly addressed as parts of a comprehensive curriculum approach. Curriculum developed through a talent development lens will include social-emotional components where students can connect what they are learning to themselves or can explore the biographies of well-known individuals in a field as they learn about certain individuals' experiences, including failures. Programs for Talented Youth curriculum (see Stambaugh et al., 2018; Stambaugh & Mofield, 2018) include opportunities for psychosocial skill development because social-emotional skills are embedded in lessons. For example, in *Interactions in Ecology and Literature* (Stambaugh et al., 2018), a unit designed for learners in second and third grade, students explore the question: How does a person's interactions with their life experiences impact the individual's future? Students are then asked to use animated films as well as the biographies of successful people like J. K. Rowling, Michael Jordan, and Walt Disney to explore how individuals interact with their own life experiences, especially failure. Students are also asked to explore the ways in which interactions impact these successful individuals' futures. In *Encounters With Archetypes* (Stambaugh et al., 2019), students explore questions such as "Do our experiences shape us, or do we shape our experiences?" and "How do encounters with archetypes in real life and fiction allow for a deeper understanding of ourselves and of our world?" Several short stories and clips are used as a launching point for discussion of these questions. The important thing to keep in mind when teaching psychosocial skills is that teaching these skills should not be void of content or context. If you are teaching engineering, talk about perseverance by studying famous engineers who have biographies that include failures. If you are talking about mindset, read a short story that relates to the unit you are teaching and allows for discussion about how the character's mindset impacted their success. Students need opportunities to recognize psychosocial factors at work and to discuss the impact of these factors on individuals' success and apply this information to their own lives. The Affective Jacob's Ladder Reading Comprehension Program (Stambaugh & VanTassel-Baska, 2018, 2020; VanTassel-Baska & Stambaugh, 2018, 2020) also focuses on affective needs of gifted students through the use of theoretical frameworks and scaffolds for discussing resiliency, motivation, achievement, stress management, and other psychosocial factors through the common curricula sources and popular media, biography, poetry, and fiction. Other works, such as Mofield and Parker Peters's (2018) *Teaching Tenacity, Resilience, and a Drive for Excellence*, may also be helpful in the development of psychosocial skills if you are looking for separate skill-development lessons.

Conclusion

When you teach through a talent development lens, you are asking yourself to not just see your students' current talents but to explore what could be their talents. To successfully explore your students' perceived and potential talents, it is important to consider: (a) what is taught, (b) how the material is organized, (c) what students are ready to learn, and (d) what students already know at a given point in time. Teaching through a talent development lens should involve having students apply models and processes that experts use to solve problems. Students should be introduced to content, concepts, and issues in a field of study, be taught the thinking habits of experts, and be asked to create authentic products. Ultimately this approach will promote engagement and expertise. This approach also allows educators to see their students' strengths and talents more easily, which, in turn, sets students up for future success in a given field of interest. Taken all together, teaching through a talent development lens provides a foundation for future interests, a cultivation of strengths, and opportunities for students to think and create in a way that encourages expertise and creative production. Designing lessons through a talent development lens is a philosophy and compilation of interwoven components that work together.

As a teacher, you hold the power in helping students recognize their skill set, determine their interest, and hone their craft so they are building toward being an expert in whatever field they choose. Who knows, you may have the next Nobel Prize winner, *New York Times* best-selling author, or Pulitzer Prize recipient. You may have a future scientist who will develop a new cure, a mathematician who will solve a proof, a doctor or nurse who will save lives, or a teacher with a talent for inspiring students. We hope you are excited about the possibility of helping students find their passion and discover their strengths, and we also hope that you now have more tools in your always growing toolbox to develop your students' talents.

End-of-Chapter Discussion/ Reflection Questions

1. What does it mean to "think about teaching using a talent development lens"? What are the key principles guiding teaching using a talent development lens?
2. How can curriculum serve as a catalyst for the development of student talent? Cite specific examples.
3. Discuss the connection between the development of expertise and talent development.
4. Review Passow's (1982) "Would, Could, Should" test described in this chapter. What are important considerations in using the "Would, Could, Should" test in the development of expertise and creative production?
5. Which of the examples of a talent development curriculum would you start with in your classroom, and why? Provide an outline of how you would get started.

References

Cawelti, G. (2006). The side effects of NCLB. *Educational Leadership, 64*(3), 64–68.

Csikszentmihalyi, M., Rathunde, K., & Whalen, S. (1993). *Talented teenagers: The roots of success and failure*. Cambridge University Press.

Dai, D. Y., & Chen, F. (2013). Three paradigms of gifted education: In search of conceptual clarity in research and practice. *Gifted Child Quarterly, 57*(3), 151–168. https://doi.org/10.1177/0016986213490020

Duckworth, A. (2016). *Grit: The power of passion and perseverance*. Scribner.

Horn, C. V. (2015). Young Scholars: A talent development model for finding and nurturing potential in underserved populations. *Gifted Child Today, 38*(1), 19–31. https://doi.org/10.1177/1076217514556532

Kettler, T. (2014). Critical thinking skills among elementary school students: Comparing identified and general education student performance. *Gifted Child Quarterly, 58*(2), 127–136. https://doi.org/10.1177/0016986214522508

Milner, H. R., IV. (2014). Scripted and narrowed curriculum reform in urban schools. *Urban Education, 49*(7), 743–749. https://doi.org/10.1177/0042085914549685

Mofield, E., & Parker Peters, M. (2018). *Teaching tenacity, resilience, and a drive for excellence: Lessons for social-emotional learning for grades 4–8*. Prufrock Press.

Mofield, E., & Stambaugh, T. (2016). *Finding freedom: ELA lessons for gifted and advanced learners in grades 6–8*. Prufrock Press.

National Council for the Social Studies. (2013). *College, Career, and Civic Life (C3) Framework for Social Studies State Standards: Guidance for enhancing the rigor of K–12 civics, economics, geography, and history*. https://www.socialstudies.org/c3

NGSS Lead States. (2013). *Next generation science standards: For states, by states*. The National Academies Press.

Passow, A. H. (1982). Differentiated curricula for the gifted/talented: A point of view. In S. Kaplan, A. H. Passow, P. H. Phenix, S. Reis, J. S. Renzulli, I. Sato, L. Smith, E. P. Torrance, & V. S. Ward, *Curricula for the gifted: Selected proceedings of the First National Conference on Curriculum for the Gifted and Talented* (pp. 4–20). Ventura County Superintendent of Schools Office.

Renzulli, J. S. (1977). *The enrichment triad model: A guide for developing defensible programs for the gifted and talented*. Creative Learning Press.

Rogers, K. B. (2007). Lessons learned about educating the gifted and talented: A synthesis of the research on educational practice. *Gifted Child Quarterly, 51*(4), 382–396. https://doi.org/10.1177/0016986207306324

Stambaugh, T. (2007). *The effects of the Jacob's Ladder Reading Comprehension Program on third, fourth, and fifth graders' reading comprehension and critical thinking in rural, Title I schools* [Unpublished doctoral dissertation]. William & Mary.

Stambaugh, T. (2012, November). *Patterns of curriculum effectiveness for students from low income backgrounds* [Paper presentation]. National Association for Gifted Children Annual Conference, Denver, CO, United States.

Stambaugh, T. (2013, February). *Gifted students and the Common Core: Implications for practice* [Keynote address]. Vanderbilt Gifted Education Institute, Programs for Talented Youth, Nashville, TN, United States.

Stambaugh, T. (2018). Curriculum and instruction within a talent development framework. In P. Olszewski-Kubilius, R. F. Subotnik, & F. C. Worrell (Eds.), *Talent development as a framework for gifted education: Implications for best practices and applications in schools* (pp. 95–128). Prufrock Press.

Stambaugh, T. (2020a). A curriculum design model for students from low-income households. In T. Stambaugh & P. Olszewski-Kubilius (Eds.), *Unlocking potential: Identifying and serving gifted students from low-income households* (pp. 109–125). Prufrock Press.

Stambaugh, T. (2020b). Designing curriculum for gifted learners. In J. H. Robins, J. L. Jolly, F. A. Karnes, & S. M. Bean (Eds.), *Methods and materials for teaching the gifted* (5th ed., pp. 147–172). Prufrock Press.

Stambaugh, T., Fecht, E., & Mofield, E. (2018). *Interactions in ecology and literature: Integrated science and ELA lessons for gifted and advanced learners in grades 2–3*. Prufrock Press.

Stambaugh, T., & Mofield, E. (2018). *Space, structure, and story: Integrated science and ELA lessons for gifted and advanced learners in grades 4–6*. Prufrock Press.

Stambaugh, T., & Mofield, E. (2021). *A teacher's guide to curriculum design for gifted and advanced learners: Advanced content models for differentiating curriculum* [Manuscript in preparation]. Prufrock Press.

Stambaugh, T., Mofield, E., Fecht, E., & Knauss, K. (2019). *Encounters with archetypes: Integrated ELA lessons for gifted and advanced learners in grades 4–5*. Prufrock Press.

Stambaugh, T., & VanTassel-Baska, J. (2018). *Affective Jacob's Ladder Reading Comprehension Program: Grades 6–8*. Prufrock Press.

Stambaugh, T., & VanTassel-Baska, J. (2020). *Affective Jacob's Ladder Reading Comprehension Program: Grade 2*. Prufrock Press.

Subotnik, R. F., Olszewski-Kubilius, P., & Worrell, F. C. (2011). Rethinking giftedness and gifted education: A proposed direction forward based on psychological science. *Psychological Science in the Public Interest, 12*(1), 3–54. https://doi.org/10.1177/1529100611418056

Taba, H. (1967). *Teachers' handbook for elementary social studies*. Addison-Wesley.

Treffinger, D. J., & Selby, E. C. (2009). Levels of service: A contemporary approach to programming for talent development. In J. S. Renzulli, E. J. Gubbins, K. S. McMillen, R. D. Eckert, & C. A. Little (Eds.), *Systems and models for developing programs for the gifted and talented* (2nd ed., pp. 629–654). Prufrock Press.

VanTassel-Baska, J., & Stambaugh, T. (2018). *Affective Jacob's Ladder Reading Comprehension Program: Grades 4–5*. Prufrock Press.

VanTassel-Baska, J., & Stambaugh, T. (2020). *Affective Jacob's Ladder Reading Comprehension Program: Grade* 3. Prufrock Press.

3

One Path to Talent Development

An Instructional Model for Talent Development

Julie Dingle Swanson

How can guiding principles of talent development be integrated into daily practice in your school? This chapter describes an instructional model gleaned from a research project called Talent Development Academies (TDA; Swanson et al., 2019, 2020). The chapter explains the instructional model's foundations and components. Because research and demonstration projects funded by the Jacob K. Javits Gifted and Talented Education Program offer evidence-based practices and curricula, the TDA project built on what was learned from previous Javits work (e.g., Bracken et al., 2007; Coleman et al., 2007; Gavin et al., 2008, 2009; Kim et al., 2012). Drawn from the work done through TDA, the instructional model offers guidance for schools, teachers, and administrators committed to implementation of a talent development philosophy. Thus, the model shows how to more effectively work with culturally, linguistically, and ethnically diverse (CLED) learners, including how to tap and grow their potential through a talent focus.

Beginning with my professional journey and the start of the TDA project, this chapter describes the lessons learned from TDA as one path to begin talent development-focused teaching in your school or district. This chapter explores how to build your talent development school using evidence-based practices effective with underserved students. Areas of concentration for teacher learning and how those areas connect to Subotnik et al.'s (2011) Talent Development Megamodel follow. Elements of the instructional model and how those elements relate to talent development and talent spotting are then explicated. Additional details of the model are explored in subsequent chapters.

My Professional Journey

The journey toward the TDA project began in the late 1980s when I was working in a rural part of my school district with primarily students from low-income households. This district had one high school, one middle school, and four elementary schools. All of the schools were designated as Title I schools, meaning that students attending came from underresourced households. The students served were about 98% African American, with a few White and Latino students. In the entire district of several hundred students, only *one* student was identified as gifted and talented.

This "in-your-face" underrepresentation in gifted programs made it possible for the district's superintendent to garner special funding for an alternative program for the district's brightest elementary students. I was hired to work with the selected students at each of the four elementary schools in what now would be called a talent development program. What quickly became evident in my work with these young students was that the schools they attended were underresourced, too. The teachers in these elementary schools focused on remedial and skills-based work, improving the basic skills test scores, and what the students did *not* have. Curriculum and materials were skill-and-drill focused. As a result, the students never got to the rich and interesting study often experienced by many in schools serving middle- and upper-income students. The bright and capable students I worked with were starving for intellectual stimulation and engagement with interesting and authentic learning. Their exposure to school smarts was neither deep nor broad, but their curiosity, interests and passions, leadership abilities, knowledge of the natural world, and many more strengths were clear.

As educators, many of us have had such an experience where you see so much potential in young people that is gradually eroding because of a lack of an authentic, interesting learning environment that values, supports, and nurtures what students *do* have. My experience allowed me to see and understand inequity in a way that I had not previously understood. For example, Herman was a bright student who had been nominated for gifted and talented program screening more than once, but he never met the threshold for eligibility. Closer investigation revealed ongoing health issues that contributed to a high rate of absence. Herman was chronically absent because he was often unwell. This situation created gaps in his learning that had to be addressed in creative ways and no doubt contributed to the difficulty of him being identified as gifted.

Fast-forwarding to later years, I was in a university position where I was able to collaborate with the gifted and talented coordinator of a large school district. Together we developed a gifted and talented education (GTE) graduate certificate program for teachers from Title I schools. This effort was based on the notion that talent spotting and development go hand in hand. The GTE program's goal was to challenge the widely held beliefs of many White teachers from middle-class backgrounds. Teachers learned how giftedness and talent manifests differently in CLED learners and how teachers' own beliefs and expectations posed barriers for students. Designed to teach educators not only how to see the diversity in giftedness but also how to scaffold learning and create interesting and rigorous learning to tap into students' interests and passions, the GTE program enabled participating teachers insight into ways to shift their perceptions and beliefs. To illustrate, teachers took a special topics course called "Promising Learners From Poverty," drawing upon the most current studies of what was known about underrepresentation. Completing an in-depth case study on a CLED student was eye-opening for many. Teachers created a school-based project to grow their students' potential. Each had to present and persuade their building leadership to implement their ideas.

These and other professional experiences helped me to understand that breaking through assumptions and beliefs about who has high ability and who does not takes a combination of (1) gaining the knowledge and skills about potential that exists in students and how to tap that potential so that it grows, (2) having a willingness to see students' strengths as the starting point for learning, and (3) being part of something bigger that extends beyond your classroom, that is, being part of a faculty that believes in the notion of talent development.

The Talent Development Academies Project

Out of my own professional journey and in collaboration with like-minded professional colleagues, a plan for talent development to nurture and grow students' potential was born. Schools that were interested in deepening understanding of how to raise the bar for all of their students, and whose teachers were committed to engaging in professional learning about how to scaffold and challenge their students' learning, were the schools that joined TDA in the effort to become talent development academies. Resources were provided to grow teacher talent development and to teach the faculty members how to raise the interest and rigor in their teaching, tap into the motivation and engagement of learners, and in so doing, become talent spotters of the potential talents in their students. Over time, powerful tools and strategies for looking for and growing emergent talent were added to the TDA teachers' instructional toolbox.

The Talent Development Instructional Model

In this guidebook, talent development is defined as growing students' strengths, interests, and passions into knowledge, skills, and abilities. The goal of the talent development process is exceptional performance and, ultimately, high accomplishment. As Horn (2018) noted, "A talent development model acknowledges that without learning experiences that elicit interests and potential, the talent of many students goes unrecognized and unrealized" (p. 129). Teaching with a talent development philosophy means identifying students' passions, interests, and potential to excel, and providing learning experiences that grow that potential into performance.

The Talent Development Megamodel (Subotnik et al., 2011, 2019) is the umbrella over the Talent Development Instructional Model (TDIM), a model of practice. The megamodel, described in depth in Chapter 1, has the following components: (1) abilities are domain-specific and malleable, (2) talent domains have differing trajectories for development, (3) opportunities to develop talent are essential and must be taken, (4) mental and social skills are important in talent development, and (5) thinking and planning over the long term is essential to reach high performance (Subotnik et al., 2011). The TDIM allows educators to put talent development into practice and enables a systematic plan based on a school's individual profile to be developed and implemented.

Figure 3.1 illustrates the Talent Development Instructional Model. Foundational to the model are four essential propositions schools need to become talent development focused: (1) schoolwide buy-in, (2) resources to support and sustain the effort, (3) leadership to guide the work, and (4) compatible innovations that complement and enhance the talent development

Figure 3.1
Talent Development Instructional Model: A Model for Practice

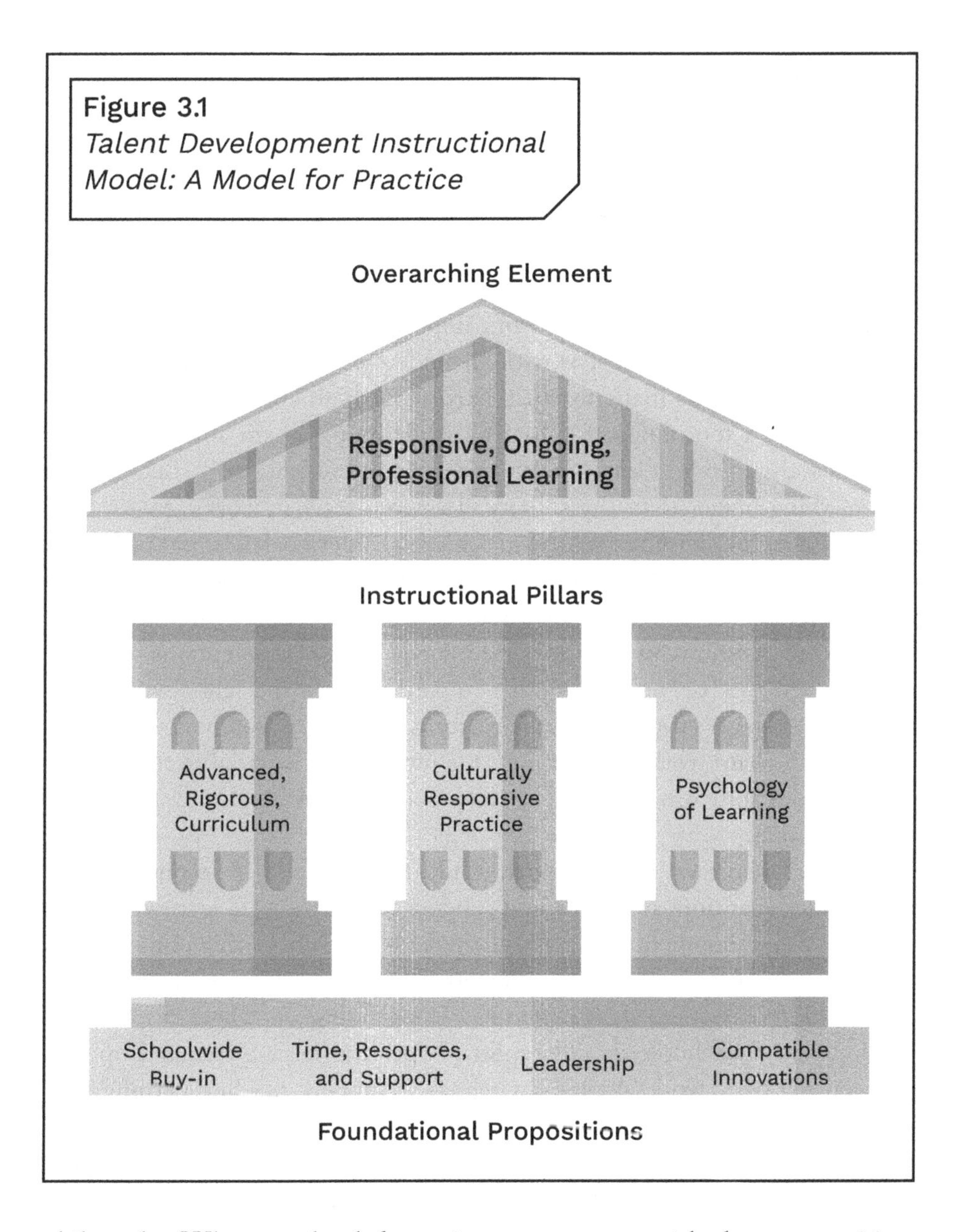

philosophy. When a school determines congruency with these propositions that support a talent development philosophy, professional learning can begin. In the TDIM, professional learning is responsive and ongoing, and builds understanding of advanced and rigorous curriculum designed to engage and enrich learners in relevant, authentic ways, is comprised of deepening culturally responsive teaching, and employs principles of the psychology of learning.

Foundational Propositions

The following propositions are foundational to the TDIM. Examples from the TDA project (Swanson et al., 2019) illustrate how each proposition was reflected in that work. The TDA examples help teachers, administrators, and schools think about how the propositions might be reflected in your unique setting.

Schoolwide Buy-In. First is the importance of schoolwide buy-in to using a talent development lens with all students. Buy-in is essential because of the implicit beliefs many teachers have about high ability and who has it. Committing to the philosophy that all students really are able means that teachers and staff take a leap of faith to engage in the hard work. Being a part of something bigger than the solitary classroom teacher, working with like-minded colleagues within a school to achieve a larger goal, is a part of how to build buy-in. In the TDA project (Swanson et al., 2019), schools interested in talent development met together, discussed the work entailed in becoming a TDA, asked questions, raised issues, examined their own perceptions, and ultimately voted "yes" or "no" on whether to participate in the schoolwide effort. Up to 75% buy-in ensured that the majority of faculty members were committed to the hard work and learning. The buy-in was essential to the school's philosophical shift toward talent development. Buy-in is a necessary part of any innovation.

Time, Resources, and Support. Linked to buy-in is a second foundational belief: that time, resources, and support are necessary in learning how to use a talent development lens with all students. A shift to this philosophical orientation happens over time as teachers learn more, see how their students respond differently, and gain confidence. Depending on where teachers are developmentally, schools should expect to spend at least a year and up to 3 years on the basic work. A plan for materials support, teacher learning supports, and time for teachers to practice, gain feedback on progress, and learn how to teach with talent in mind are key in the process. In the TDA project, instructional coaches supported teachers' learning in school and out of school. Demonstration of the value and importance of the work is evident (or not) in the resources provided. When schools buy in to this philosophical shift, if they do not plan for and garner resources in the form of funding and expertise, it is difficult to support the necessary professional learning for teachers. To illustrate, the TDA project brought grant funding to support professional learning, curriculum and student materials, and expertise to guide and grow teachers. TDA project teachers were provided with time to learn and practice. They received a stipend to attend intensive sessions during the summer months and then were provided release time during the school day to attend follow-up sessions to deepen and extend their learning. Materials in the form of specialized curriculum and classroom support materials were provided so that teachers had the rich and complex instructional resources needed to teach with talent in mind. Full implementation of TDA was planned over a 2-year period, with schools gradually becoming independent and talent focused. Resources are a necessary part of the work.

Leadership. Leaders, including the building administrator, teachers on the faculty, and administrators at the district level, are necessary to meet the challenges of learning to become a talent-focused school. Leadership enables progress toward the goal and steers needed resources for support. Shared and distributed leadership ensures that, if a principal leaves the school, when new teachers are hired, or if a superintendent change occurs (as all of these types of changes happen regularly in schools and districts), the effort is not derailed and stays on track. "Puddle jumper" teachers are defined as those risk-takers who jump in enthusiastically and test out new strategies with the expectation that they will learn from doing. In the TDA project, teachers who were high adopters led the way as puddle jumpers and showed their more skeptical, less enthusiastic colleagues that teaching for talent was doable. The puddle jumper teachers were doing practices and letting others see their work and the results with students. When tough decisions had to be made, district and building administrators lent authority to the work.

Compatible Innovations. Compatibility of other innovations with talent development strengthens the talent-focused school. Often, schools have multiple innovations underway, potentially creating fragmentation of effort and confusion among teachers. Choosing compatible and complementary innovations shows that the underlying philosophy driving school-based decisions is cohesive and congruent with the values and beliefs of those in the school. For example, in TDA, a school adopted an arts-based integrated curriculum. This approach was completely compatible with talent development, as exposure and enrichment allowed students to experience rich, interesting learning through the arts and, in some cases, discover their passions. Cohesiveness and compatibility of school innovations matter.

For schools interested in becoming talent development schools, examination of the foundational propositions—the degree of buy-in, the necessary resources to support the effort, leadership to guide the work, and compatibility of other innovations with talent development—is the first step in determining readiness. Once readiness is assessed and a determination is made to become a talent development-focused school, planning for teacher learning is next. Teachers must learn how to teach with talent development in mind, about instruction focused on talent spotting and development, and how to integrate these components into daily practice.

Overarching Element: Professional Learning

Professional learning that is responsive and ongoing, that builds teachers' understanding and ability to teach in ways to support and encourage talent development, is the element that arches over the TDIM model. Professional learning that is responsive and ongoing assumes that teachers start where they are. Learning is developmental, varied, and tiered. Specifically, professional learning is varied in both form and content, starts with whole group, moves on to small group, and then moves on to individual learning. Planning for teacher learning in responsive ways uses a feedback loop so that professional opportunities involve teachers in new and relevant learning. The content of professional learning includes three instructional pillars described next: advanced curriculum, culturally responsive teaching practices, and neuroscience and psychology of learning.

TDA Professional Learning: Learning the Instructional Pillars

In TDA, teachers were introduced to the big picture of talent development and the three instructional pillars in an intense multiday summer immersion conference. During the conference, teachers learned broadly about the concept of talent development. They were reintroduced to neuroscience concepts relevant to student motivation—persistence and grit—and how those concepts connected to emergent talent. They reviewed and discussed components of a culturally responsive classroom, beginning to explore ways in which their beliefs, expectations, and perceptions opened or blocked students' opportunity to learn. They learned about high-level, advanced curricula and instructional strategies. Specifically, teachers were introduced to and practiced the embedded instructional models within the William & Mary English language arts (ELA) and science (Project Clarion) units (e.g., Literature Web, concept development, Scientific Wheel of Reasoning), as well as the "talk moves" strategy found in the Mentoring Mathematical Minds (M^3) and Mentoring Young Mathematicians (M^2) math units developed at University of Connecticut.

Based on the whole- and small-group learning, teachers set instructional talent development-focused goals for the beginning of the school year based on (a) one of the academic content areas of ELA, science, or math; (b) culturally responsive teaching; and (c) application of how students learn.

The summer conference introduced the basic instructional pillars of the TDIM to teachers. Ongoing and sustained professional learning guided planning for growing teacher understanding and ability. Throughout the school year, TDA teachers participated in several planned half-day follow-up sessions with the whole group and with small groups. Starting with effective curriculum for underserved students (Stambaugh & Chandler, 2012), professional learning extended to deepening initial understanding of advanced, rigorous curriculum and strategies. Specific psychosocial strategies of how to teach students how to increase their grit and academic persistence were introduced (Gutshall, 2014). Teachers learned about TOPS, or Teacher Observation of Potential in Students (Coleman et al., 2010), and how to use TOPS in spotting student talent. Teachers explored observable behaviors in TOPS indicative of potential, including whether a student learns easily, shows advanced skills, displays curiosity and creativity, has strong interests, shows advanced reasoning and problem solving, displays spatial skills, shows motivation, shows social perceptiveness, and displays leadership (Coleman et al., 2010).

In the second half of the first year of learning, after teachers had been practicing, supported with instructional coaching and demonstration teaching in their classrooms, high-adopter teachers shared successes with curriculum and strategies in a breakout session format. As teachers gained proficiency in use of instructional strategies, more in-depth development included additional prescriptive training in the use of William & Mary ELA and Clarion units and M^3 and M^2 units. As a follow-up to teacher training in units, instructional coaches provided sustained, individualized sessions through individual meetings with teachers to coplan, demonstrate in individual teachers' classrooms, coach and observe with feedback.

TDIM and the Megamodel

The TDIM offers foundational propositions that schools can use to gauge readiness to become talent development focused. Further, the instructional pillars are described and exemplified. Connections of TDIM to the Talent Development Megamodel (Subotnik et al., 2011) are evident in the focus on revealing emergent talent, providing enrichment for all students, and seeing what is visible. This emergent talent focus in TDIM ties back to the issue of underdeveloped potential and how to grow and nurture existing potential, in particular with CLED learners. Horn (2018) stated:

> Enrichment should begin as early as possible. Early identification coupled with early intervention, in an enriched and engaging learning environment, fosters a growth mindset in students and teachers (Dweck, 2006). When this becomes the norm, teachers soon realize that it is not possible to know what students are capable of learning and achieving in specific domains unless they are exposed to an educational pedagogy that elicits and nurtures the development of talent. When young children actively participate in authentic learning tasks that require problem solving and a high level of thinking, their self-efficacy increases, and they are better prepared for challenging work as they progress in grade level. (p. 130)

With the focus on emergent talent, TDIM is recommended for use with early childhood and elementary schools. In a district adopting a talent development philosophy, long-term planning for talent development in middle and high schools should be part of a comprehensive approach.

TDIM, drawing on the Talent Development Megamodel, recognizes the malleability and domain specificity of talent, in that instruction using rich, challenging, and enriching curriculum in specific domains to find and grow emergent talent is a key instructional pillar. At a minimum, schools should tap into language arts, mathematics, and science. In the TDA project, early childhood and elementary teachers chose the language arts and literacy curriculum as their first choice, math as their second choice, and science third. In TDIM, opportunities to develop talent are essential and must be open to all learners.

This model advocates for schoolwide adoption and use with all learners, and this opportunity connects to the TDIM pillar of culturally responsive teaching. Teachers who know their students, see their strengths, and begin with what students can do are the most effective in spotting talent and encouraging it. The TDIM psychology of learning pillar connects with the Talent Development Megamodel principle that mental and social skills are important in talent development. The examples from the TDA project illustrate the TDIM. Part II of this book unpacks how the use of rich, challenging, and enriching curriculum looks in a talent-focused classroom. Part III of the book goes deeper into culturally responsive practice and what teachers can do to strengthen their practice with diversity in mind. Part IV explains how teachers learned about the psychology of learning as applied to talent development and offers examples of how teachers implemented that pillar of the TDIM in their classrooms.

Assessing school and district readiness for a talent development focus is guided by the TDIM foundational propositions. To review, the important propositions for assessing readiness include buy-in, planning for and garnering resources to support and sustain the work, ensuring the leadership is ready and responsive, and combining talent development with compatible innovations. Once these propositions are met, providing teachers with opportunities to grow instructional practices congruent with and necessary to their students' talent development follows.

Lessons to Build On

What has been learned from the application of TDIM in schools building a talent development philosophy? It is important to develop a broad base of support for the work in becoming a talent development school. Inclusion of gifted and regular education professionals from the school, district, and higher education community helps to ensure issues are tackled from multiple perspectives. Using multiple perspectives and including many voices in decision making strengthens the effort to transform schools into places where talent is recognized and developed.

Schools becoming talent focused should expect and be ready for change. Expect and plan for teacher and principal turnover. Planning means that schools have a process for bringing new teachers and principals up to speed on the TDIM. Be aware that results take time and know that everything takes longer than expected. For example, asking teachers to choose one content area to start with, to take on smaller tasks in their initial development, has been an effective way to build teacher confidence in learning and teaching with a talent development lens. It takes a consistently positive and encouraging attitude to get teachers to take what they see as a leap of faith. A focus on building relationships and identifying "puddle jumpers" and teacher leaders encourages trust and risk-taking and builds capacity from within.

Conclusion

Right now, the field often provides an approach to gifted education that is rooted in past conceptions of intelligence—you either have it or you don't. As educators, we now know from brain research how malleable intelligence is. We spend time on the psychological and social factors because we now know how important these factors are to learning and motivation. What if we thought of the development of giftedness into talent into high accomplishment or eminence as our mission? What if we sought out and searched for talent that was both easy and hard to spot? What if schools, districts, and teachers sought to provide pathways to grow talent? As you work to improve learning in your school and district, think about how to move your gifted and talented services toward a more inclusive and comprehensive approach, to one of spotting and developing talent. The world needs talent now as much or more than any other time in history.

End-of-Chapter Discussion/ Reflection Questions

1. In what ways has your professional *or* personal journey led you to a talent-focused approach to teaching?
2. Examine the foundational propositions of Talent Development Instructional Model (TDIM). If you were ranking these propositions from most important to least important, how would you rank them, and why?
3. How do each of the instructional pillars of TDIM relate to the Talent Development Megamodel?
4. Reflect on how you might move your gifted and talented services toward a more inclusive, comprehensive, and talent-focused approach. In what ways does TDIM guide your thinking about next steps in this process?

References

Bracken, B. A., VanTassel-Baska, J., Brown, E. F., & Feng, A. (2007). Project Athena: A tale of two studies. In J. VanTassel-Baska & T. Stambaugh (Eds.), *Overlooked gems: A national perspective on promising students of poverty* (pp. 63–67). National Association for Gifted Children.

Coleman, M. R., Coltrane, S. S., Harradine, C., & Timmons, L. A. (2007). Impact of poverty on promising learners, their teachers, and their schools. *Journal of Urban Education: Focus on Enrichment, 6*, 59–67.

Coleman, M. R., Shah-Coltrane, S., & Harrison, A. (2010). *U-STARS~PLUS: Teacher's observation of potential in students: Individual student form*. Council for Exceptional Children.

Dweck, C. S. (2006). *Mindset: The new psychology of success*. Ballantine Books.

Gavin, M. K., Casa, T. M., Adelson, J. L., Carroll, S. R., Sheffield, L. J., & Spinelli, A. M. (2008). Project M^3: Mentoring mathematical minds: A research-based curriculum for talented elementary students. *Journal of Advanced Academics, 18*(4), 566–585. https://doi.org/10.4219/jaa-2007-552

Gavin, M. K., Casa, T. M., Adelson, J. L., Carroll, S. R., & Sheffield, L. J. (2009). The impact of advanced curriculum on the achievement of mathematically promising elementary students. *Gifted Child Quarterly, 53*(3), 188–202. https://doi.org/10.1177/0016986209334964

Gutshall, C. A. (2014). Pre-service teachers' mindset beliefs about student ability. *Electronic Journal of Research in Educational Psychology, 12*(3), 785–802.

Horn, C. V. (2018). Serving low-income and underrepresented students in a talent development framework. In P. Olszewski-Kubilius, R. F. Subotnik, & F. C. Worrell (Eds.) *Talent development as a framework for gifted education: Implications for best practices and applications in schools* (pp. 129–152). Prufrock Press.

Kim, K. H., VanTassel-Baska, J., Bracken, B. A., Feng, A. X., Stambaugh, T., & Bland, L. (2012). Project Clarion: Three years of science instruction in Title I schools among K-third grade students. *Research in Science Education, 42,* 813–829. https://doi.org/10.1007/s11165-011-9218-5

Stambaugh, T., & Chandler, K. L. (2012). *Effective curriculum for underserved gifted students*. Prufrock Press.

Subotnik, R. F., Olszewski-Kubilius, P., & Worrell, F. C. (2011). Rethinking giftedness and gifted education: A proposed direction forward based on psychological science. *Psychological Science in the Public Interest, 12*(1), 3–54. https://doi.org/10.1177/1529100611418056

Subotnik, R. F., Olszewski-Kubilius, P., & Worrell, F. C. (2019). High performance: The central psychological mechanism for talent development. In R. F. Subotnik, P. Olszewski-Kubilius, & F. C. Worrell (Eds.), *The psychology of high performance: Developing human potential into domain-specific talent* (pp. 7–20). American Psychological Association.

Swanson, J. D., Brock, L., Van Sickle, M., Gutshall, C. A., Russell, L., & Anderson, L. (2020). A basis for talent development: The integrated curriculum model and evidence-based strategies. *Roeper Review, 42*(3), 165–178. https://doi.org/10.1080/02783193.2020.1765920

Swanson, J. D., Russell, L. W., & Anderson, L. (2019). A model for growing teacher talent scouts: Decreasing underrepresentation of gifted students. In S. R. Smith (Ed.), *Handbook of giftedness and talent development in the Asia-Pacific* (pp. 1–20). Springer. https://doi.org/10.1007/978-981-13-3021-6_55-1

Part II

Application of High-End, Research-Based Curriculum, Strategies, and Models With All Students

4

Talent Development in Language Arts

Samantha E. Blake

Many educators associate giftedness in reading with high scores on standardized tests or reading levels that indicate above-grade-level ability. However, there is much more to identifying and developing talent in language arts. When properly trained to integrate high-end strategies and models into reading and writing curriculum, educators will be able to see students' thinking throughout the reading and writing processes. Talent Development Academies (TDA; Swanson et al., 2020), a Javits grant recipient based in Charleston, SC, prepared teachers to implement the Integrated Curriculum Model (ICM; VanTassel-Baska, 2017) that included the use of high-end strategies and models within the language arts curriculum that would aid educators in developing talent through specific and targeted professional learning. This chapter explores the use of content-based, high-end strategies and models for talent spotting, the research behind the tactics, and implementation examples from four of these strategies and models within a fifth-grade classroom.

Why an Integrated Curriculum Model Approach?

As explained by VanTassel-Baska (2017), the ICM approach to curriculum development is comprised of three distinct, yet intermingled, dimensions: (1) advanced content knowledge that frames disciplines of study, (2) higher order thinking and processes, and (3) learning experiences centered "around major issues, themes, and ideas that define both real-world applications and theoretical modeling within and across areas of study" (pp. 21–22). Think of these three dimensions as physically intersecting or overlapping. Practically speaking, this means that elements of all three dimensions must be accounted for during instructional planning when implementing a true integrated curriculum. When implemented correctly, such an approach allows educators to develop units of study that integrate multiple subject areas while developing specific skills and content knowledge more deeply. Curriculum and instruction delivered in this integrated approach allows for a better transfer of learning and an increase in long-term learning (National Research Council, 2000).

Given the wide range of student ability levels in classrooms, the ICM becomes a relevant approach to maintaining a high level of rigor within the curriculum. The thinking models used within the ICM allow for scaffolding and the development of talent among students of all ability levels. Four of these thinking models are introduced in the subsequent sections of this chapter: the Vocabulary Web, a reasoning model, a concept development model, and the Literature Web. Each thinking model is explained, and classroom examples are included that illustrate its use within a specific language arts context, as well as within an integrated unit of study.

Language Arts Strategies

Using a Vocabulary Web to Deepen Understanding

According to Beck et al.'s (2013) *Bringing Words to Life*, students learn a word and retain it in their own repertoire only after frequent, rich, and extended instruction. Rich instruction goes beyond simple definitions, pushing students to investigate the meaning of, and build connections or associations between, groups of words. The Vocabulary Web (see Figure 4.1), developed by the Center for Gifted Education at William & Mary, is the perfect tool to begin the process of providing students with rich vocabulary instruction.

Figure 4.1
Vocabulary Web

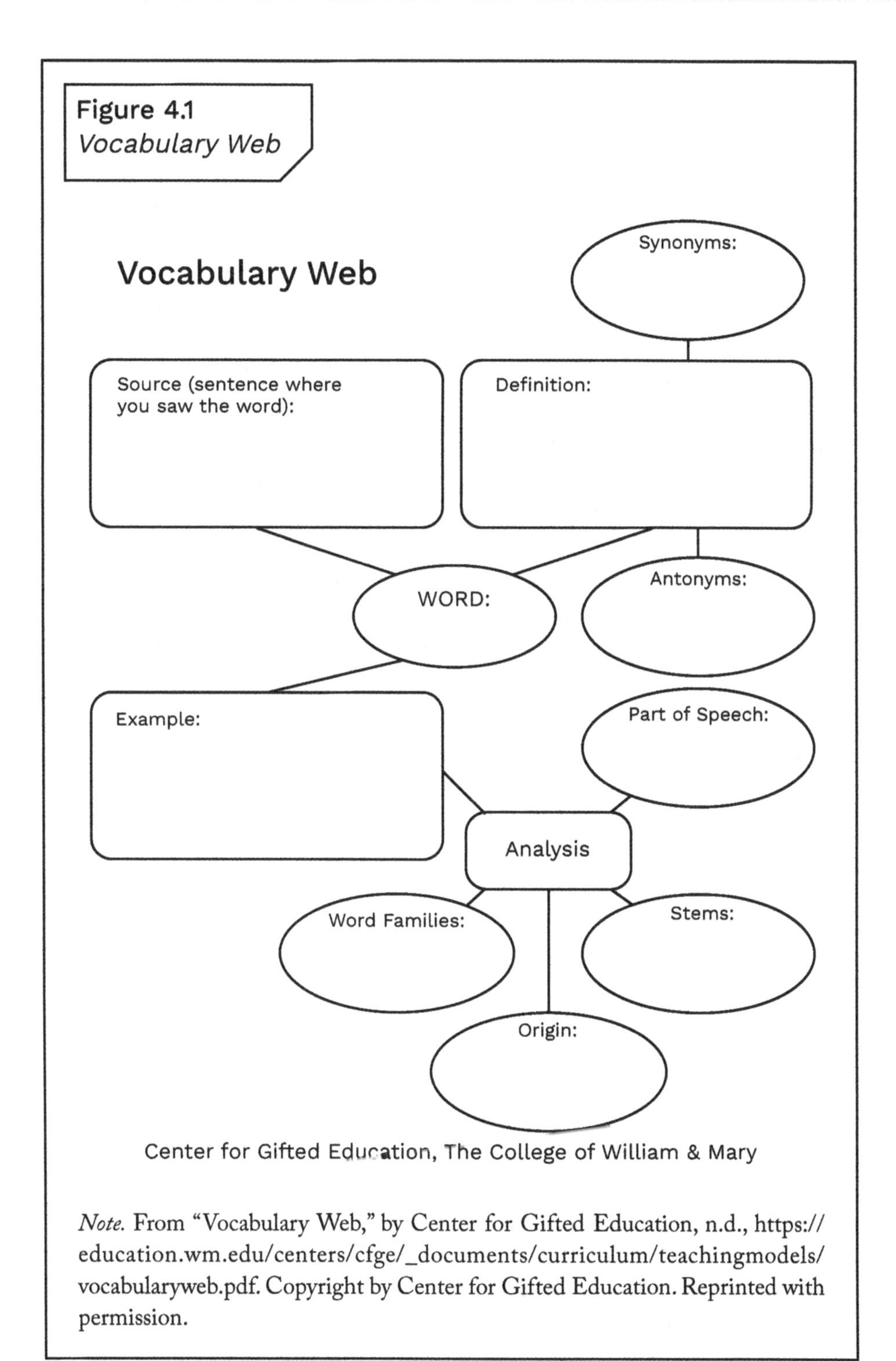

Note. From "Vocabulary Web," by Center for Gifted Education, n.d., https://education.wm.edu/centers/cfge/_documents/curriculum/teachingmodels/vocabularyweb.pdf. Copyright by Center for Gifted Education. Reprinted with permission.

Looking at Figure 4.1, notice the components of the Vocabulary Web that allow for a deeper understanding of the word, beyond the definition. Particularly important for a deep understanding is the source, or context, in which a word is found. The context in which a word is used often provides nuance to the meaning of the word and is vital to its correct interpretation. Additionally, understanding the synonyms and antonyms of a word provide a deeper understanding of the shades of meaning. Finally, notice the other components of the web that allow for connections and associations to be made: source, examples, word families, origin, stems, and part of speech. These components not only continue to develop a depth of knowledge about the word, but also help students find similarities and differences between new words and their existing vocabulary. In the following sections, I will first share how the Vocabulary Web was used to introduce a research unit, deepening and expanding students' understanding of the act of research through analysis of the word *research*. Then I will share how the Vocabulary Web was used to enhance students' understanding of the concept of conflict prior to engaging in a study of conflict through a United States history unit.

Classroom Connection. In many classrooms, students receive a weekly list of 10–20 vocabulary words related to content areas, texts being read, or even Greek and Latin roots. With this approach to vocabulary instruction, asking students to complete a Vocabulary Web with each word would be a daunting task. However, using the Vocabulary Web can be powerful when used with intention at the beginning of a unit of study, for example, allowing students to access background knowledge to create context and build connections. To better understand how a Vocabulary Web can enhance instruction, consider the following examples from a fifth-grade classroom of heterogeneous students who have either been identified as gifted and talented or spotted as having that potential.

Informational text and research are often a unit with which many students struggle. One of the things I have noticed about students and their attempts at research is that, after we work to generate carefully crafted research questions and validate sources for credibility, students simply write down the first answer they come across and proclaim themselves done with their research. This is something that has frustrated me throughout my career, that students do not understand the perseverance required for true research.

After working with the Talent Development Instructional Model (TDIM) in recent years, I began to incorporate many of the thinking models used in TDIM into my own curriculum design. One major change to my instructional process was to begin using the Vocabulary Web to open units, helping students to focus on key concepts or vocabulary within the unit. Using the graphic organizer to explore the word *research* was a strategy employed to open the writing component of an integrated ELA and science unit that focused on informational text and research.

The Vocabulary Web, with only the word *research* in the middle, was presented to students. Many students commented that they already knew the word and could use it in a sentence but were prompted to think about how using the Vocabulary Web to analyze the word *research* would provide a better understanding of what the action of research entails. The class discussion began by building context as students shared where they had previously seen or heard the word. Most had encountered the word in school or within some kind of print or digital nonfiction text. From there, students were asked to share examples of the word being used in correct context, either by explaining how research is used or conducted, or by providing an example of the word used accurately in a sentence. Throughout this discussion, students' responses were recorded on the class anchor chart and students were also encouraged to record responses on their personal copy of the Vocabulary Web (see Figure 4.2 for an example student response). This part of the discussion illustrated the baseline knowledge of what students already knew about the word and, more importantly, the process of research. As expected, many students knew the meaning of the word *research*, but not what it meant to conduct research.

With a broad understanding of students' background knowledge, the class moved on to the next component of the Vocabulary Web, the definition of *research*. A variety of dictionaries, both print and digital (e.g., American Heritage Dictionary, Dictionary.com, etc.), were brought out to begin to dig into the meaning of the word and find definitions, synonyms, and antonyms. The use of a variety of dictionaries provided an opportunity to discuss differences in dictionaries and how using multiple sources to cross-reference information provides a more robust understanding. The goal was for students, through firsthand experience in seeking and using multiple sources, to transfer the act of seeking multiple sources to their own research process. The multiple definitions were utilized to write a unique definition of the word and tailor that definition of *research* to the purpose of the unit of study. Without prompting, or even having to use the dictionaries, students began generating synonyms. When a word came up, such as *google*, discussions ensued. Students compared words they generated to the definition they wrote, and ultimately decided whether the word qualified as a synonym, an antonym, or neither. In the case of the word *google*, students determined that it was an antonym because it does not require one to search again and again, and therefore would not qualify as

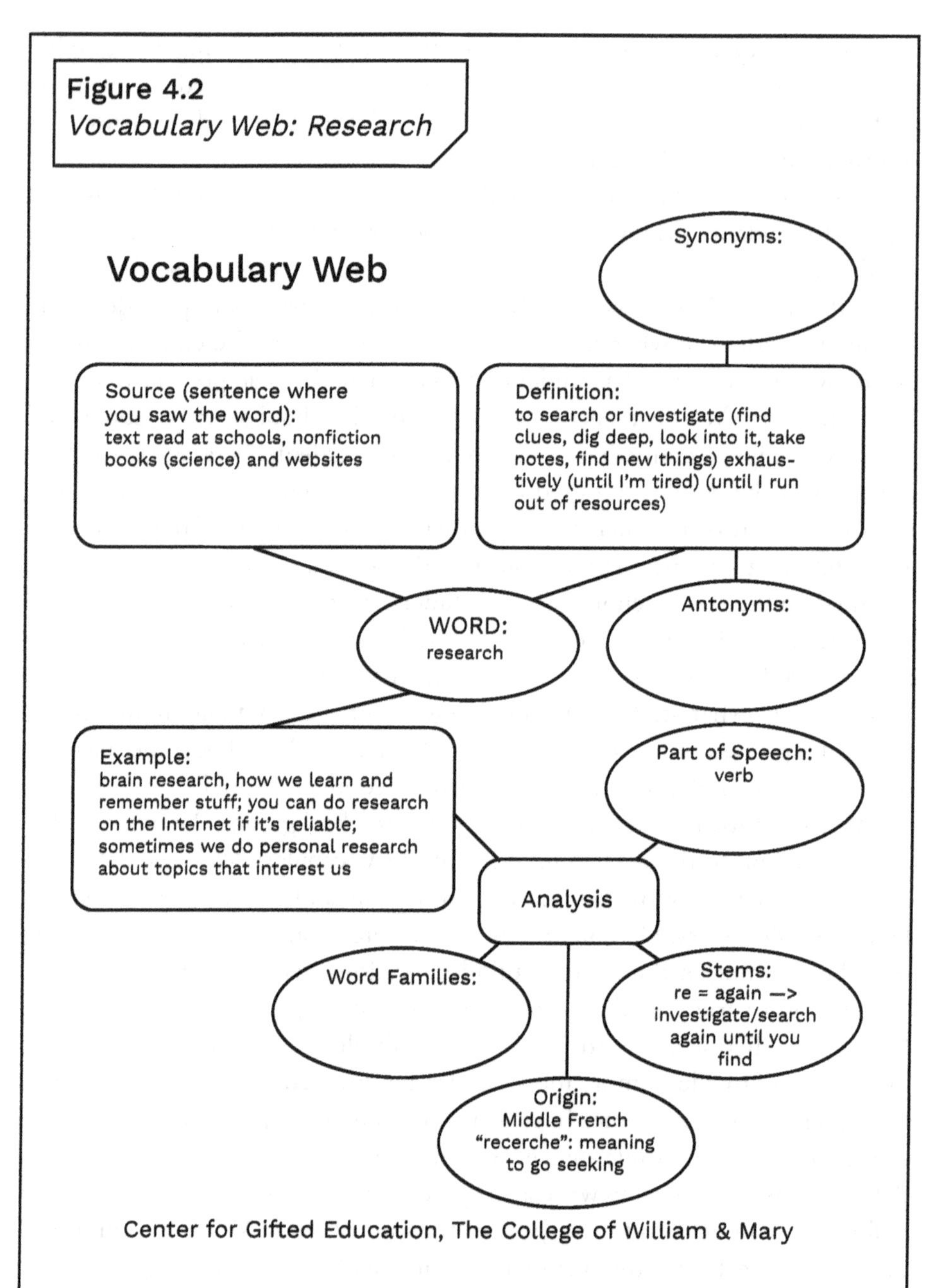

Figure 4.2
Vocabulary Web: Research

Note. The student responses are included with permission of the author. The Vocabulary Web is from "Vocabulary Web," by Center for Gifted Education, n.d., https://education.wm.edu/centers/cfge/_documents/curriculum/teachingmodels/vocabularyweb.pdf. Copyright by Center for Gifted Education. Reprinted with permission.

research. Throughout the discussion, pertinent student examples, such as *google*, *find*, *investigate*, and *explore*, were added to the class anchor chart and students' personal Vocabulary Webs.

As the analysis of the word *research* continued, the dictionaries were also used to find out about the word's origin, part of speech, stems, and word families. Interesting conversations also stemmed from the part of speech, in this case, because of the word's use as a noun and a verb. The result of the discussion was that research is being used as a verb, according to the students' definition, because of the need to actually do something, such as a physical search for information. Equally as interesting was the discussion of stems. Students found the prefix "re-" in the word and knew that prefix means "again." Immediately students started to connect *again* to the search for information, saying, "You have to keep searching for information, again and again, until you find it all." Once students made this connection between the prefix "re-" and the word *exhaustive* in the definition, it was apparent that they had a better understanding of what research actually entails and would be better prepared for the research process moving forward.

The class anchor chart proved a useful reminder throughout the research process. Students who proclaimed themselves done were encouraged to reflect on whether they had exhausted their resources, examine how many sources they had used to locate information, and investigate until they could not investigate further. The product of the students' research process yielded much more impressive results than in years past, which can be attributed to beginning the unit with an analysis of the word *research*.

An Integrated Example. Language arts is not the only subject in which a strong understanding of vocabulary produces a better understanding of the content. Therefore, using the Vocabulary Web in other subjects with key concepts and words is beneficial to talent development.

Figure 4.3 is an example of the Vocabulary Web that was used as an opening activity for a fifth-grade social studies unit on conflict. The unit was designed around the concept of conflict and the essential question that students were attempting to answer, "What causes conflict within and between nations?" Before students could begin to respond to the essential question, they had to understand the concept of conflict, and that began with understanding the word *conflict*. The Vocabulary Web was presented in much the same way as the web for the word *research*, and the discussion elicited much the same results. For example, once students used multiple sources to develop a meaning of *conflict* appropriate for the context of the unit of study, they were able to better determine the synonyms and antonyms that would further define con-

Figure 4.3
Vocabulary Web: Conflict

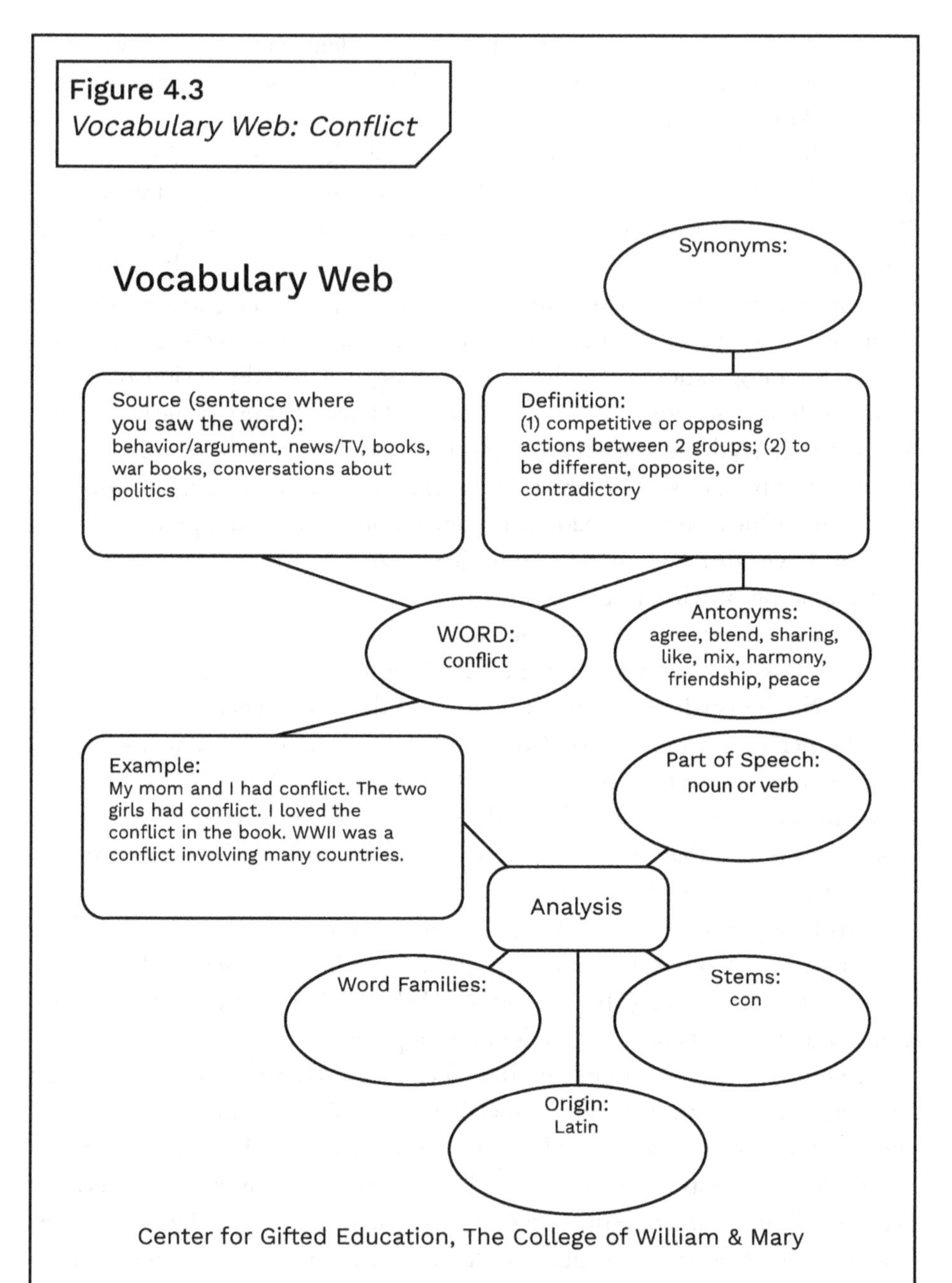

Note. The student responses are included with permission of the author. The Vocabulary Web is from "Vocabulary Web," by Center for Gifted Education, n.d., https://education.wm.edu/centers/cfge/_documents/curriculum/teachingmodels/vocabularyweb.pdf. Copyright by Center for Gifted Education. Reprinted with permission.

flict so that they could apply that meaning as they studied conflicts throughout American history.

In the discussion of the word *research*, students' references came solely from academics, but during the discussion of the word *conflict*, the sources relied more on personal associations. Both discussions had a crucial element in common (students' connections), but the type of connection differed in each conversation, one being academic and the other personal. The source and example components were the most important piece of the Vocabulary Web during the introduction of the social studies unit. Content area information is often not retained or transferred due to a lack of personal connection to the material. However, when you begin with a personal connection to a concept, the material will be easier to retain and transfer throughout the unit. This retention occurs because students have that critical personal connection as a foundation. In this particular example, students' sources and examples of the word *conflict* related more to their personal lives than to a school setting. Students connected to arguments between friends or with parents first and then branched out further, connecting to the news or television shows and finally to examples from the subject area (war and politics). Throughout the unit, references were often made to the personal examples that students first generated during the analysis of the word *conflict*. For example, during a discussion about alliances in World Wars I and II, students talked about what would happen if someone had a conflict with a family member or friend. They immediately responded with examples of times they had jumped in to defend a loved one who had a conflict with an individual who was totally unconnected to them personally. This personal connection helped students better understand why countries would jump into a war when they seemingly had no connection to the countries involved.

The Vocabulary Web is a powerful analysis tool that allows students to become active investigators, moving beyond the definition to the intended meaning of word in a variety of contexts. The analysis of words' meanings and parts allows students to better understand the vocabulary embedded within the content they are studying. This, in turn, helps students to better understand and be able to make connections to the content. The Vocabulary Web is also versatile, allowing educators to use the same format across subject and content areas. When students are able to use this tool across disciplines to deepen their analysis of words and concepts, then their thinking becomes visible and allows educators to spot talent where it may have been previously overlooked.

Using a Reasoning Model to Guide Critical Thinking

As educators, we understand that teaching thinking skills is an important part of developing a well-rounded student. Students' ability to reason through a problem and articulate their thought process is indicative of higher order thinking skills. Therefore, it is becoming more important to integrate critical thinking and reasoning into instruction as we prepare students for their future careers—in some cases, careers that do not currently exist. However, critical thinking is often a component that is watered down or even missing from curriculum. In this case, it is the educator's responsibility to enhance the curriculum by integrating critical thinking skills. Dr. Richard Paul and Dr. Linda Elder (2019) spent many years researching, developing, and sharing the importance of critical thinking skills. Paul and Elder explained that, "a well cultivated critical thinker: raises vital questions and problems . . . gathers and assesses relevant information . . . comes to well-reasoned conclusions and solutions . . . thinks open mindedly within alternative systems of thought . . . and communicates effectively with others" (p. 2).

The Center for Gifted Education at William & Mary adapted Paul and Elder's elements of reasoning into a graphic organizer that can be used to guide students through the critical thinking process. A close look at the elements of reasoning in Figure 4.4 reveals the eight elements of thought that play a crucial role in critical thinking: point of view, purpose, question at issue, information and evidence, interpretation and inference, concepts, assumptions, and implications and consequences. This tool is an excellent, concrete graphic organizer that will engage students' critical thinking skills as they reason through a specified issue. In the following sections, I will first share how the elements of reasoning were used throughout a document-based question (DBQ) unit to guide students' thinking about an essential question so that they could gather evidence that would ultimately support their argument in a debate. Then I will share how the elements of reasoning were adapted to focus on a specific event and used to frame a class discussion about Chinese immigrants during the time of westward expansion in the United States.

Classroom Connection. Preparing students to think critically about a situation can seem overwhelming. The first time I thought about and planned to integrate the elements of reasoning into my instruction, I lacked confidence that I, or my students, could manage the entire process. Therefore, I decided that I would only use parts of the elements of reasoning during my students' initial exposure to the web and reasoning process.

Figure 4.4
Reasoning Web

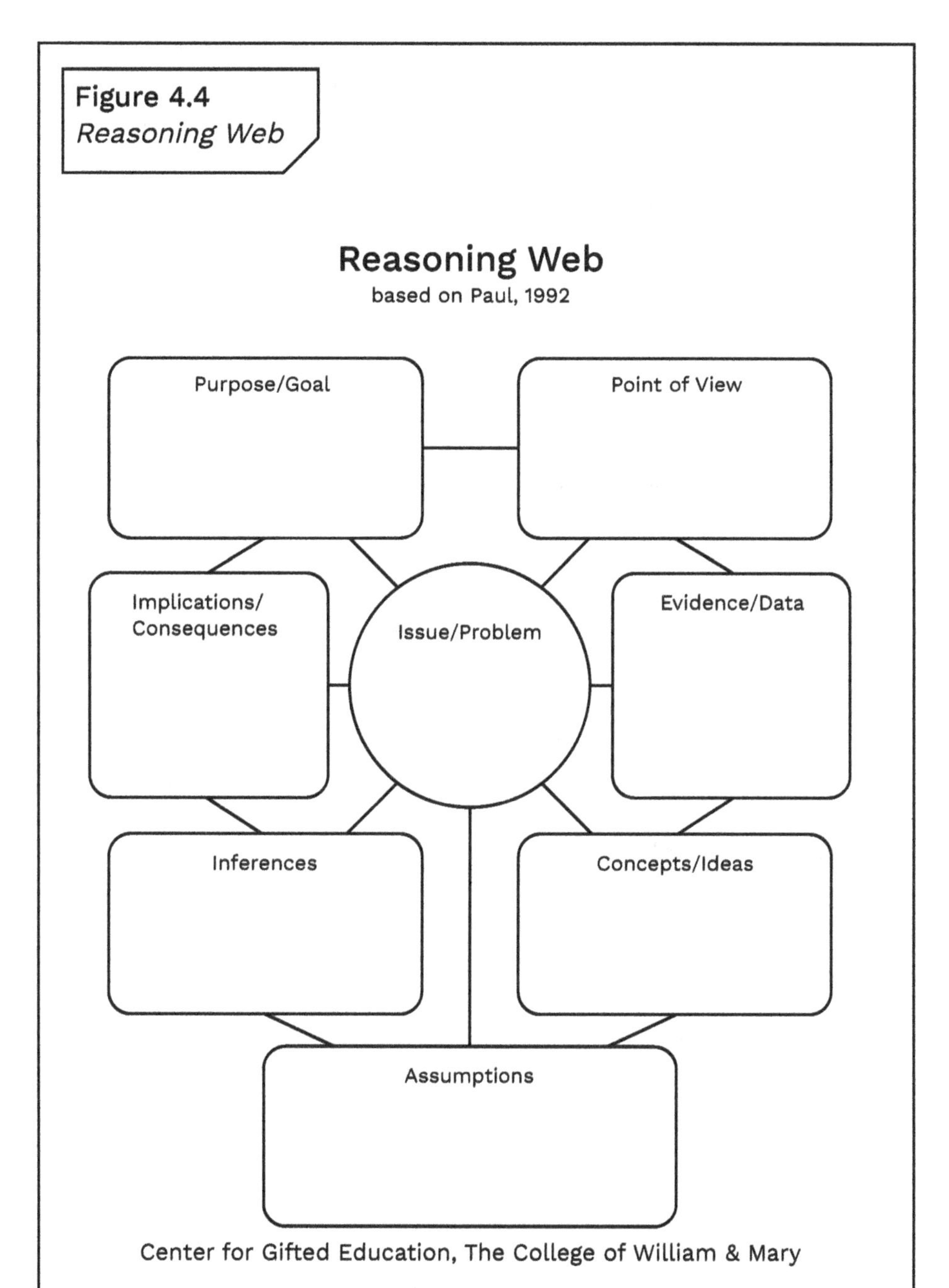

Note. From "Reasoning Web," by Center for Gifted Education, n.d., https://education.wm.edu/centers/cfge/_documents/curriculum/teachingmodels/reasoningweb.pdf. Copyright by Center for Gifted Education. Reprinted with permission.

A DBQ unit was selected to introduce the elements of reasoning because these units integrate literacy and social studies through the analysis of primary and secondary sources, with the goal of students forming arguments in response to an essential question and then using their document analysis to support those arguments. In this particular unit, students would examine five or six primary and secondary sources related to Andrew Carnegie and his philanthropy. The essential question, or issue, at the heart of the unit was, "Does Andrew Carnegie's philanthropy make him a hero?" The elements of reasoning were used with this DBQ unit for two reasons: (1) Students needed a visual guide to think about the sources differently so they could move beyond simply reading text, and (2) teachers commonly find that students often form opinions based on what friends think or an initial reaction to a situation. Therefore, students often have difficulty developing differing opinions into well-supported arguments that can then be articulated and defended. The goal of the DBQ unit was to have students work as teams to debate this issue, and the elements of reasoning would provide a concrete method of preparation and analysis of the issue, allowing students to defend their arguments with evidence, data, and information.

The "issue" was the first piece of the elements of reasoning that was tackled. Students discussed the essential question of the DBQ unit by first analyzing the words *philanthropy* and *hero*. A discussion ensued in which students shared their views of what makes a hero, who they consider heroes in their lives, and why. Once the issue at hand was understood, each student added the essential question to their elements of reasoning graphic organizer, using words that helped them understand the question being asked.

The next step in the process was to set a "purpose" for thinking. Students had to determine how they would address the essential question by analyzing and thinking through all of the sources they were going to investigate related to Andrew Carnegie. Students had some background knowledge about Carnegie, and many had already started forming opinions based on their limited knowledge. One student explained that students had to "figure out if Carnegie was still a good person, even though he hurt people's feelings." In her words, she incorporated the essential issue, as well as background knowledge, and was already thinking ahead about her task throughout the process.

With the purpose set, students began the analysis of the primary and secondary sources. As each source was investigated, students gathered evidence that could then be used to develop and support arguments. The "evidence" piece of the elements of reasoning graphic organizer was a place where students documented this information. Because multiple sources were used, the graphic organizer was adapted by students in a variety of ways. Some students wanted to work within the confines of the graphic organizer and simply used multiple graphic organizers to house the evidence that was collected from sources. Other students chose not to limit themselves to the graphic organizer and used index cards that were labeled as evidence, leaving that component of the graphic organizer blank. Although the graphic organizer is a helpful tool for students to visualize the process, it is important to allow students flexibility and ensure that the focus remains on the thinking process. Otherwise, the graphic organizer simply becomes a worksheet and the value of the reasoning process becomes watered down to a procedure that students follow in order to complete an assignment. Figure 4.5 shows how a student started recording evidence in the web about Carnegie's time working for the railroads.

"Inferences" was the final component of the elements of reasoning that was used during this initial experience. Although students can become efficient collectors of evidence, using that evidence to draw their own conclusions can be somewhat challenging. After investigating each source, a lot of time was devoted to discussing evidence collected and what that evidence revealed related to the issue and purpose. In Figure 4.5, the evidence about Carnegie's railroad work helped this student determine that Carnegie was a hard worker who started at the bottom and worked his way up. This work ethic would later reinforce the student's initial opinion and provide evidence to support her argument for the heroism of Carnegie.

In some cases, however, students found evidence that, once interpreted, changed their initial opinions of Carnegie's heroism. One student in particular began the DBQ unit with the opinion that Carnegie was very heroic because he not only had a lot of money, but also gave a lot of it away. The student thought this was very noble of Carnegie and that because Carnegie was looking out for poor people, he must be a hero. However, this student's opinion began to shift when he analyzed a political cartoon "Forty-Millionaire Carnegie in His Great Double Role" from *The Saturday Globe* (1892). This particular political cartoon started the wheels turning in this student's mind about exactly how Carnegie made his millions. After realizing that Carnegie was cutting corners with the working class, the student went back to a previous source of information, a table that listed the charities to which Carnegie donated, as well as how much was donated. The student found some donations to be what he considered valuable (e.g., teachers' pensions, Carnegie Peace Endowment), but others were thought to be very frivolous after a second look (e.g., church organs, creating a lake at Princeton University). After a thorough analysis and interpretation

Figure 4.5
Reasoning Wheel: Andrew Carnegie

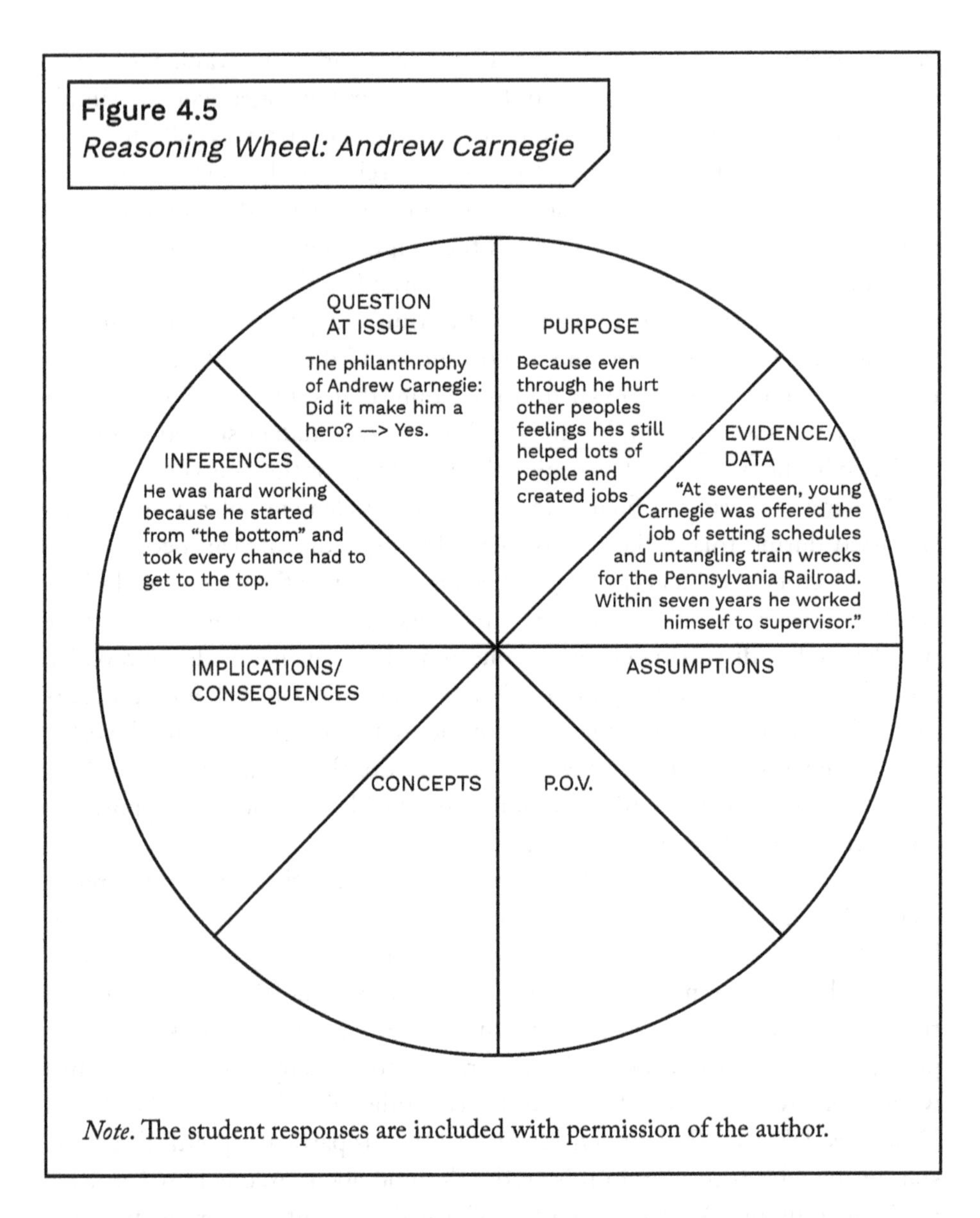

Note. The student responses are included with permission of the author.

of the evidence, this student reversed his initial opinion of Carnegie's heroism and ultimately argued against it during the final debate.

Once students finished gathering evidence and making inferences about Andrew Carnegie, they prepared for the live debate by writing arguments based on their analysis of the sources. Students went through the full writing process—planning, drafting, and revising their arguments. Quite a bit of time was spent providing peer feedback. This component was important to the critical thinking process because it required students to reflect on their analysis of source evidence and how the evidence was used to support their arguments. To stretch that reflection and thought process, students were asked to peer review arguments from the opposing team's point of view. Although this introductory delve into the elements of reasoning did not include the "point of view" component, the peer review process provided students with a small taste of how point of view can impact one's interpretation of the evidence collected. Many students found that their peers were using similar evidence, but the analysis of that evidence supported an opposing argument. Also, as a part of the peer review process, students would leave each other comments about where their peers' arguments were weak. Being able to think critically requires students to consider alternate views and, essentially, find holes in arguments. The peer review step of the writing process embedded these crucial elements of critical thinking. In Figure 4.6, the student arguing for Carnegie's heroism because of his work ethic received feedback about the use of some evidence that may not be the strongest to support her argument.

After students refined their arguments, they engaged in a live debate, with each team member presenting one argument for or against Carnegie's heroism and the team's anchor concluding with a rebuttal argument that was based on evidence presented throughout the debate rounds. Once the debate concluded, students' critical thinking skills continued through the self-reflection process.

In Figure 4.7, the student responds to the second question saying, "I think I should improve the way I explain my evidence." This was a key learning moment for the student. This particular student did not take the advice from the peer revision process to strengthen her supporting evidence. When she presented her argument in the debate, the opposing team's rebuttal revealed the weaknesses of her argument in a way she now felt the need to address. Her reflection showed that she was able to identify flaws in and draw conclusions about her argument and evidence, not needing the teacher to point that out. This moment of reflection indicates that this student will likely retain this particular lesson, so as not to make the same mistake in the future.

An Integrated Example. Perhaps the most obvious place to integrate the elements of reasoning, other than language arts, would be in a social studies unit. Another visual adaptation of Paul and Elder's (2019) critical thinking work was made by the Center for Gifted Education at William & Mary specifically for reasoning about events. This graphic organizer is shown in Figure 4.8. A significant difference between the two graphic organizers—the Reasoning Web (Figure 4.4) and the Reasoning About a Situation or Event organizer—is that the Reasoning Web takes students through all eight elements of thought, whereas the Reasoning About a Situation or Event organizer focuses on point

Figure 4.6
Student Opinion Writing: Andrew Carnegie

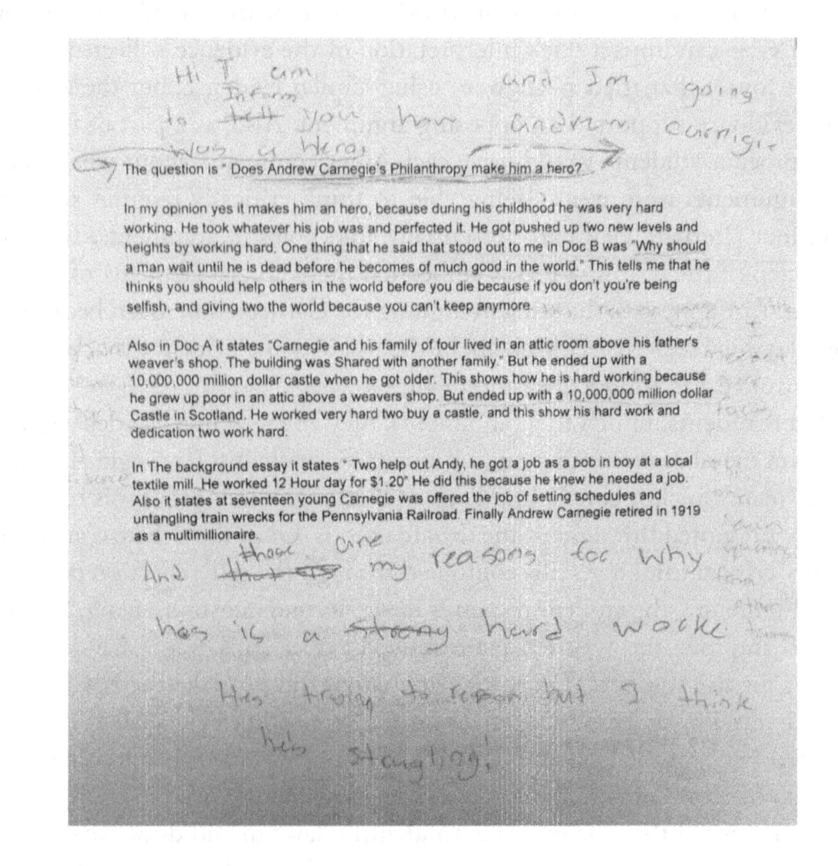

The question is " Does Andrew Carnegie's Philanthropy make him a hero?

In my opinion yes it makes him an hero, because during his childhood he was very hard working. He took whatever his job was and perfected it. He got pushed up two new levels and heights by working hard. One thing that he said that stood out to me in Doc B was "Why should a man wait until he is dead before he becomes of much good in the world." This tells me that he thinks you should help others in the world before you die because if you don't you're being selfish, and giving two the world because you can't keep anymore.

Also in Doc A it states "Carnegie and his family of four lived in an attic room above his father's weaver's shop. The building was Shared with another family." But he ended up with a 10,000,000 million dollar castle when he got older. This shows how he is hard working because he grew up poor in an attic above a weavers shop. But ended up with a 10,000,000 million dollar Castle in Scotland. He worked very hard two buy a castle, and this show his hard work and dedication two work hard.

In The background essay it states " Two help out Andy, he got a job as a bob in boy at a local textile mill. He worked 12 Hour day for $1.20" He did this because he knew he needed a job. Also it states at seventeen young Carnegie was offered the job of setting schedules and untangling train wrecks for the Pennsylvania Railroad. Finally Andrew Carnegie retired in 1919 as a multimillionaire.

Note. The student responses are included with permission of the author.

of view, assumptions, and implications. This difference is precisely why I prefer the second graphic organizer when guiding students' critical thinking about historical events. When thinking about historical events, the focus should be on the stakeholders involved and how their perspectives shape their actions during a particular event.

One of the most effective ways to integrate this adaptation into social studies is through literature, for example, with the book *Coolies* by Yin (2003). During our study of westward expansion, this book was used as a read aloud so that students could engage in discussions about immigration during the

Figure 4.7
Student Reflection: Andrew Carnegie

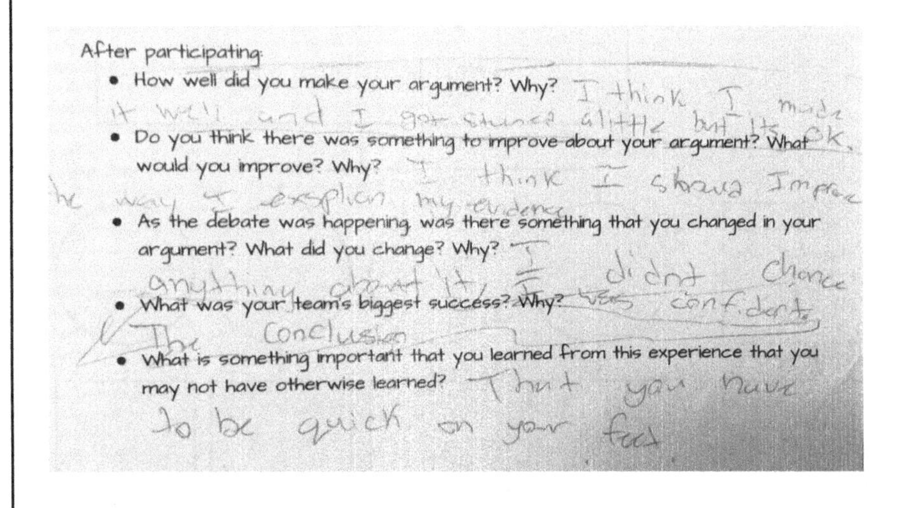

After participating:

- How well did you make your argument? Why? I think I made it well and I got stuck alittle but its ok.
- Do you think there was something to improve about your argument? What would you improve? Why? I think I should Improve the way I explain my evidence
- As the debate was happening, was there something that you changed in your argument? What did you change? Why? I didnt change anything about it, I was confident.
- What was your team's biggest success? Why? The conclusion
- What is something important that you learned from this experience that you may not have otherwise learned? That you have to be quick on your feet

Note. The student responses are included with permission of the author.

time period. The Reasoning About a Situation or Event organizer was used to guide and record students' discussions. Throughout the entire unit, additional books were read that revealed the point of view of various stakeholder groups and allowed ongoing discussion, using the graphic organizer as a guide. At the conclusion of the unit, students spent time reflecting on patterns that they saw by using the graphic organizer to frame their discussions. Students often found themselves coming back to these completed graphic organizers as similarities were revealed in subsequent time periods. One common thread that was revealed was discrimination. During the *Coolies* discussion, students made connections to slavery because of the way the Chinese immigrants were treated by White people, to the Civil Rights Movement because the Chinese immigrants went on strike after discovering the discrepancies in wages, and to the modern-day immigration debate because of the assumptions made about the Chinese immigrants due to their differing cultures.

Having a guide to help students through the critical thinking and reasoning processes is impactful on talent development. Students who may not be typically seen as gifted critical thinkers in their classroom have the opportunity to shine with a scaffold that guides the thinking process. They are better able to

Figure 4.8
Reasoning About a Situation or Event

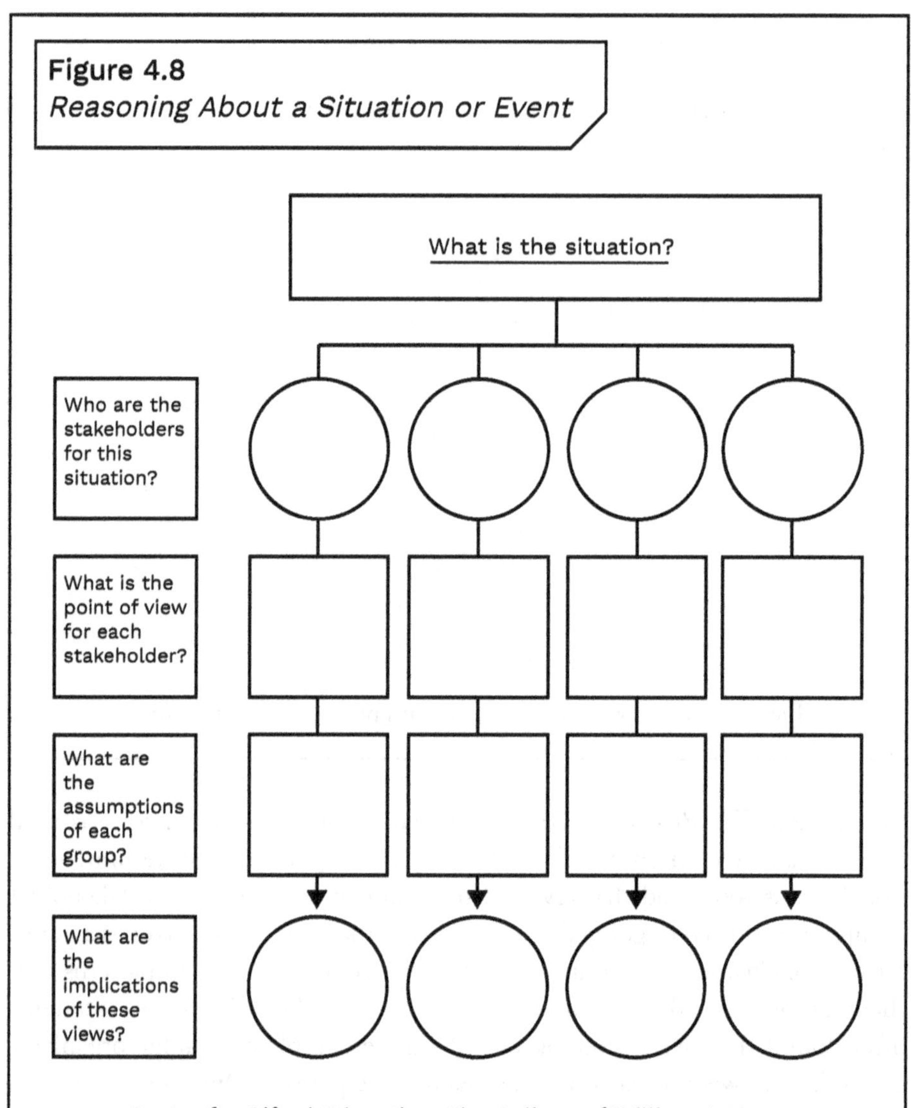

Center for Gifted Education, The College of William & Mary

Note. From "Reasoning About a Situation or Event," by Center for Gifted Education, n.d., https://education.wm.edu/centers/cfge/_documents/curriculum/teachingmodels/reasoningevent.pdf. Copyright by Center for Gifted Education. Reprinted with permission.

articulate their thinking because these graphic organizers encourage students to slow down and reflect on what they have learned, considering others' opinions and perspectives, as they develop their own. The retention and transfer of knowledge is evident by students' use of the elements of reasoning as a reference tool throughout the year.

Using a Concept Development Model to Connect Big Ideas

One of the dimensions of the ICM (VanTassel-Baska, 2017) is concepts and themes, and this dimension is often difficult for students to identify and understand, especially across content areas. Hilda Taba (1962), a curriculum theorist and teacher educator, developed a method of inductive learning that allows students to more easily develop concepts by first listing examples and nonexamples, then categorizing information, before finally synthesizing information to develop generalizations about the concept as a whole:

1. **Listing:** Students list everything that they know about the topic. (Suggestion: Encourage students to write their knowledge on separate pieces of paper or sticky notes to make grouping easier in the next step.)
2. **Grouping:** Students group similar items from their lists.
3. **Labeling:** Students label their groups and explain how they decided to assign items to each group.
4. **Regrouping:** Students reconsider the item placement in each group, move items to different groups, or make new groups altogether.
5. **Synthesizing:** Students synthesize the information by summarizing the information they have gathered and forming generalizations about the topic.

This process is effective because students begin with what they know. As students look for similarities and differences while grouping in the next step, they are further analyzing and thinking about their initial information. Once students categorize and classify, and even reclassify information, they look for patterns within and across their categories. Those patterns then develop into generalizations so that students can better understand the overarching concept. In the following sections, I first share how Taba's concept development model was used to develop an understanding of the autobiography genre. Then I share how Taba's model can be used as a tool to develop an understanding of concepts found in the study of U.S. history, with specific examples from units on movement and discrimination.

Classroom Connection. When thinking of a way to integrate Taba's (1962) concept development model into my curriculum and instruction, I brainstormed lessons that were typically taught by giving students a list of characteristics or generalizations about a topic. Some of the first lessons that came to mind were those related to genre studies. Many educators know about mentor texts and how to use them as models for writing lessons. Mentor texts are books, or other types of texts, that teachers and students use as a mentor to aid in the understanding or writing of similar texts. For example, when studying autobiographies, I read *Knots in My Yo-Yo String* by Jerry Spinelli (1998) as a class read aloud. His autobiography serves as a mentor text to students as they learn more about reading and writing autobiographies. Students return to his autobiography as an example of how to organize their writing, how to select important moments from their lives to include in their writing, and so on. The more I thought about the purpose of mentor texts, the more I realized they would serve as excellent texts for genre analysis by way of Taba's concept development model. I chose to begin this experiment with an autobiography unit that I adapted from the Center for Gifted Education's (2011) *Autobiographies and Memoirs.*

The first step in the concept development model is to generate a list of ideas, examples related to, or information about the topic. To begin this step, students were divided into four groups and each group was given a different mentor text, an excerpt from an author's autobiography. Students in each group read their autobiography excerpt together and highlighted anything that seemed important to include in an autobiography. As I watched students working in their groups, I noticed that one student had highlighted the first sentence of her assigned excerpt and wrote a note in the margin of the text that autobiographies "normally start before the person was an author."

This example showed strong understanding by the student who found it and clearly exemplifies the goal of the lesson for students. However, it quickly became clear that this student was the exception and not the norm. Moving from group to group to listen in on conversations, it became evident that many students were highlighting and noting evidence specific to the text, not the genre. For example, another student highlighted "Chinatown" in an excerpt from Lawrence Yep's autobiography and noted that autobiographies take place in Chinatown. This observation led to guiding conversations to help students see the bigger picture, such as that autobiographies include places important to the author, rather than specific details. Once students caught on to thinking more broadly about the text, they were better able to identify other characteristics of the genre and ultimately form a list of traits commonly found in this

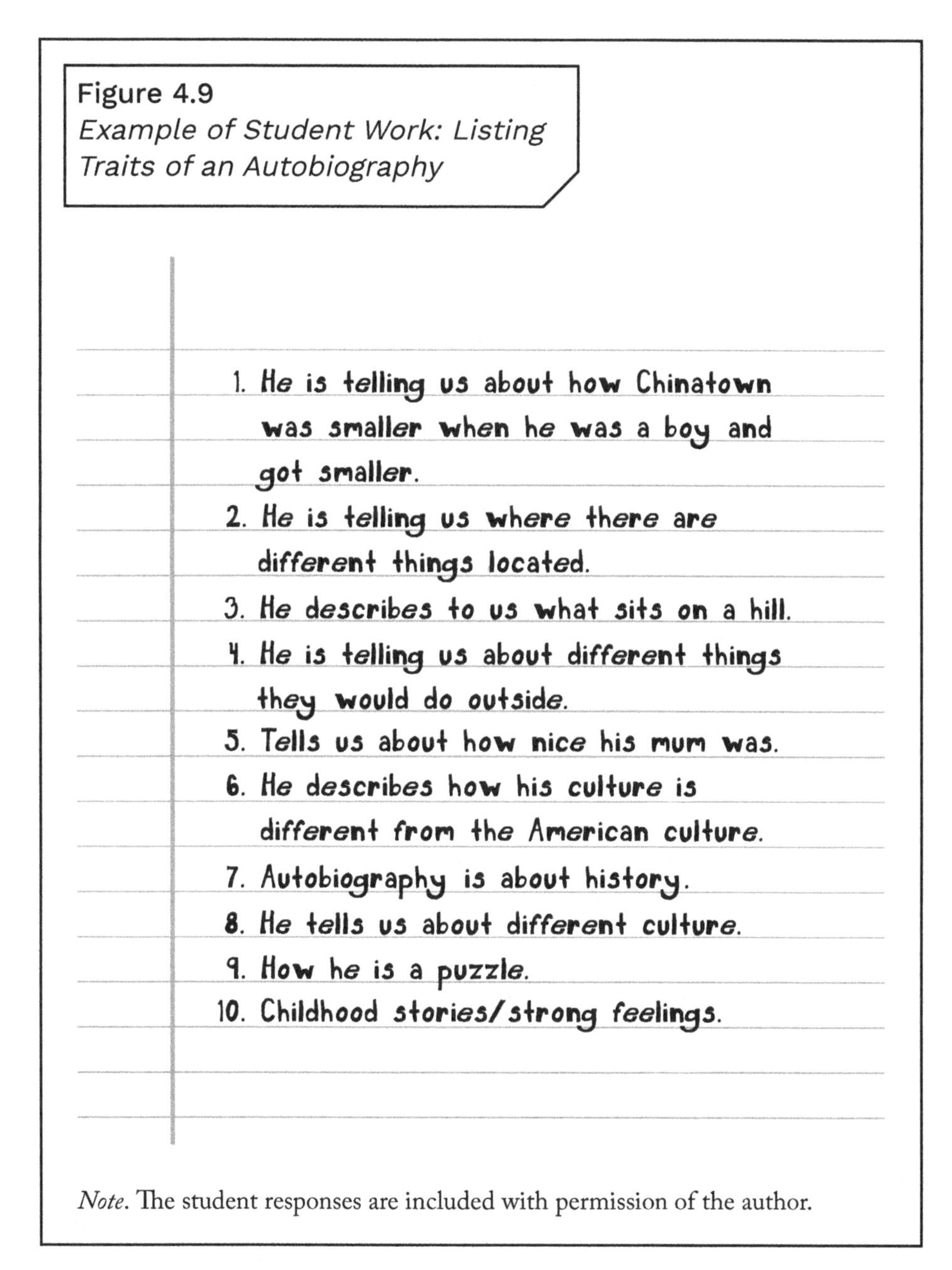

1. He is telling us about how Chinatown was smaller when he was a boy and got smaller.
2. He is telling us where there are different things located.
3. He describes to us what sits on a hill.
4. He is telling us about different things they would do outside.
5. Tells us about how nice his mum was.
6. He describes how his culture is different from the American culture.
7. Autobiography is about history.
8. He tells us about different culture.
9. How he is a puzzle.
10. Childhood stories/strong feelings.

Figure 4.9
Example of Student Work: Listing Traits of an Autobiography

Note. The student responses are included with permission of the author.

genre. Figures 4.9 and 4.10 show examples of lists generated by two student groups during this phase of the process.

Once students had generated their traits lists, groups were reconstituted to compare notes. For the second grouping, one student from each of the first groups comprised the new group so that each mentor text was represented.

Figure 4.10
Example of Student Work: Listing Traits of an Autobiography

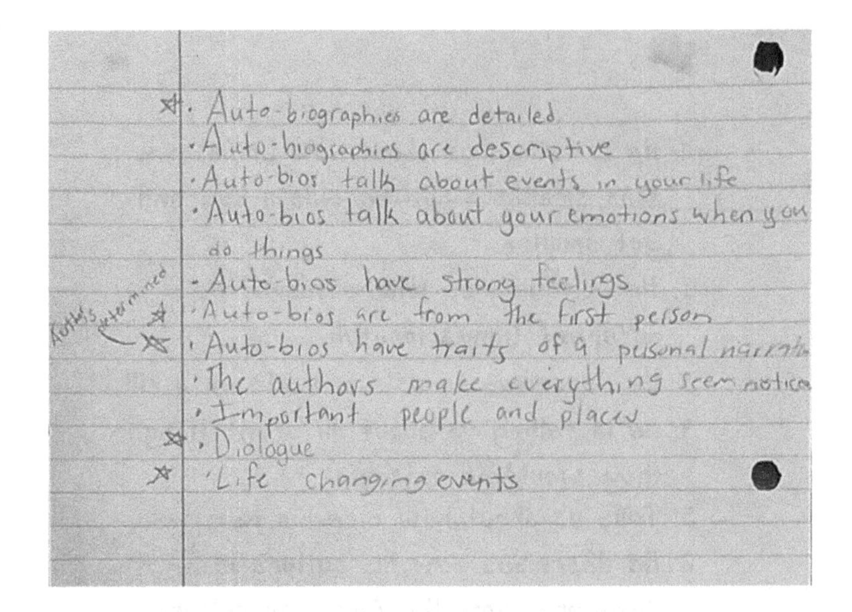
- Auto-biographies are detailed
- Auto-biographies are descriptive
- Auto-bios talk about events in your life
- Auto-bios talk about your emotions when you do things
- Auto-bios have strong feelings
- Auto-bios are from the first person
- Auto-bios have traits of a personal
- The authors make everything seem
- Important people and places
- Diologue
- Life changing events

Note. The student responses are included with permission of the author.

Students were asked to compare their lists of traits and begin discussing how to categorize their traits. Students sorted traits into categories that included writing style, such as writing in narrative form, using first-person point of view, and including descriptive detail; content, such as including life-changing events or important places; and organization, such as focusing each chapter on one major event or time in the author's life and writing chronologically. Once students had categorized their genre traits, the groups were asked to select the most important trait from each category that was unique to an autobiography and set it apart from other genres. The groups created a chart with their most important genre traits and included evidence from the mentor texts that exemplified that trait and explained their reasoning. One group's example of key traits and supporting evidence is included in Figures 4.11–4.14.

Each group explained its categories and justifications for sorting its traits, and groups shared their most important traits. At that time the class decided, as a whole, what made an autobiography an autobiography. Students had a

Figure 4.11
Example of Student Work: Important Traits of an Autobiography

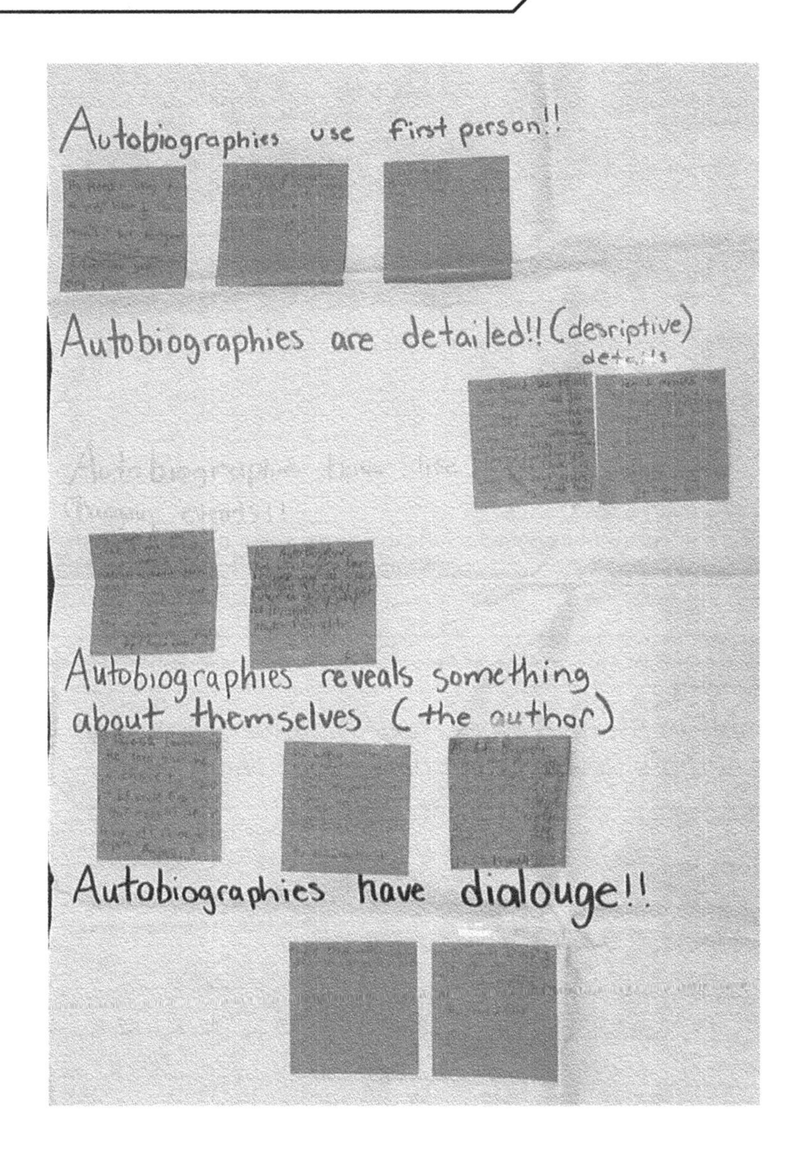

Note. The student responses are included with permission of the author.

Figure 4.12
Example of Student Work: Text Evidence Supporting the Descriptive Detail Trait

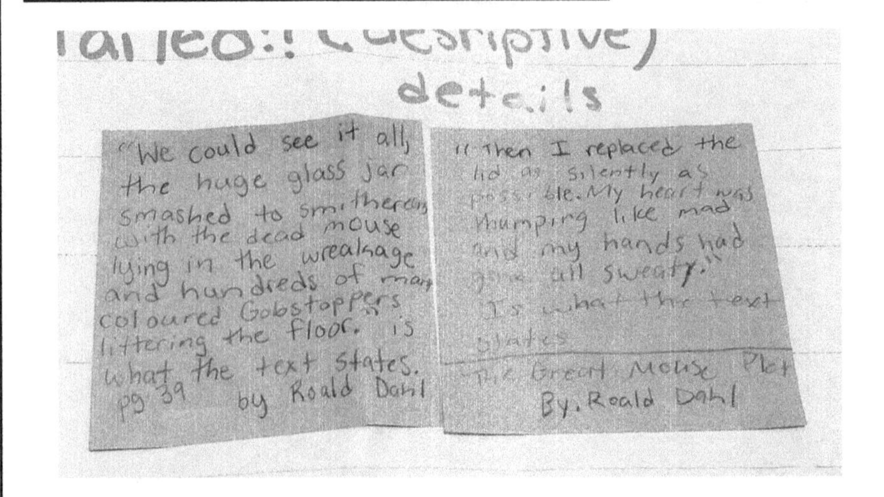

Note. The student responses are included with permission of the author.

Figure 4.13
Example of Student Work: Text Evidence Supporting That Authors Reveal Something About Themselves

Note. The student responses are included with permission of the author.

Figure 4.14
Example of Student Work: Text Evidence Supporting That Authors Include Life-Changing Events

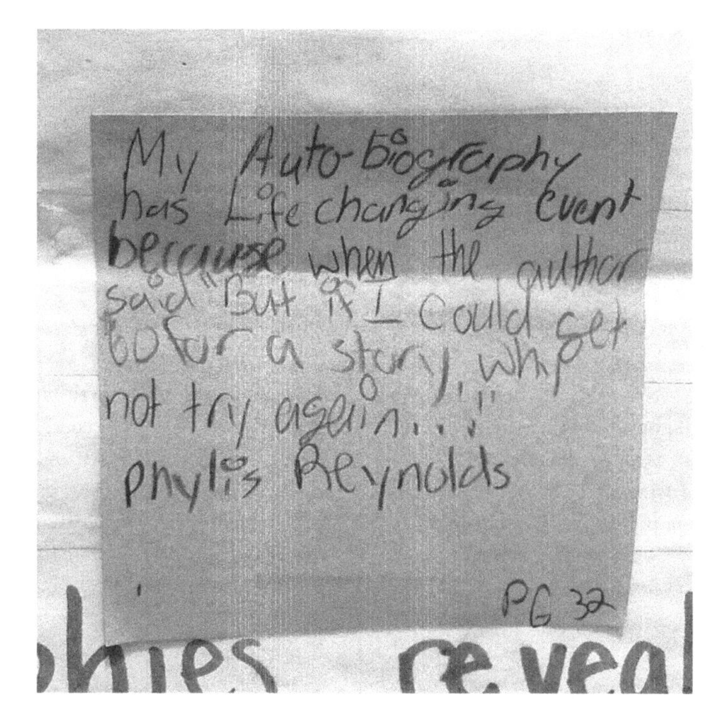

Note. The student responses are included with permission of the author.

wide-ranging discussion that included many differing opinions about the traits on which each group placed importance. Eventually, students came to a consensus about the categories and the most important traits in each category. The genre-defining traits were agreed upon after students pointed out that some of the traits that they deemed important could be found in many genres and they wanted to instead focus on the traits that were found more often in autobiographies. For example, it was important to students that they include the trait that autobiographies are narratives written in first-person point of view because the authors are writing about themselves, and that is different than many other genres. Students used the agreed-upon traits to define an autobiography and create a rubric by which they would evaluate and critique their own autobiographical writing (see Figure 4.15).

Figure 4.15
Student-Developed Rubric to Evaluate Autobiographical Writing

Author's Name: ____________________

Autobiography Rubric

The following components were developed together as a class. Your autobiography is being critiqued using the rubric that you helped to create.

Generalizations	Got It	Getting There	Not Yet
Most autobiographies are written as narratives using first-person point of view.	▪ Uses words like *I, me, my, mine, we, us.* ▪ Written like a story with characters, setting, and a plot. ▪ The author is the main character.	▪ Not using first-person point of view consistently. ▪ Some elements of a story, but not all (e.g., no setting, just a list of things that happened, etc.).	▪ Writing in second- or third-person point of view. ▪ Written more like an informational or opinion piece. ▪ No evidence of characters, setting, or plot.
Most autobiographies included memories or lessons learned from the author's childhood.	▪ Includes time and transition words to indicate when the memory happened. ▪ Uses transition words to show cause and effect for lessons learned.	▪ Talks about real life, but we don't know when it happened or memory is incomplete. ▪ Timeline of events, but no story to explain the memory. ▪ Starts with a real memory but mixes in details that didn't actually happen.	▪ The memory is made up, didn't really happen.

Figure 4.15, *continued*

Generalizations	Got It	Getting There	Not Yet
Most autobiographies include strong emotions, dialogue, and descriptive detail.	▪ Shows emotion through characters' actions, thoughts or dialogue. ▪ Uses the five senses to describe the setting, characters, and events. ▪ Uses figurative language. ▪ Conversation between characters, using quotation marks correctly.	▪ Just telling how I feel. ▪ Just listing what I see. ▪ Tried to have characters talk, but no quotation marks.	▪ No emotion included. ▪ No detail at all, just a list of things that happened. ▪ No dialogue, no talking by characters.
Most autobiographies are organized into chapters that focus on one strong memory.	▪ Each memory or lesson is a separate chapter. ▪ Writes multiple paragraphs and pages per chapter. ▪ Each chapter has a title related to the memory and a chapter number. (Add a table of contents to tell what page it starts on.) ▪ Includes graphics (photos, maps, etc.) that go with the chapter.	▪ Chapters can get off topic in some places, but it doesn't confuse the reader.	▪ No chapters at all, written in one long paragraph. ▪ Story goes off topic and gets confusing. ▪ Story doesn't conclude; it just ends. ▪ The book or chapter title and picture doesn't match the story.

Figure 4.15, *continued*

Generalizations	Got It	Getting There	Not Yet
Most authors follow grammar and spelling conventions.	▪ Punctuate all sentences. ▪ Complete sentences. ▪ Use commas in long sentences. ▪ Separate ideas by paragraph. ▪ Correct spelling. ▪ Use text features to draw attention to important words. ▪ No abbreviations or texting.	▪ Mistakes don't confuse the reader.	▪ So many mistakes the reader can't understand the writing.

Areas of Growth: ______________________________

____

____

____

____

Keep Working On: ______________________________

____

____

____

____

Note. Reprinted with permission of the author.

The use of the Taba (1962) concept development model was successful in developing students' understanding of the genre compared to years past when an anchor chart with the traits of an autobiography was simply presented during a class discussion. Students' writing of their own autobiographies was more descriptive, and their content steered away from the "on the day I was born" or "on my ninth birthday" stories, instead focusing on more impactful events in their lives. The quality of not only the writing but also the peer feedback improved. Because students developed the rubric with which they evaluated one another's writing, they were familiar with the expectations. They had already identified exemplars of each expectation within mentor texts and were able to clearly articulate whether or not a peer was meeting the expectations of each trait.

An Integrated Example. Experiencing significant student results with Taba's (1962) concept development model in the reading and writing units prompted me to look into other areas that would be enhanced by its use. I recently revised all of the American history social studies units, and, instead of teaching them chronologically, I chose to teach them by overarching themes and concepts. This curriculum revision was the perfect opportunity to integrate the concept development model. What follows is a general overview of how a social studies unit progressed.

The unit opens with a vocabulary analysis web of the concept word for the unit (movement, discrimination, conflict, etc.), and students use the concept development model to explore generalizations about the concept based solely on their background knowledge. During the unit opener, students jot down anything they know about the concept word onto sticky notes. They then work as a class to sort those sticky notes into categories as they see fit. This sorting and resorting process creates a rich discussion, as students argue for or against a sticky note going in a certain category. Once they finish, students are invited to present their final categories and explain how they classified the ideas in each category. These explanations are placed on an anchor chart as generalizations. They are not always related to social studies—and that is okay. For example, in the first unit, movement, students' initial generalizations were mostly science based because they were studying force and motion at the time. In another unit, conflict, students' initial generalizations were personal because their minds went immediately to intrapersonal relationships when they thought of the word *conflict*. During this opening session, any and all generalizations about the concept were accepted and added to the anchor chart.

As the unit progressed, each lesson focused on an event in American history that would expand the students' understanding of the concept. For example, in the movement unit the lessons included westward expansion, industrial era immigration, and modern-day immigration. As students learned about movement in each time period, we used the Reasoning About a Situation or Event organizer to focus on key stakeholder groups during each time period. Students examined a variety of sources, including primary and secondary sources, to learn about the time period and what caused each stakeholder group to move, as well as the effects of their movement.

This process of collecting information and observations was important because, to conclude the unit, students used the concept development model to sort all of their observations made throughout the unit and refine their understanding of the concept based on what they learned throughout the unit. By doing this, students learned the habits of the discipline and how to think like historians. For example, in our discrimination unit, students were asked to focus on two main questions throughout the unit: (1) Why are people discriminated against? (2) How does discrimination affect our community? Figures 4.16 and 4.17 show how two groups classified the same information found throughout the unit into different categories.

Groups interpreted the information differently and placed different emphasis on key parts of the information. For example, in Figure 4.16, notice that the observation, "Forced to move into internment camps to live, not like concentration camps, not tortured, just captured," was placed in the category for "disloyalty and difference" because students in that group placed emphasis on the fact that Americans viewed Japanese Americans with distrust during World War II and therefore placed them in internment camps. However, in Figure 4.17, another group placed the same piece of information into the category "forced" because the Japanese Americans were forced to move to internment camps against their will. The first group focused more on the cause of the discrimination, while the second group focused more on the effect of the discrimination.

Highlighting these moments of different thought processes and reasoning lead to deeper discussions about the historical event, the time period, and the differing viewpoints of each stakeholder group. Teaching in this manner, through overarching themes and concepts, and using Taba's (1962) concept development model to do so, has led to a deeper understanding of American history and how different perspectives of the same event are possible. Students have been able to make more personal connections, often because we start the unit building the concept from what students already know and then refine that understanding at the end of the unit using what they learned. They interact with the information multiple times throughout the unit, which allows for

Figure 4.16
Classification of Information and Observations About Discrimination

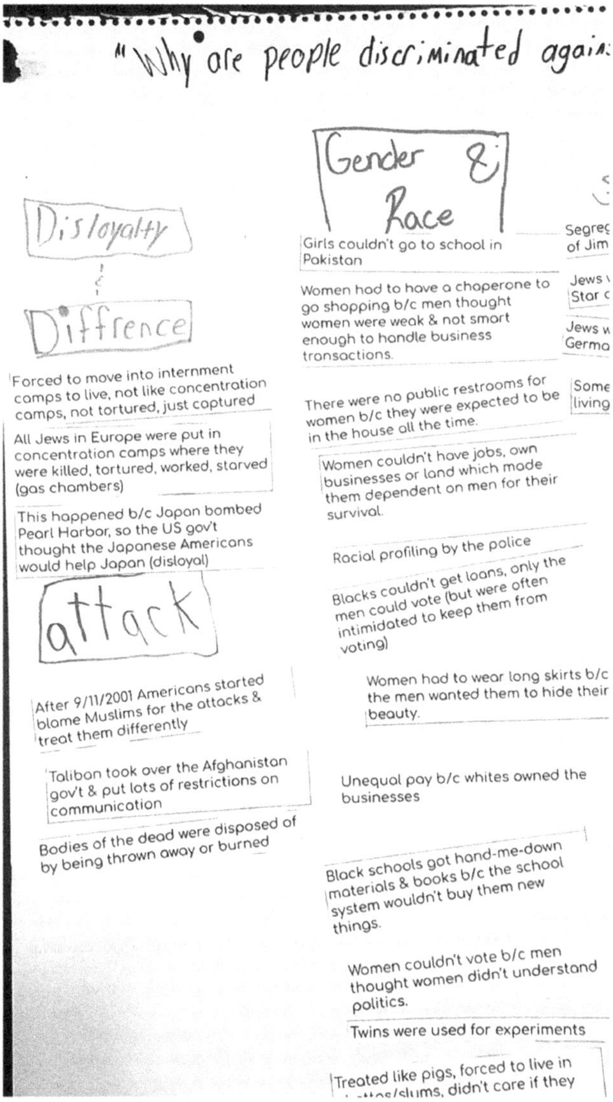

"Why are people discriminated agai

Disloyalty

Diffrence

Forced to move into internment camps to live, not like concentration camps, not tortured, just captured

All Jews in Europe were put in concentration camps where they were killed, tortured, worked, starved (gas chambers)

This happened b/c Japan bombed Pearl Harbor, so the US gov't thought the Japanese Americans would help Japan (disloyal)

attack

After 9/11/2001 Americans started blame Muslims for the attacks & treat them differently

Taliban took over the Afghanistan gov't & put lots of restrictions on communication

Bodies of the dead were disposed of by being thrown away or burned

Gender & Race

Girls couldn't go to school in Pakistan

Women had to have a chaperone to go shopping b/c men thought women were weak & not smart enough to handle business transactions.

There were no public restrooms for women b/c they were expected to be in the house all the time.

Women couldn't have jobs, own businesses or land which made them dependent on men for their survival.

Racial profiling by the police

Blacks couldn't get loans, only the men could vote (but were often intimidated to keep them from voting)

Women had to wear long skirts b/c the men wanted them to hide their beauty.

Unequal pay b/c whites owned the businesses

Black schools got hand-me-down materials & books b/c the school system wouldn't buy them new things.

Women couldn't vote b/c men thought women didn't understand politics.

Twins were used for experiments

Treated like pigs, forced to live in ghettos/slums, didn't care if they

Segreg of Jim

Jews Star

Jews Germa

Some living

Note. The student responses are included with permission of the author.

Figure 4.17
Classification of Information and Observations About Discrimination

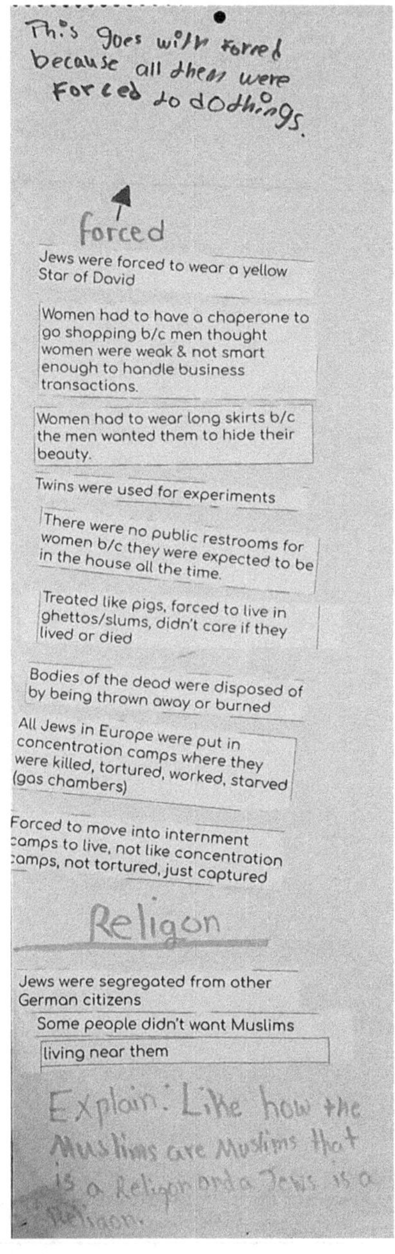

Note. The student responses are included with permission of the author.

better retention of knowledge. As the year progressed and students dug into more and more themes throughout history, they began making connections between units as well. When students discussed discrimination throughout history, they went back to the movement unit and were able to make connections between the treatment of African Americans during the Jim Crow era and the treatment of Chinese Americans during westward expansion. It is a moment like this, when students make a connection, that illustrates the power of thinking models such as Taba's (1962) concept development model. Being able to see the big picture through the process of making generalizations and inductive thinking highlights students' ability to make connections across content areas and time periods in a way that deepens their understanding of the content and develops talents that may not have been previously spotted.

Using a Literature Web to Visualize the Analysis Process

Many educators teach groups of students with varying ability levels. This range of abilities can make it challenging to find a thinking model that allows students to analyze a piece of literature in depth without excluding some students from the conversation. The Literature Web, developed by the Center for Gifted Education at William & Mary, however, provides literature analysis with multiple points of entry so that students of all ability levels are able to participate in the process. The Literature Web (see Figure 4.18) has five components: key words, feelings, images and symbols, structure, and ideas, which will be explored in further detail in the subsequent sections. The web, as a whole, is scaffolded so that students at any level can analyze. Students who struggle with reading may actively contribute to the identification of key words, while students who are more gifted in reading will be thinking deeply about the symbolism or themes found in the text. Therefore, the advantage of using the Literature Web is that every student in the class can participate, and because they are all participating, the discussion of the text is enriched, benefiting every student. In the following sections, I will first share how the Literature Web was used to analyze a read-aloud text during the launch of a research unit. Then I will share how the Literature Web can be used with media other than text, such as art and music, to deepen students' understanding of the analysis process.

Classroom Connection. During an integrated science and language arts unit, *The Lorax* by Dr. Seuss (1971) was read aloud to engage students in thinking about problems in their community and how they could solve them. The

Figure 4.18
Literature Web

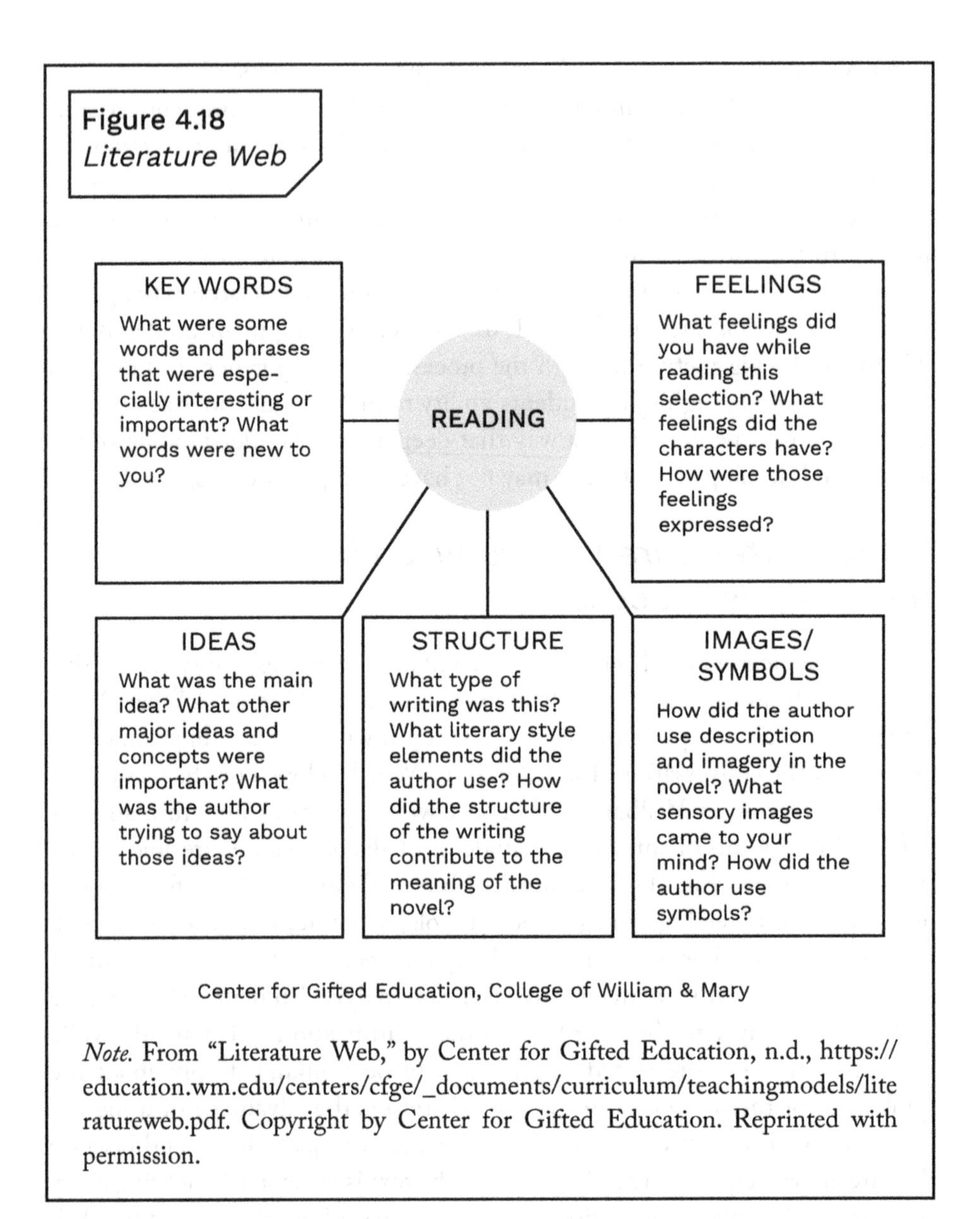

Note. From "Literature Web," by Center for Gifted Education, n.d., https://education.wm.edu/centers/cfge/_documents/curriculum/teachingmodels/literatureweb.pdf. Copyright by Center for Gifted Education. Reprinted with permission.

book was used as a catalyst to launch a research project, but also as a quality piece of text that students would benefit from analyzing. The Literature Web was an ideal thinking model to use in this situation. What follows is an overview of the lesson in which students analyzed *The Lorax*.

The lesson began with an interactive read aloud of *The Lorax*, during which students engaged in discussions about both the text and the illustrations. Following the read aloud, a blank Literature Web was posted on the board and the analysis process began with the key words component. This component was used to begin the process because it is the best entry point for students who struggle as readers. During this component students were encouraged to call out words that they thought were important to the text or important to them as the reader. Everything that students shared was recorded on the Literature Web; this was not the time to discuss whether a word was right or wrong. If a word seemed like an odd choice, students were encouraged to explain their responses. Their explanation gave insight into a student's understanding of the text that could be noted for inquiry or instruction at a later point in time.

Once students sufficiently discussed and added key words to the Literature Web, the class moved on to feelings. This bubble is physically split in half on the web, reserving half of the bubble for the author or characters' feelings and half of the bubble for the readers' feelings. Again, students were encouraged to share any feelings that they have as readers and then the feelings of the characters or authors, and everything was recorded on the Literature Web. Starting this component with students' personal feelings is another way to engage struggling readers early in the process and also is an important opportunity for students to make personal connections to the text. Often, students will notice and begin to discuss similarities or differences between the feelings of the author or characters and their own feelings. During the analysis of *The Lorax*, students began to look for similarities between themselves and one character over another. Some students empathized with the Once-ler because, as one student explained, "He is running a business and needs to give his employees work to do." Other students connected more with the Lorax because he "is trying to save the forests," as another student pointed out. Making and articulating these personal connections to a character at this point in the analysis process helped students identify images and symbols, and later develop big ideas.

Images and symbols are the third component of the Literature Web. This is the point at which the higher level readers begin to dominate the discussion. Teachers should encourage these students' leadership at this point, but also make sure to temper their dominance so that all readers can use what they have contributed thus far to the Literature Web to build their analysis to the next, more abstract level of thinking. In analyzing *The Lorax*, students built from the more concrete symbols, such as the tired look on the animals' faces representing their reaction to the loss of their habitat, to the more abstract symbols, such as the factory workers being laid off representing the extinction of the Truffula trees. As they added symbols to the Literature Web, it was important that students shared their thinking because this was also when students started making connections between the components of the Literature Web. The student who contributed the symbol of the tired look on the animals' faces was prompted by the sad feelings expressed by the characters that were noted when we discussed characters' feelings. As students shared their thinking, lines were physically drawn to connect ideas that were pointed out in their explanations.

The final two components discussed were structure and big ideas. These components required students to think about the text as a whole, putting all of the puzzle pieces together, so to speak. When students discussed structure, this was an opportunity to bring in text structures, grammatical structures, or even word structures. Teachers can lean on this component to steer the discussions toward a teachable moment. With *The Lorax*, it was important for students to see the nonlinear timeline that Dr. Seuss used to tell his story. Therefore, the discussion was steered toward the impact of the storytelling by beginning and ending the story in the present day with a big flashback in the middle. Discussing text structure in this way was more authentic and students were better able to grasp the reasoning behind the author's craft, compared to through an out-of-context mini-lesson on all text structures at once. From this discussion students learned that the author wanted readers to see the consequences of an action at the beginning and end, because that is usually what is remembered most, with the middle of the story focused on the causes. This discussion led to big ideas, or themes, based on cause and effect, such as "think before you act" and "don't be greedy." The act of teaching theme was simplified because students were able to discuss all of the small parts of the text, making connections along the way, so that when it came time to think about the big picture, all of the pieces had been put together. Figure 4.19 shows the completed Literature Web from *The Lorax* discussion.

An Integrated Example. The Literature Web, I have found, also works beautifully for the analysis of a variety of other mediums. In fact, when introducing the Literature Web itself, one may find it simpler to use the web with a piece of art or an illustration from a book, rather than an entire text. In this way, students become familiar with the components of the web and the analysis process without feeling the pressure of having to analyze an entire piece of text. In the previously mentioned autobiography unit, I also used different mediums to inspire students as they thought about writing their own autobiography. Visual arts and music were integrated into this unit, offering self-portraits and song lyrics for students to analyze as an alternate form of autobiography. The Literature Web was used to aid the analysis process.

Norman Rockwell's *Triple Self-Portrait* (1960) is full of symbolism for students to uncover and is a great example of a nontraditional autobiography. This self-portrait was selected to help students think about what they might include

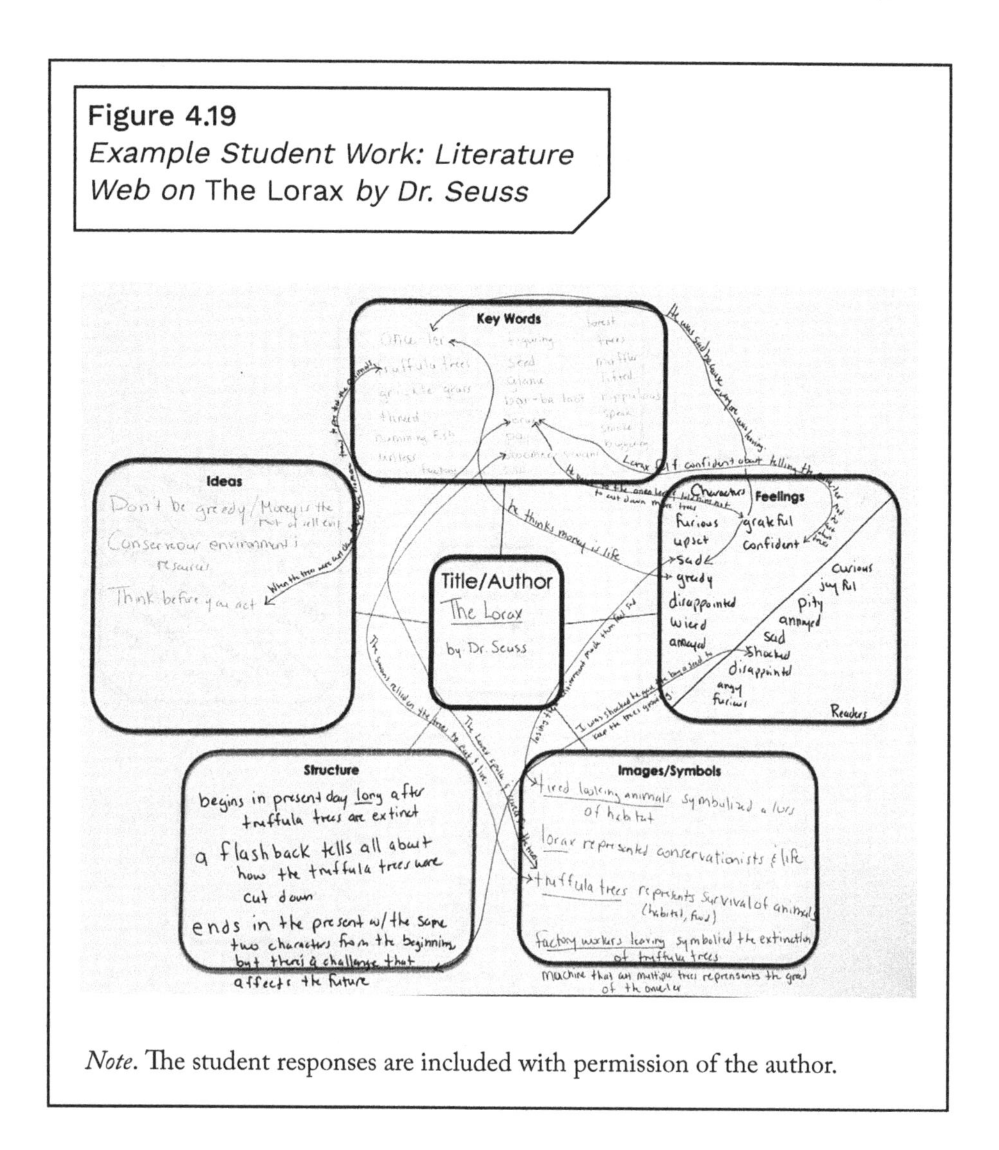

Figure 4.19

Example Student Work: Literature Web on The Lorax *by Dr. Seuss*

Note. The student responses are included with permission of the author.

first in a self-portrait and, ultimately, in an autobiography. During the analysis process, and using the Literature Web as a guide, students discussed the size and placement of various objects within the portrait to uncover their potential importance in Rockwell's life. Students related this particular finding from the artwork to the writing process. They discussed how an author should add or eliminate important events in their lives so that readers get a clear understanding of who they are based on what they decided to include, and emphasize, within their autobiography. Figure 4.20 shows that students made a wide range of analyses, again illustrating how the Literature Web allowed students of differing ability levels an opportunity to contribute.

Figure 4.20
Example Student Work: Literature Web on Triple Self-Portrait *by Norman Rockwell*

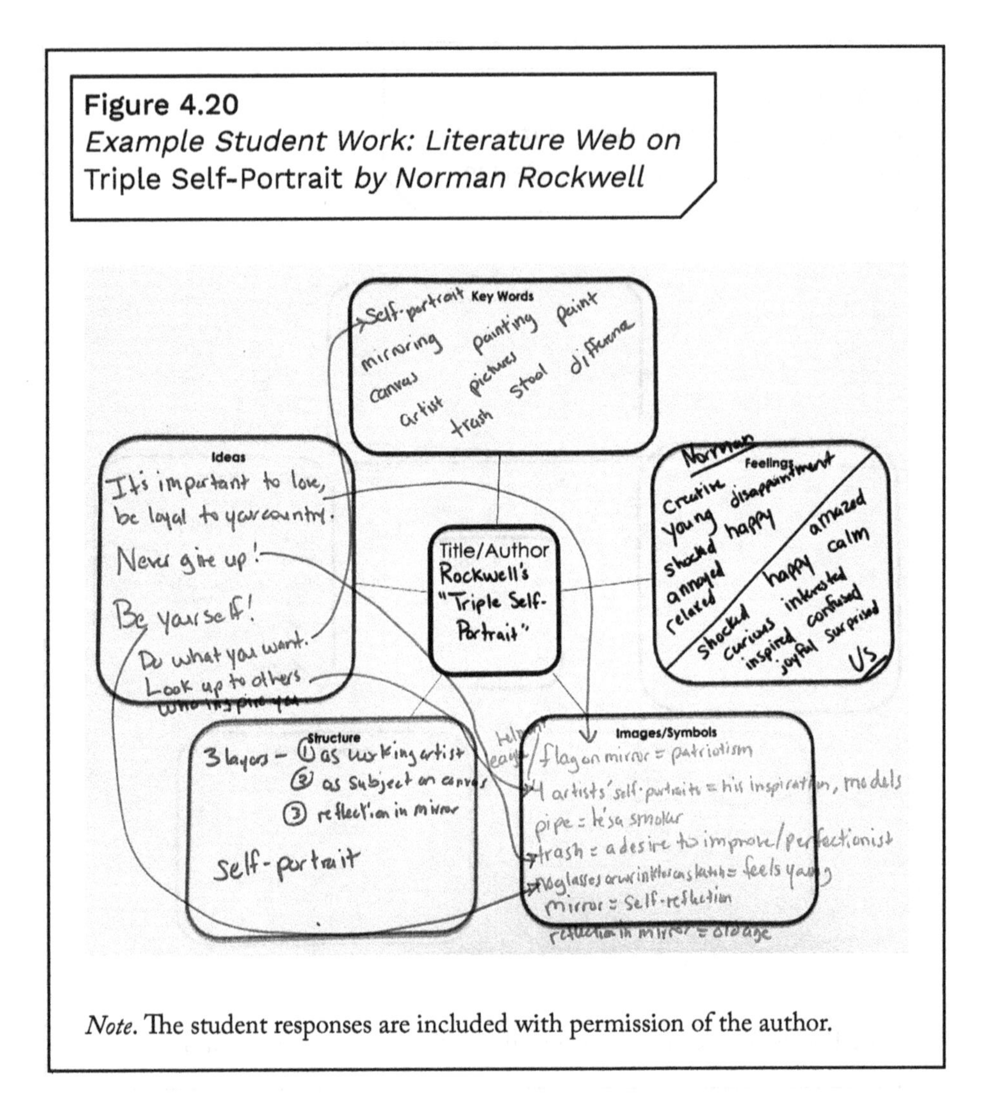

Note. The student responses are included with permission of the author.

Finally, lyric analysis through a Literature Web offered another opportunity for students to engage in thinking about their own autobiographies in a unique way. Students analyzed the song lyrics of several well-known musicians, and discussions began with a conversation about the song topic. Students discussed why the musician may have selected that topic to write and/or sing about. Students were encouraged to do quick background research to find out about the time period or the musician to determine what may have inspired the song. Then, they began their analysis of the lyrics, using the Literature Web as a guide. Figure 4.21 shows students' analysis of John Lennon's "Imagine."

This group's analysis of the lyrics shows they were able to really discover the person behind the song and determine that John Lennon, according to the

Figure 4.21
Example Student Work: Literature Web on "Imagine" by John Lennon

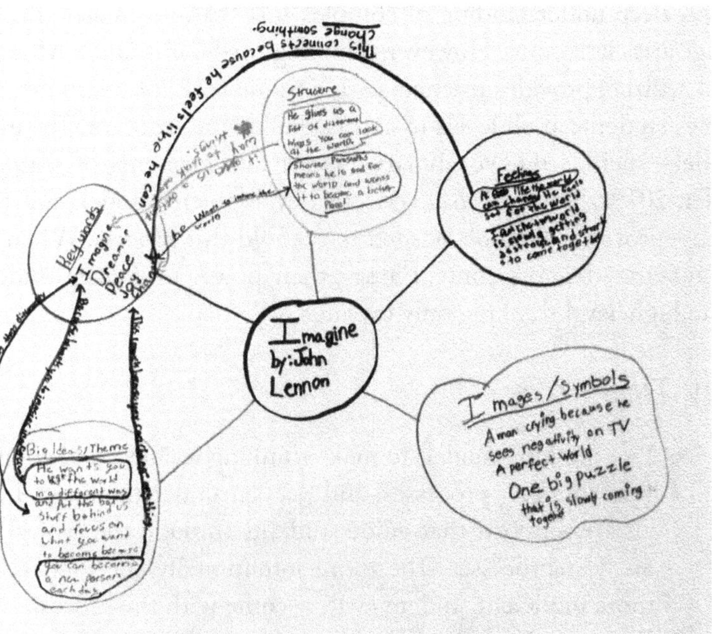

Note. The student responses are included with permission of the author.

students' analysis of theme, "wants you to look at the world in a different way and put the bad stuff behind us and focus on what you want to become because you can become a new person each day." This analysis process was important to students' writing process because they used these themes, or big ideas, as a common thread throughout their writing. As students selected different events from their lives to include in their autobiographies, they had to keep in mind their big idea, just as John Lennon had to focus on his big idea from one verse of the song to the next.

Like the other thinking models that have been discussed throughout this chapter, the Literature Web is an opportunity to scaffold critical thinking and make the process visible. When students have the opportunity to use a tool consistently and across disciplines, they will not only become familiar with the tool itself, but also the thinking process that the tool is designed to guide.

Knowing how to think critically about texts and content across subject areas provides students with opportunities to let their talents shine.

Summary

A deep understanding of complex texts can be challenging in many language arts classrooms. However, the Integrated Curriculum Model (VanTassel-Baska, 2017) provides teachers with a framework for instructional design that allows students at all levels to access challenging content. The use of thinking model—such as the Vocabulary Web, Paul's elements of reasoning (Paul & Elder, 2019), Taba's (1962) concept development model, and the Literature Web—provides the tools needed to scaffold this process. When these models are integrated across content areas, their power to engage students and promote high-level thinking only expands.

Key Tips

- Use thinking models to make thinking visible, build connections, scaffold thinking processes, and deepen understandings. Thinking models are supports that guide students through the critical thinking and analysis processes. The more intentionally the models are used, the more proficient students will become with the processes.
- Be strategic about the use of the thinking models. Overuse of any strategy can become disengaging. Therefore, teachers should use the thinking models described when addressing complex texts or concepts that may require scaffolds for students. Consider what kind of thinking students will be doing in order to select the most appropriate thinking model for the task and text.
- Integrate thinking models into other content areas. Thinking models can be easily introduced through literacy lessons. Once students have an understanding of how to use the thinking model, it can then be transferred to other content areas to support critical thinking across the curriculum.

Conclusion

Too often, students attending high-poverty schools, especially students of color, are not identified as gifted and talented. In fact, these groups of students are widely underrepresented in gifted and talented classes and programs. Unfortunately, that can be due to the teachers' inability to develop and spot talent. The Talent Development Instructional Model was designed with this issue in mind and dedicated to training teachers to develop and spot talent and provide them with support, such as these thinking models and tools. By using these thinking models, teachers are better able to support their students through the thinking processes, develop critical thinkers, and ultimately develop talent. In the next chapter, you will explore similar tools and models to engage students in high-level thinking specifically within mathematics.

End-of-Chapter Discussion/ Reflection Questions

1. What are some significant reasons for using the Integrated Curriculum Model in talent-focused teaching?
2. In this chapter, the Vocabulary Web is described as a tool to deepen understanding of words and their meanings. What makes this tool important in talent-focused teaching? Explain using details and examples to illustrate why.
3. Review the descriptions and applications of both the reasoning model and the concept development model. How might you integrate one of these models into a unit of study you currently teach? Why are these thinking models important in a student's talent development?
4. In this chapter, the author writes, "Like the other thinking models that have been discussed throughout this chapter, the Literature Web is an opportunity to scaffold critical thinking and make the process visible." Why is making the process visible to students key to their talent development?

References

Beck, I. L., McKeown, M. G., & Kucan, L. (2013). *Bringing words to life: Robust vocabulary instruction* (2nd ed.). Guilford Press.

Center for Gifted Education. (n.d.-a). *Literature web*. https://education.wm.edu/centers/cfge/_documents/curriculum/teachingmodels/literatureweb.pdf

Center for Gifted Education. (n.d.-b). *Reasoning about a situation or event.* https://education.wm.edu/centers/cfge/_documents/curriculum/teachingmodels/reasoningevent.pdf

Center for Gifted Education. (n.d.-c). *Reasoning web.* https://education.wm.edu/centers/cfge/_documents/curriculum/teachingmodels/reasoningweb.pdf

Center for Gifted Education. (n.d.-d). *Vocabulary web.* https://education.wm.edu/centers/cfge/_documents/curriculum/teachingmodels/vocabularyweb.pdf

Center for Gifted Education. (2011). *Autobiographies and memoirs* (2nd ed.). Kendall Hunt.

Dr. Seuss. (1971). *The Lorax.* Random House.

National Research Council. (2000). *How people learn: Brain, mind, experience, and school* (Expanded ed.). The National Academies Press. https://doi.org/10.17226/9853

Paul, R., & Elder, L. (2019). *The miniature guide to critical thinking concepts and tools* (8th ed.). Rowman & Littlefield.

Rockwell, N. (1960). *Triple self-portrait.* Saturday Evening Post.

The Saturday Globe. (1892). *Forty-millionaire Carnegie in his great double role.* http://digitalexhibits.libraries.wsu.edu/items/show/5569

Spinelli, J. (1998). *Knots in my yo-yo string.* Knopf.

Swanson, J. D., Brock, L., Van Sickle, M., Gutshall, C. A., Russell, L., & Anderson, L. (2020). A basis for talent development: The integrated curriculum model and evidence-based strategies. *Roeper Review, 42*(3), 165–178. https://doi.org/10.1080/02783193.2020.1765920

Taba, H. (1962). *Curriculum development: Theory and practice.* Harcourt, Brace & World.

VanTassel-Baska, J. (2017). Introduction to the integrated curriculum model. In J. VanTassel-Baska & C. A. Little (Eds.), *Content-based curriculum for high-ability learners* (3rd ed., pp. 15–32). Prufrock Press.

Yin. (2003). *Coolies* (C. Soentpiet, Illus.). Puffin Books.

5

Talent Development in Math

Denise E. Zacherl

> The student most neglected, in terms of realizing full potential, is the gifted student of mathematics. Outstanding mathematical ability is a precious societal resource, sorely needed to maintain leadership in a technological world. (National Council of Teachers of Mathematics [NCTM], 1980, p. 18)

How does one cultivate a love of math in the classroom? Math in today's classroom should not be static, passive, or worksheet driven, but should transform how students engage in mathematical thinking and problem solving. A nurturing classroom focused on talent development creates a space where multiple solutions are shared and discussed. Replacing rote learning with rich, in-depth understanding unleashes mathematical potential.

In developing students' emergent potential in mathematics, a broadened view recognizes and develops traditionally underserved students, including high-potential students from diverse or underserved backgrounds as well as those traditionally identified as gifted (Sheffield, 1999). An emphasis on disciplinary thinking aligns with the NCTM (2000) Process Standards and the

Standards for Mathematical Practice of the Common Core State Standards (National Governors Association Center for Best Practices [NGA] & Council of Chief State School Officers [CCSSO], 2010). Research from NCTM and the Common Core State Standards supports the use of math curricula that are concept-based and rich with inquiry and productive discussion.

This chapter explicates a specific set of curricula developed by researchers at University of Connecticut led by Dr. Kathy Gavin called the Mentoring Mathematical Minds Project (Project M^3; e.g., Gavin et al. 2006) for grades 3–5 and the Mentoring Young Mathematicians Project (Project M^2; e.g., Gavin et al., 2010) for grades K–2. Instructional practices in this set of curricula provide a catalyst to transform students from passive learners into actively practicing mathematicians and have shown effectiveness with diverse learners (Gavin & Casa, 2012; Gavin et al., 2006, 2007, 2009). This chapter discusses specifics on these curricula, examples of their use in Talent Development Academies (TDA; Swanson et al., 2019), and the connection to talent development.

The Curriculum

The IRIS Center, a federally-funded program at Vanderbilt University's Peabody College, provides evidence-based practices for teachers that improve student outcomes, especially for struggling learners and those with disabilities. With regard to quality mathematical instruction, the IRIS Center (n.d.) noted that:

> The most effective way to teach concepts and procedures is to implement evidence-based practices (EBPs)—practices and strategies that have been shown to be effective through rigorous research. When teachers implement EBPs along with a standards-based curriculum, they are providing high-quality mathematics instruction. (p. 3)

Use of curricula and strategies with a research base of effectiveness with all learners is a key pillar in implementing the Talent Development Instructional Model (TDIM) in your school.

Gavin et al. (2009) found that students using M^2 and M^3 curricula demonstrated mathematical growth, both in promise and equity outcomes. Findings with diverse learners indicated that these materials fostered a passion for mathematics through inclusion of evidence-based practices. The EBPs of conceptual inquiry, teaching for depth of understanding and complexity through embedded differentiation, and productive communication (both oral and written) promoted a growth orientation toward learning. These instructional practices (Gavin et al., 2009) tap into and grow mathematical talent. Colangelo et al. (2004) promoted the use of grade acceleration, but others (Robinson et al., 2007) have disagreed. For example, Robinson et al. (2007) found that although acceleration allows for efficient content coverage, acceleration alone does not provide the high-level thinking needed to develop the in-depth understanding characteristic of mathematically promising students. In Projects M^2 and M^3, the combination of gifted education best practices like enrichment and acceleration (Renzulli et al., 2000; Tomlinson et al., 2002) and NCTM standards provide a unique way to ensure that students learn through tasks that real-world mathematicians face (Sriraman, 2004). Using the practice of mathematical inquiry, students learn the epistemology of mathematics, identifying what they do and do not understand as they build deep and enduring learning.

Project M^3 Design and Effectiveness

How is this powerful and effective math curriculum that works well in the TDIM organized and designed? What does research report about its effectiveness? Project M^3 is organized to allow teachers flexibility in the implementation of the curriculum units. There are 12 units, with four units at each of three levels—grades 3, 4, and 5. Each unit addresses mathematical ideas from one of the NCTM content strands: (a) algebra, (b) data analysis or probability, (c) geometry or measurement, or (d) numbers and operations. The content is accelerated one to two grade levels, with a focus on in-depth investigation. Math process standards are embedded in conceptual inquiry, and the lessons demand high-level thinking. In addition, the creation of products encourages students to apply what they learn in varied ways, such as creating games and culminating projects. Verbal and written communication, based on important mathematical concepts (NTCM, 2000), are central to the design. Students regularly use NCTM processes of problem solving, reasoning, making connections, and creating and using representations.

Gavin et al.'s (2009) research on student impact used multiple measures of mathematics achievement to evaluate the effectiveness of the Project M^3 curriculum. Researchers found statistically significant differences between the experimental and comparison groups. Results indicated that the mathematics was learned at a statistically significant level among both learners from low-income households and the mathematically talented learners.

Project M² Design and Effectiveness

Project M², built upon the success of Project M³, focuses similarly on in-depth mathematics using research-based practices and standards from math and early childhood education. Project M²'s main goal is to help primary students learn more complex and in-depth geometry and measurement concepts, thus increasing student achievement. Fuson (2004) noted that "increasing learning in the early grades will make it easier to be more ambitious at the upper grades where U.S. students are considerably behind" (p. 109). Like M³, each Project M² unit addresses mathematical ideas from the NCTM (2000) content strands of algebra, geometry, and measurement, all identified as needing additional instructional time at the primary level. Further, algebra, geometry, and measurement are listed as critical areas at the primary grades in the Common Core State Standards (NGA & CCSSO, 2010). Project M² curriculum was designed to challenge all primary-level students in the classroom, not to be used in a gifted pull-out program or special class. This opens access to all students in a school's talent pool, allowing classroom teachers to become talent developers and scouts early in their students' mathematical learning.

In conclusion, results for Project M² revealed that field-test groups in kindergarten, first grade, and second grade showed significant gains from pre- to post-testing across all schools on the open-response assessment that measured growth in geometry and measurement. At each grade level the effect size was large, indicating that the students from all backgrounds were 1–3 years ahead of the comparison group of similar ability and demographics in terms of grade-level equivalence (Gavin & Casa, 2012; Gavin et al., 2013).

Evidence-Based Practices for Talent Development

Although there are other challenging math curricula that work to enable talent development, this chapter highlights experience with Projects M² and M³ in TDA schools (Swanson et al., 2019) using the Talent Development Instructional Model. Projects M² and M³ were chosen because of their evidence base of effectiveness in student learning and the utilization of evidence-based practices supported by professional mathematics organizations. This section describes the evidence-based practices found in Projects M² and M³, including conceptual inquiry, embedded differentiation for depth and complexity, and talk moves/talk frames to grow mathematical written and oral communication.

Conceptual Inquiry

What is conceptual inquiry? In this context, conceptual inquiry is defined as a combination of using concepts for thinking and learning with in-depth, teacher-guided mathematical inquiry. EBPs in Projects M^2 and M^3 allow teachers to develop student understanding of mathematical concepts (National Research Council, 2001, 2005) through teacher-guided inquiry. Further, this curriculum includes advanced content (Renzulli et al., 2000) for high-ability learners by focusing on structures of knowledge, basic principles, functional concepts, and methods of inquiry in particular disciplines. Inquiry encourages students to move beyond their comfort level to embrace and struggle with new problems (Vygotsky & Cole, 1978). Included in the conceptual inquiry are Type II and III activities (Renzulli & Reis, 2014), providing students opportunities to think and act like professional mathematicians. In Type II learning, students learn problem finding, problem solving, critical thinking, and reasoning with evidence. In Type III learning, students are able to pursue a mathematical area of interest, going beyond the classroom inquiry into self-directed inquiry.

In each Project M^2 or M^3 lesson, the heart is the "Think Deeply" question(s) to promote mathematical thinking. "Think Deeply" questions address a concept that ties directly to the important mathematical idea in the lesson. Teachers in TDA schools used "Think Deeply" questions to guide students though conceptual inquiry to grapple with difficult mathematical concepts. This grappling, an example of Type II learning, is a springboard that enables students to learn to track their moment-to-moment understanding or lack of understanding, to coordinate the ideas and understandings, and to engage in thinking or solving problems. "Think Deeply" questions, too, can be used by teachers as formal and informal assessment tools to gauge what students are learning and understanding.

Examples From Practice. Conceptual inquiry proves to be highly effective within the talent development model because it helps teachers to spot potential in students. An example of one teacher's "aha" moment was shared in an interview of TDA teachers in schools using the Talent Development Instructional Model. This teacher shared her experiences and reflections from implementation of the Project M^3 curriculum. She modified a lesson from the fifth-grade Project M^3 unit *Treasures From the Attic* (Gavin et al., 2015b), changing the order in which she taught fractions by teaching fractions before teaching division. She described one student who was struggling with math. The student worked and worked on a fractions problem, dividing the newspaper pages into fractional pieces, using page after page to explore possible solutions. The teacher was amazed that the student persisted. When he reached a solution, the student was proud and excitedly shared the solution with others in the class.

In making this change to her sequence of instruction, the teacher discovered the power of conceptual inquiry—that once students understood the concept of fractions as part of a whole, division became more easily understood as they divided a whole (dividend) into parts of a whole (by the divisor). She added more concept-based activities, like making a human (student) number line and then having the students act as fractions of the line. By allowing students to explore fractions conceptually and acting as a guide with thoughtful questions, the teacher found that students persevered in problem solving using different approaches. Their task commitment was an eye opener for her. Student mathematicians became passionately involved (J. Rowe, personal communication, June 15, 2020). In talent development, finding one's passions and interests matters.

In Project M^2's *Designing a Shape Gallery: Geometry With the Meerkats* (Gavin et al., 2010), students investigate two- and three-dimensional shapes and the relationships between them. Using van Hiele's (1999) model of geometric thinking, the unit encourages students to move beyond van Hiele's visual level, identifying shapes by appearance: "It must be a triangle because it looks like one" (Gavin et al., 2013, p. 482). Students are exposed to different scenarios from which they deduce different shape properties. For example, in the "Think Deeply" questioning prompts, students are given two sets of shapes and asked to identify which set is the set of triangles and to explain why. Moving the focus to a deeper level, students begin identifying shapes by their characteristics, such as having three sides and three vertices. This level requires careful analysis and understanding of the definition of a triangle. For teachers in schools using a talent development model, class discussion focused on the different shapes in both sets and required students to conduct close analysis and define what a triangle is. Many students do not achieve this level of proficiency with geometric shape characteristics until middle school. According to Clements and Sarama (2009), "Children can learn richer concepts about shapes if their educational environment includes four features: varied examples and nonexamples, discussions about shapes and their attributes, a wider variety of shape classes, and a broad array of geometric tasks" (p. 133). This deep study through inquiry focused on the mathematical idea of triangles is part of the Project M^2 unit.

Project M² and M³ lessons engage students in sensemaking, reasoning, and problem solving. As the teachers in TDA schools using the Talent Development Instructional Model guided students using conceptual inquiry focused on the lesson's mathematical idea, students practiced the disciplinary thinking needed to reason through and solve mathematical problems. Teachers learned to guide, providing students opportunities to struggle and persevere. The conceptual inquiry helped teachers to see students' talents, easily missed without this rich interaction of teachers guiding while students grappled.

Embedded Differentiation: Scaffolds, Depth, and Complexity

Depth of understanding and complexity embedded in Projects M² and M³ allows students to study mathematics intensely and realize the layers and connectivity among the concepts. How can the curriculum be high-level and advanced and still meet the needs of all learners in a classroom? The embedded differentiation in Projects M² and M³ provides advanced curriculum that raises the bar beyond what is typical at a grade level. With resources for the TDA teachers to easily differentiate lessons matched to student needs, the teachers were able to make advanced learning accessible for all. The embedded differentiated resources are "Hint Cards" and "Think Beyond Cards."

Hint Cards were used to scaffold students who were struggling. They provided differentiation for students who did not have the necessary background or prior experiences to move forward in their mathematical thinking (Gavin et al., 2006). Hint Cards posed questions to guide students' thinking in smaller steps in order to bring them to a more complex understanding. Think Beyond Cards focused on questions promoting high-level thinking and mathematical discussion with students who had a firm grasp of the concepts presented and were ready for increased challenges. The Think Beyond cards expanded student knowledge by requiring deeper, more complex reasoning.

Examples From Practice. In the Project M³ unit *Awesome Algebra: Looking for Patterns and Generalizations* (Gavin et al., 2015a), student mathematicians explore patterns and determine how the patterns change, how they can be extended or repeated, and/or how they grow. Students organize and analyze patterns to draw generalizations about the mathematical relationships they found. For teachers in TDA schools, class discussion focused on how to verbalize these generalization(s). The unit's embedded differentiation through Hint Cards to scaffold students helped break down the pattern problem into questions such as "What patterns do you see? Does the pattern repeat or grow? How do you know what comes next?" (Gavin et al., 2015a, p. 82). Think Beyond Cards provided questions that carefully scaffolded the learning for those who were challenged by the content. The wide variety of the Hint and Think Beyond Cards at each level made individualization easier for the teachers and provided students rich opportunities to develop an interest and love for the topic through new experiences and new learning.

The embedded differentiation (Renzulli et al., 2000) was not busywork or a task similar to what students were already doing in class. This differentiation supported talent development, starting where students are, building on interests with relevant and engaging learning tasks within the developmental reach of learners. The Hint and Think Beyond cards expanded students' knowledge, requiring deeper and more complex reasoning. By scaffolding or challenging students based on need, teachers had many opportunities to see the potential of their students.

Talk Moves and Talk Frame: Oral and Written Communication

Chapin et al.'s (2013) model of classroom discussions called "talk moves" is a tool to grow students' reasoning and problem-solving abilities in Projects M^2 and M^3, enabling students to develop conceptual understanding through talking through their approaches to problem solving. The TDA teachers used talk moves in combination with conceptual inquiry via "Think Deeply" questions (described previously) to build deep mathematical understanding first through discussion.

As an instructional strategy, talk moves transformed passive learning (e.g., students completing a worksheet) to active learning (e.g., students reasoning through a problem). Students learned to communicate orally (i.e., talk moves) and in written forms (i.e., talk frame) to make meaning of the mathematics they were learning. The goal was to increase not only classroom discussion, but also the amount of quality talk, specifically mathematically productive talk (Chapin et al., 2013). Setting up the classroom as a supportive learning community was essential. Students learned to be listeners, be supportive in sharing ideas, and talk about their mathematical thinking without fear of ridicule. Students learned how to avoid ridiculing others in their discussions, so that trust necessary for mathematically productive talk was built. As students were asked to discuss or write about the concept being taught, they learned to recognize gaps, incomplete or flawed reasoning in their knowledge.

In implementing the Projects M^2 and M^3 curriculum, talk moves was used in two ways. Directly, the classroom discussion gave students access to others' ideas, allowing them to see different perspectives as well as relationships among ideas, strategies, procedures, facts, mathematical history, and mathematical thinking. Indirectly, classroom discussions developed a powerful learning community. A learning community grew that supported and encouraged students who were respectful of others as equal partners in thinking, conjecturing, exploring, testing, and sharing ideas. In mathematically productive dialogue, students learned to revoice each other's ideas on a peer-to-peer level and among the whole class, as well as state their own contributions for clarification. Students learned respectful communication through practicing speaker and listener roles.

The listener roles included asking speakers to speak up, showing speakers one was listening, and asking questions to understand an idea. The speaker roles included these talk moves: repeat/rephrase one another's ideas, agree/disagree with why, use mathematically valid evidence, use partner talk to discuss ideas and solutions, and use wait time for organizing thoughts (Chapin et al., 2009). Teaching students both speaker and listener roles was crucial, as the roles work hand in hand in productive discussion. Teacher strategies for using the talk moves in mathematically productive classroom discussions included:

- focusing on an important mathematical idea;
- using an open-ended problem with multiple solutions;
- requiring students to think deeply, going beyond recall;
- encouraging students to reason and to justify responses with evidence; and
- encouraging different solution strategies and/or various correct answers.

An essential transition between verbal discourse using talk moves and written understanding to capture mathematical thinking from the class was developed using the talk frame (Casa, 2013). The talk frame established the topic of discussion in written form. Each idea shared orally through discussion was summarized and added to the talk frame in written language by the teacher. All ideas, both correct and incorrect, were summarized and written on the talk frame. Productive discussion via talk moves ensued to make sense of the multiple solutions and/or current misconceptions among students. Using talk moves, students offered claims, were asked for evidence to support their claims, or discussed and analyzed, as a group, counterexamples to the claim for consideration and clarification. The talk frame was a visual, written record of the discussion.

Conceptual inquiry and talk moves were used in tandem in the lessons. Specifically, the lesson's "Think Deeply" question, along with the talk frame, helped students connect their verbal thinking out loud with the development of writing as a way to communicate mathematically. While using the talk frame, teachers gathered different student perspectives, not judging their validity. By encouraging students to make sense of the mathematical concepts themselves, correct and incorrect ideas were considered on the talk frame. The instructional goal was for students to consider and clarify ideas in a way similar to mathematicians: through examining reasoning and evidence as a class.

Examples From Practice. TDA teachers implemented talk moves and saw the power of this instructional strategy. An instructional coach modeled lessons for teachers using talk moves and followed up with the teachers to plan and develop lessons using talk moves. Teachers learned to engage students with math content using the list of strategies for using the talk moves (discussed previously) to guide the lesson development. As teachers gained experience in using talk moves with their students, instructional coaches introduced the Project M^2 and M^3 units to the individual grade levels. In other words, teachers learned how to conduct discussions using talk moves before teaching the math units. TDA teachers shared the following comments:

> [Talk moves] is beginning to become part of the classroom culture. I have also been encouraging students to respectfully explain their thinking as well as why they disagree with another student's idea. (as cited in Kessler, 2016, para. 6)

> I have been using the talk moves around open-ended problems during the math block to deepen the students' thinking. The students are really getting used to using agree and disagree in their sentences. . . . Students are now using it without me having to prompt them and I love it. (as cited in Kessler, 2016, para. 7)

Talk moves can be used as a discussion tool in other content areas as well. Once students have learned talk moves, they are able to have productive dialogue around literary selections and literary analysis. A TDA teacher shared the following about her use of talk moves with her students in discussion of a literary selection the class read:

> I have also been using [talk moves] when discussing *Yolanda's Genius*. We have really been stressing using agree/disagree with [another student's] "idea" and not just that person. So far, it has shown that students are being more respectful in their discussions, and more students are offering up ideas and concepts in discussion. I have also been working on wait time and my poker face, which I have found to be difficult but seems to slow the discussion down and allows more students to process and take ownership of what we are learning. (as cited in Kessler, 2016, para. 11)

Next, observations from the classroom of a first-grade teacher implementing a Project M^2 lesson at a TDA school are described. After teaching the math lesson and capturing the learning/understanding on the whiteboard using the talk frame, the teacher was amazed that students' distinct understandings came out in individual writing in student math journals. The teacher thought the "Think Deeply" journal writing would be too hard, but her thinking was wrong. In their math journals, the first graders displayed academic risk-taking, showing understanding using the talk frame to explore and communicate their thinking in writing.

At this point, capturing the discussion on the talk frame allowed the first-grade students to return to discussion to use talk moves and to explore evidence and validity of the ideas captured. In a give and take, students debated the ideas and evidence, and came to consensus on ideas to be accepted and/or discredited based on reasoning supported by evidence. Through practice, the teacher and students created a classroom environment in which students learned to listen to each other, freely contribute to the dialogue, provide evidence for their claims, and offer counterevidence for conflicting ideas or solutions. Lastly, the teacher guided students to reach a mathematical understanding and summarize the mathematically valid conclusion upon which the class agreed. Through this process, when given time to debate and justify their ideas, students learned to notice the errors in their thinking.

Students do not arrive at the classroom knowing how to communicate mathematically. Providing students with rich tasks does not guarantee that they know the skills of oral and written communication in mathematics. Often in mathematics, students are so busy getting to the "right" answer that there is little thought or discussion of the mathematical thinking behind their answers. As teachers in schools using the Talent Development Instructional Model learned the skills of implementing productive mathematical discussions using rich tasks, students learned to be more observant and reflective thinkers, better listeners, and capable of participating in mathematical thinking. Consider these thoughts from @NCTM Blog:

> Meaningful assistance encompasses more than fixing a careless error related to poor study habits, such as misreading directions, miscopying a numeral, or forgetting a sign. Although we can easily and explicitly address careless errors in our instruction, it can be more challenging—but potentially much more rewarding—to address errors that fall into the special category of productive mistakes. These are the mistakes that have the potential to promote rich learning. (Gojak, 2013, para. 3)

Talk moves and talk frame are tools for thinking and reasoning that illustrate how this curriculum taps into and grows mathematical talent. Through the discussion process, students were able to bring to light discrepancies in their own and others' thinking. Productive discussion uncovered partial understandings or misunderstandings, allowing for student self-correction by listening and responding to others through speculation, investigating different ideas or solutions, and presenting viable solutions.

Learning of mathematical language was evident, as students became more precise in mathematical discussions. Teachers using Projects M^2 and M^3 created a vocabulary word wall to support students and teachers in using the language of a mathematician. Modeling the language of the discipline is essential for students to develop their mathematical potential and grow talent. Oral and written communication is tied directly to talent development, allowing teachers to formatively assess their students' thoughts and understanding through mathematically productive discussion and writing.

Connected Instructional Practices: A Summary

Description and illustration of conceptual inquiry through "Think Deeply" questions, scaffolds and extensions through embedded differentiation, and talk moves and talk frame show the power of these instructional strategies as individual components. In fact, the conceptual inquiry uses talk moves and the talk frame to guide students as they construct meaning. Through ongoing formative assessment, teachers identify which students need differentiated instruction and draw upon the Hint Cards and Think Beyond Cards to meet individual learners where they are. The connectedness of the instructional components is illustrated so that educators better understand the unique design of Project M^2 and M^3 curriculum units that were implemented by teachers in schools using the talent development model.

Mathematical writing is uncommon in most elementary classes, so thoughtful modeling of the process starting with mathematical concepts began with a discussion of the "Think Deeply" question from the lesson. Opening with conceptual inquiry centered on the "Think Deeply" question, teachers guided students to formalize the deeper understanding orally through talk moves. Capturing the discussion visually on the board via talk frame allowed students to reread and reflect on what was discussed—priming students for mathematical writing.

Mathematicians in practice use pictures, examples, graphs, charts, and mathematical language to explain their thoughts, so students learned to use these means to communicate mathematically. Teachers found that, at times, it was important to discuss the "Think Deeply" question first and then ask students to write about it by summarizing the discussion and adding their own interpretations. Other times, students brainstormed ideas on the "Think Deeply" questions and wrote down ideas first, partner shared, and, finally, presented their findings in a class discussion. These partner-to-partner "Think Deeply" discussions were followed up with a written summary and concluding thoughts by students in math journals.

As students progressed, the teacher employed the embedded differentiation, using Hint Cards for students needing a bridge and Think Beyond Cards for students who needed more complexity and depth. With the opportunity to play with mathematical ideas though the verbal give and take, many students developed a love for mathematics and true enjoyment for "doing" math. These approaches of "doing math" differ greatly from "doing computation." Utilization of processes that mathematicians actually employ enabled student understanding of the skills/processes needed to discover new mathematical thinking and concepts.

Conclusion

Learning Environment

What makes a supportive and nurturing classroom environment essential? Teachers in TDA schools supported and nurtured students by using teaching strategies, such as embedded differentiation tailored to student needs, talk moves, conceptual inquiry, and evidence-based discussions. Teachers took care to build relationships with and among students. Through the rich and interesting inquiry and discussion, students' minds and hearts were fed. Through use of rules of engagement, those in the classroom learned to respect the individual's rights to share diverse perspectives and ideas. Students began to value precision, clarity, intellectual honesty, effort, and thoroughness—intellectual traits often evident in scientists and mathematicians.

The classroom transformed into a safe, supportive learning community where students learned how to think, question, and develop their own ideas and thoughts through conversations grounded in evidence, not opinion. As Chapin et al. (2009) stated, "Unless we are put in a situation where we must talk or write about the concept, we may never come to realize that our knowledge is incomplete, shallow, or passive" (p. 7). It is easy for teachers to supply students with answers or point out errors. In classrooms using Projects M^2 and M^3, student learning grew out of struggle, challenge, and effort, all essential to growing potential. In teaching, how educators "respond to productive errors can encourage or discourage student thinking and learning" (Gojak, 2013, p. 2). Student errors and mistakes as a platform for learning provided teachers with ongoing formative assessment and offered a basis to promote richer learning.

The following vignette illustrates how powerful math curriculum can impact the teacher's ability to see talent. A teacher at a TDA school shared that although students wrote daily, they did not know automatically how to write in math. The students were good at sharing the steps and solutions aloud in discussion, but they froze when asked to write the same information in response to the "Think Deeply" question. The teacher explicitly modeled and taught her students how to write in math. She was excited to share how essential the strategies were for talent spotting:

> I chose children to be tested [for the gifted program] that I would never have picked because of the way they processed and applied themselves to the tasks presented to them. I looked at how they applied themselves to the task, figured out what to do, and explained their thinking [in writing and orally]. Some of these children, I would not have picked [as high-potential had I not been using the curriculum/strategies because I would not have seen them doing this sort of application and thinking. (J. Rowe, personal communication, June 15, 2020)

As a result of developing a learning environment where students think aloud and in writing, this teacher was able to better spot talent. The powerful curriculum provided by Projects M^2 and M^3 was essential in the Talent Development Instructional Model implementation, as the hard-to-see talents of students became visible.

Key Tips

Projects M^2 and M^3 were written using a talent development lens, broadening mathematical talent to one inclusive of mathematical promise and equity. The primary instructional strategies embedded in the curricula foster a passion for mathematics in students. Mathematical talent development power is evident in the curricular strategies. Teachers in TDA schools made the journey with their students as they approached teaching of mathematics differently; the teaching approach in Projects M^2 and M^3 revealed talents in both teachers and students. Supported by a strong math curriculum, teachers saw student engagement and growth in mathematical understanding.

Advice for teachers beginning to implement this powerful, conceptual, and inquiry-based math curriculum to develop and identify talent follow:

- **Build a community of learners with the strategies and models of talk move discussions, along with the talk frame, to help students build connections and deepen their thinking and understanding in conceptual inquiry.** The transformation of the classroom into a safe, supportive, and responsive learning community allows students to share their mathematical thinking, including misunderstanding and misconceptions. Take the time with your students to develop their understanding of speaker and listener responsibilities, as well as how to engage in productive discussion using rules to guide the learning.
- **Model both the reasoning process (ideas on how to solve the problem) and product (the answers) as valuable.** Overall, the reasoning process should be more highly regarded than the answer. Reasoning must be grounded in evidence, and it is critical for students to explain reasoning with details and examples.
- **Embrace (i.e., do not be afraid of) students' struggle to clarify and understand.** Too many times, teachers unwittingly steal the opportunity for learning by providing students with the answer too soon. According to Fisher and Frey (2017), teachers do not want students to struggle, but that struggle is where student learning happens. Grappling and challenge as part of a classroom culture are import-

ant in talent development, so teaching yourself and your students that challenges are essential to growth makes a difference.

For teachers who are more advanced in use of inquiry with learners, be aware that you are the most significant influence on student learning. You have much control of the classroom culture and the extent to which diverse ideas are welcomed, nourished, or shunned. You influence the degree to which challenge, struggle, and academic risk-taking are embraced. Application of the talent development found in Projects M^2 and M^3 provided TDA teachers with powerful mathematics strategies and curriculum. Teachers who expect the unexpected as they cultivate the love of math open the door for mathematical potential to shine and to grow into mathematical talent. Noteworthy is that, before beginning their use of the advanced math curriculum, many TDA teachers did not think their students could perform at the higher levels embedded within the Projects M^2 and M^3 curriculum. After undertaking the learning journey with their students, their new perspective provided them with an effective way to spot the talent in their students.

End-of-Chapter Discussion/ Reflection Questions

1. What are similarities and differences in Projects M^3 and M^2?
2. Discuss conceptual inquiry as used in mathematics. What is it, and why is it important in development of mathematical talent?
3. In the curricula explicated in this chapter, Hint Cards and Think Beyond Cards are examples of differentiation strategies. Describe each strategy and its connection to emerging talent.
4. Why is it important for teachers using a talent-focused approach to teaching to embrace students' struggle to clarify and understand, and to allow students to grapple with difficult and challenging questions?

References

Casa, T. M. (2013). Capturing thinking on the talk frame. *Teaching Children Mathematics, 19*(8), 516–523. https://doi.org/10.5951/teacchilmath.19.8.0516

Chapin, S. H., O'Connor, C., & Anderson, N. C. (2009). *Classroom discussions: Using math talk to help students learn, grades 1–6* (2nd ed.). Math Solutions.

Chapin, S. H., O'Connor, C., & Anderson, N. C. (2013). *Classroom discussion in math: A teacher's guide for using talk moves to support the Common Core and more, grades K–6* (3rd ed.). Math Solutions.

Clements, D. H., & Sarama, J. (2009). *Learning and teaching early math: The learning trajectories approach*. Routledge.

Colangelo, N., Assouline, S. G., & Gross, M. U. M. (2004). *A nation deceived: How schools hold back America's brightest students* (Vol. 2). The University of Iowa, The Connie Belin & Jacqueline N. Blank International Center for Gifted Education and Talent Development.

Fisher, D., & Frey, N. (2017). Show and tell: A video column/the importance of struggle. *Educational Leadership, 74(*8), 85–86.

Fuson, K. C. (2004). Pre-k to grade 2 goals and standards: Achieving 21st-century mastery for all. In D. H. Clements & J. Sarama (Eds.), *Engaging young children in mathematics: Standards for early childhood mathematics education* (pp. 105–148). Erlbaum.

Gavin, M. K., & Casa, T. M. (2012). Nurturing young student mathematicians. *Gifted Education International, 29*(2), 140–153. https://doi.org/10.1177/0261429412447711

Gavin, M. K., Casa, T. M., & Adelson, J. L. (2006). Mentoring mathematical minds: An innovative program to develop math talent. *Understanding Our Gifted, 19*(1), 3–6.

Gavin, M. K., Casa, T. M., Adelson, J. L., Carroll, S. R., & Sheffield, L. J. (2009). The impact of advanced curriculum on the achievement of mathematically promising elementary students. *Gifted Child Quarterly, 53*(3), 188–202. http://doi.org/10.1177/0016986209334964

Gavin, M. K., Casa, T. M., Adelson, J. L., Carroll, S. R., Sheffield, L. J., & Spinelli, A. M. (2007). Project M^3: Mentoring mathematical minds: A research-based curriculum for talented elementary students. *Journal of Advanced Academics, 18*(4), 566–585. https://doi.org/10.4219/jaa-2007-552

Gavin, M. K., Casa, T. M., Adelson, J. L., & Firmender, J. M. (2013). The impact of challenging geometry and measurement units on the achievement of grade 2 students. *Journal for Research in Mathematics Education, 44*(3), 478–510. https://doi.org/10.5951/jresematheduc.44.3.0478

Gavin, M. K., Casa, T. M., Chapin, S. H., & Sheffield, L. J. (2010). *Project M^2: Level 2: Designing a shape gallery: Geometry with the meerkats, teacher guide*. Kendall Hunt.

Gavin, M. K., Chapin, S. H., Dailey, J., & Sheffield, L. J. (2015a). *Project M³: Level 3–4: Awesome algebra: Looking for patterns and generalizations, teacher guide*. Kendall Hunt.

Gavin, M. K., Chapin, S. H., Dailey, J., & Sheffield, L. J. (2015b). *Project M³: Level 4–5: Treasures from the attic: Exploring fractions, teacher guide*. Kendall Hunt.

Gojak, L. M. (2013). *The power of a good mistake*. @NCTM Blog. https://www.nctm.org/News-and-Calendar/Messages-from-the-President/Archive/Linda-M_-Gojak/The-Power-of-a-Good-Mistake

IRIS Center. (n.d.). *High-quality mathematics instruction: What teachers should know*. https://iris.peabody.vanderbilt.edu/module/math

Kessler, L. (2016, January 9). *Teachers grow their knowledge and skills in the first semester 2016*. Talent Development Academies: Project Talentum Academe. http://blogs.cofc.edu/talent-development-academies/2017/01/09/teachers-grow-their-knowledge-and-skills-in-the-first-semester

National Council of Teachers of Mathematics. (1980). *An agenda for action: Recommendations for school mathematics for the 1980s*. https://www.nctm.org/Standards-and-Positions/More-NCTM-Standards/An-Agenda-for-Action-(1980s)

National Council of Teachers of Mathematics. (2000). *Principles and standards for school mathematics*. https://www.nctm.org/standards

National Governors Association Center for Best Practices & Council of Chief State School Officers. (2010). *Common Core State Standards for mathematics*. http://www.corestandards.org/Math

National Research Council. (2001). *Adding it up: Helping children learn mathematics*. The National Academies Press. https://doi.org/10.17226/9822

National Research Council. (2005). *How students learn: History, mathematics, and science in the classroom*. The National Academies Press. https://doi.org/10.17226/10126

Renzulli, J. S., Leppien, J. H., & Hays, T. S. (2000). *The multiple menu model: A practical guide for developing differentiated curriculum*. Prufrock Press.

Renzulli, J. S., & Reis, S. M. (2014). *The Schoolwide Enrichment Model: A how-to guide for talent development* (3rd ed.). Prufrock Press.

Robinson, A., Shore, B. M., & Enerson, L. (2007). *Best practices in gifted education: An evidence-based guide*. Prufrock Press.

Sheffield, L. J. (1999). Serving the needs of the mathematically promising. In L. J. Sheffield (Ed.), *Developing mathematically promising students* (pp. 43–55). National Council of Teachers of Mathematics.

Sriraman, B. (2004). Gifted ninth graders' notions of proof: Investigating parallels in approaches of mathematically gifted students and professional mathematicians. *Journal for the Education of the Gifted, 27*(4), 267–292. https://doi.org/10.4219/jeg-2004-317

Swanson, J. D., Russell, L. W., & Anderson, L. (2019). A model for growing teacher talent scouts: Decreasing underrepresentation of gifted students. In S. R. Smith (Ed.), *Handbook of giftedness and talent development in the Asia-Pacific* (pp. 1–20). Springer. https://doi.org/10.1007/978-981-13-3021-6_55-1

Tomlinson, C. A., Renzulli, J. S., Purcell, J. H., Leppien, J. H., Burns, D. E., Strickland, C. A., Imbeau, M. B., & Kaplan, S. N. (2002). *The parallel curriculum: A design to develop learner potential and challenge advanced learners* (2nd ed.). Corwin.

van Hiele, P. M. (1999). Developing geometric thinking through activities that begin with play. *Teaching Children Mathematics, 5*(6), 310–316.

Vygotsky, L. S., & Cole, M. (1978). *Mind in society: The development of higher psychological processes*. Harvard University Press.

6

Talent Development in Science

Meta Van Sickle

The literature is filled with conflicting viewpoints about what works and for whom in the science classroom. In this chapter, early childhood and elementary curriculum materials are described in terms of research-based teaching practices that show efficacy for talent development, with a special focus on culturally responsive aspects of these practices. The purpose of this chapter is to elucidate ways teachers can put their culturally responsive beliefs and knowledge into practice while teaching science for talent development.

Research on Early Childhood and Elementary Science Teaching

It is difficult to find curriculum materials designed for early childhood and elementary science classrooms that emphasize culturally responsive teaching (Atwater, 2010; Ukpokodu, 2011). Two such curricular materials that have data to support their efficacy and address elements of culturally responsive science teaching practices are (1) the Project Clarion units from the Center for Gifted Education at William & Mary (Bland et al., 2010; Kim et al., 2011) and (2) the U-STARS~PLUS materials created by a group of researchers at Frank Porter Graham Early Childhood Center (Coleman et al., 2007, 2008, 2010). A component of the U-STARS~PLUS materials, the Teacher's Observation of Potential in Students (TOPS) tool helps teachers systematically observe and document the academic strengths of young students in domains such as curiosity and creativity, advanced reasoning and problem solving, motivation, and leadership (Coleman et al., 2007, 2008, 2010). Harradine et al. (2014) reviewed the use of TOPS by teachers in large studies and found that teachers who learned to use TOPS consistently identified students of color as having potential that they otherwise would not have noticed.

Project Clarion units produce positive gains in conceptual understanding, as well as science content and process attainment (Kim et al., 2009). Project Clarion units also improve students' critical thinking skills, with findings indicating that more Project Clarion units completed over the early childhood years is better (Kim et al., 2011). Students who first received Project Clarion instruction "in kindergarten and first grade and continued to receive instruction for multiple years scored higher on standardized measures of science content than students who received Project Clarion instruction for one year or less" (Kim et al., 2011, p. 51). Findings also indicate that the sky's the limit with Project Clarion—no ceiling effects were noted (Kim et al., 2011). Project Clarion acts as an equalizer. Finally, Bland et al. (2010) noted that Project Clarion is "more than the sum of its parts" (p. 51). The Project Clarion innovation improves teachers' science instruction (Bland et al., 2010).

From reviewing the Project Clarion, U-STARS~PLUS, and TOPS materials, it is apparent that teachers need to know their students and get to know them on a deep level. When teachers are taught ways to use powerful materials and choose to know students deeply, then they overcome hidden and explicit biases, prejudices, and bigotry that results in underidentification of talent. Instead, they see the potential in each child. Teachers who learn about their students and the content to be taught to this depth want to ensure each child's learning.

Talent Identification Practices

Identifying talent among students is not always easy. Students present teacher-pleasing and non-teacher-pleasing behaviors. Both can disguise the latent talent that students may have. Behaviors that do not please teachers most often hinder talent identification because students are exhibiting behaviors that a teacher may not prefer, and thus the teacher is often engaged in measures designed to control. Children who present with teacher-pleasing manners and organizational skills are often mistakenly identified as talented in a specific way. Moreover, when a student is from a culture that differs from the teacher's, it is easy to mistake a student's intent based on their action. For example, a boy who is raised to "flirt" with Momma to get her to laugh is likely to be misinterpreted in a classroom where children are expected to show a solemn face and verbally ask for forgiveness versus this child who knows he is forgiven when Momma laughs. This child is likely to be reprimanded for being sassy or unremorseful and then act out further. So, what can a teacher do to overcome the underidentification of students whose identities are not matched by the teacher's identities? I suggest two practices: (1) using your keen eyes and ears to deeply learn about the students and (2) using the TOPS tool (Coleman et al., 2010) to note areas for students that nurture talent development.

Using Your Keen Eyes and Ears

To use our keen eyes and ears as educators, we must be willing to deeply observe and listen. Once we begin this process of deep observation, we can identify our own hidden and explicit biases, prejudices, and bigotry. When I notice a non-teacher-pleasing behavior, I step back and ask myself: What is the child really trying to tell me? Is he bored? Is she expressing frustration due to tensions at home? Is he seeing the problem in a way that I am not? Is she feeling left out because all of the examples are of men? The questions that arise are innumerable. The biggest key for me is to recognize when I need to take a deeper look. I know it is time when it feels like I am in a contest with the student and trying to control them into my way of thinking instead of working with them so that they learn.

When frictions occur between you and a student, it is your job to determine how to get positive productive results without getting into a "battle" with the student. Everyone loses when the interaction becomes a win/lose confrontation. Instead, inviting the student to learn and expecting that they will engage in age-appropriate behaviors that are culturally rich will challenge you to learn more about the child—from home life, to cultural norms, to learning preferences.

TOPS

The TOPS tool is a second way to develop deeply honed observation skills about each student's potential. The instrument looks across a variety of domains in which a student might be talented: (1) learns easily, (2) shows advanced skills, (3) displays curiosity and creativity, (4) has strong interests, (5) shows advanced reasoning and problem solving, (6) displays spatial abilities, (7) shows motivation, (8) shows social perceptiveness, and (9) shows leadership (Coleman et al., 2007, 2008, 2010). This tool is best used in a variety of settings, from the classroom to the lunchroom to the home, and over multiple observations.

Using the TOPS tool helps a teacher note strengths that reflect a student's potential in one or more areas. For example, in considering teacher-pleasing and non-teacher-pleasing behaviors, the area of leadership from TOPS comes to mind: Is the student showing leadership by being disruptive, and thus no one is doing the classwork? How can this non-teacher-pleasing behavior, because the child is using a form of leadership the teacher doesn't approve of, be reframed and advance the student's skills into producing a way to generate leadership that gets students interested in a project?

A second domain with non-teacher-pleasing characteristics that I often see is displays of curiosity and creativity: What do you do when a student always has an unexpected answer and you are out of time to think through to a reasoned answer that will keep the learning momentum going? What do you do with a student who is so curious that the questions are never-ending? How do you let these passions develop and yet ensure that the student is learning all they need to during class time?

I think about both highly-honed observational skills and TOPS when I think about talent development in any classroom where I teach. It helps me not only identify more students for gifted and talented schoolwork, but also decide on the teaching practices that I employ with every lesson. Although reading and mathematics have become the focus of the elementary school classroom, other content areas are helpful when identifying talent in children. Science is an area that employs content from several domains, from reading and writing to mathematics, to the numerous fields of study within the discipline. Science actively engages students in problem finding and problem solving. That active engagement often reveals creativity and curiosity in a way not readily obvious in other content areas.

Instructional Practices That Promote Talent Development

Instructional practices that encourage talent development include knowing your students and letting them know you, and concept development through questioning strategies, such as KWHL charts, the scientific wheel of reasoning, concept mapping, and encouraging students to become the authority on the concepts. This is a list of practices that I have used and find helpful when identifying and developing the science talent in my students. Following each practice, a scenario from a classroom is described.

Knowing Your Students and Letting Them Know You

One of the most effective ways to overcome hidden and explicit biases, prejudices, and bigotry in the classroom is to learn about your students. Getting to know students helps one move past the traditional negative stories based on class, race, gender, and other identities. For example, some people wrongfully believe that girls are not good at science and that Black boys will break all of the equipment. These are biases that may prevent a teacher from identifying a student's talent. Knowing more about each student can help you move past the negative stereotypes that limited information creates. It is your job to learn more about each child in your classroom and help them develop to their potential.

Project Clarion units help teachers get to know their students because homework often requires input from adults in the child's life. For example, in *Weather Reporter: An Earth and Space Unit for High-Ability Learners in Grade 2* (Center for Gifted Education, 2010b), a homework assignment has students ask an adult at home about a time in which plans changed because the weather changed. Each student then has an opportunity to understand a reason that an adult might feel the need to change a plan. Then, when students share these stories during circle time, they learn more about each other. These stories also help the teacher better understand students and their home lives. Beyond that, the unit helps students understand weather changes from different parts of the state, the nation, and the world, which helps them comprehend that changes in weather happen all over the planet. Broadening the idea from self to the world is a skill that young children need to develop.

Weather Reporter also helps teachers and students to get to know more about each other through certain instructions (Center for Gifted Education, 2010b). The unit might ask a teacher to say, "I am going to show you ______" or "I am going to tell you something about how ______ works." Such a start gives young students an opportunity to know something about the teacher. Then the teacher can reciprocate learning about the student by stating or asking, "How would you make your own ______?" or "How would you study______ ?" It is generally most effective to ask questions in a direct manner. For example, an indirect question sounds like, "Would you come inside if the clouds were very dark?" versus a direct question, "If the clouds are dark, then what would you do?" Make sure the question cannot be answered with yes or no. It is better for the question to cause higher order thinking and require a descriptive answer. To ensure that the students know I think they can and will solve problems, I ask higher order thinking questions.

Conceptual Thinking Through Questioning

Conceptual thinking is required to do the sciences. Students must form big ideas about concepts and then link the concepts together to solve problems. This means that students must develop understanding beyond the remember and understand levels of the Bloom's revised taxonomy (Anderson & Krathwohl, 2001). Concepts take time and experience to understand, and unfortunately, students are frequently denied these opportunities. When a teacher tells students facts, students rarely end up understanding the concept. Students may be able to recite a dictionary-perfect definition but not comprehend the meaning. Students must experience the concept and develop their own words and drawings of explanation. Once the words and drawings match the text definition, then the science vocabulary development begins in earnest. There are several processes to help students with vocabulary development and concept development that are discussed in other chapters (e.g., the Taba and Frayer Models). This chapter focuses on questioning to help students develop language and concept construction.

Asking thinking questions informs students that you, as the teacher, believe that they have ideas and can think. The notion of talent development requires a teacher to have high expectations. Asking questions sets high expectations in place to help a teacher overcome hidden and explicit biases, prejudices, and bigotry by warmly demanding that students achieve. Using questions to guide students is an important skill for talent development.

The Use of *What* and *How* as Question Starters. *Young Scholars Handbook* (Advanced Academic Programs Office, 2012) noted that *who*, *what*, *when*, *where*, *how*, and *why* questions help students focus, in a productive way, on the concepts being studied. In addition, asking questions is consistent with the nature of science. Science needs to be grounded in physical, tangible data drawn from nature. The order in which one asks questions of students makes a difference in the form of answer they will create. For example, young children often express wonderful and creative—even magical—stories when asked questions that begin with *why*. If you are asking about a myth or story not related to the data/observations a student makes, then asking "Why?" first is a wonderful idea. Otherwise, I begin questions with *what* and *how*. What and how questions can be formed that meet all levels of the revised Bloom's taxonomy. This helps keep students focused on the physical data and away from magical thinking.

For example, the Next Generation Science Standards (NGSS Lead States, 2013) feature crosscutting concepts. The crosscutting concept of stability and change provides ample opportunity to use many what and how questions to help students gain a deeper understanding of a big idea. I generally start with the change aspect. Using the unifying concept of change, one can ask a question about change that specifically addresses one of the four generalizations about change. Students can remember the four generalizations about change: Change happens everywhere, change happens over time, change can be natural or human made, and change can be random or predictable. The Clarion units provide many additional ideas to ask about to get students to understand that things change in one of the four ways stated. Some ideas follow.

When starting to help students gain an understanding of the four generalizations about change, I use students as an example. When thinking about change over time, I ask questions like, "How did you look when you were a baby?" "How do you look now?" "What changed?" "How many years did the change take?" Then I ask about something from nature, such as, "What did the trees or flowers look like in the spring?" "What did they look like in the fall?" "What did they look like in the winter?" "How did they change?" "Did the change happen all at one time or during a span of time?"

Next, I work on the idea that change happens everywhere. I ask questions like, "What things do you see that change?" "What places do you see change?" Then I change to the idea that change can be random or predictable. I might ask, "In what ways does a tree change?" "Which of the ways a tree changes are predictable?" "Which are not predictable?" "How do you know?" Finally, I move to questions that will help students understand that change can be human made or natural. For this series of questions, I am likely to ask, "What are the ways I can get a room to change from dark to light?" "What happens when I dig in the ground and plant flowers?" "What happens in the garden if I don't dig out the weeds?" Questions like these help students create ideas about the crosscutting theme of stability and change.

Next, depending on the age of students, I either write a list of all of the things they think change or I have them write the words on sticky notes. I have either an anchor chart or four large wall-sized poster papers ready for use. Either way the four types of change are listed individually, one per poster. I then let students move the words to the poster that they feel best fits the change they are likely to notice. They soon notice that some words could be placed in more than one type of change. This is true! I encourage students to continue deciding where each word best fits and allow them to repeat words in different categories once they have expressed an idea that works.

If I am using the *Weather Reporter* unit (Center for Gifted Education, 2010b), I ask students to apply a category to a specific topic, such as weather, by asking, "How are any of your categories related to weather?" Again, students have the opportunity to choose any of the generalizations about change and apply it to weather (i.e., change is everywhere, change is related to time, change can be natural or human made, and change may be random or predictable). Sticking with the theme of weather, students might choose to talk about how weather changes with time, that weather is everywhere, that weather changes are natural or human made, or that weather can be random or predictable.

Scaffolding Questioning. Questioning can also use the Jacob's Ladder model of higher order thinking questions (e.g., VanTassel-Baska & Stambaugh, 2017). Using this model of questioning uses the same processes as in language arts while making the questions specific to the topic. One ladder using this model might ask students to sequence, look for cause and effect, and determine consequences and implications (see Figure 6.1). A second ladder might ask students to observe details, make classifications (pattern formation), and generate generalizations. Other ladders might ask students about how they will collect, record, and analyze data. The nature of science includes creativity, and thus another ladder might ask students to paraphrase, summarize, and synthesize what they know once the experience is complete. I generally use these ladders in conjunction with the Scientific Wheel of Reasoning, especially with the Design and Conduct Experiments portions of the wheel.

Using the sample ladder in Figure 6.1, I start with the questions at the bottom of the ladder and climb upward over time. In the case of this ladder, students have created a study. The *Weather Reporter* unit (Center for Gifted Education, 2010b), for example, has a series of lessons on what a scientist is and measuring the weather, including air pressure, wind, droughts, and tor-

Figure 6.1
Example Jacob's Ladder for Science

	Consequences and Implications
A3	▪ What happens if I do not conduct the test fairly? ▪ What happens if others gain different results? ▪ Did I disprove my hypothesis? How do you know?
	Cause and Effect
A2	▪ Does my fair test allow me to determine a cause and an effect? ▪ How do I know?
	Sequencing—Planning My Fair Test
A1	▪ Which order do I need to complete the steps of my plan to gain data about my question/hypothesis? ▪ Does the order matter? What makes the order matter?

Note. This ladder will be used in the "conduct a fair test" section of the Scientific Wheel of Reasoning. Adapted from the goals and objectives framework provided in *Jacob's Ladder Reading Comprehension Program: Grades K–1* (2nd ed., p. 3), by J. VanTassel-Baska and T. Stambaugh, 2017, Prufrock Press. Copyright 2017 by Prufrock Press. Adapted with permission.

nados. During these lessons, I ask students questions to help ensure they are thinking about aspects of doing science that matter. If the lesson is about collecting temperature data, then students need to consider the concept of change, specifically change over time. Getting students to make observations on a regular schedule helps them see that temperature changes over time, during a day, as well as across the seasons of the year.

Classrooms often have daily weather boards, and I encourage the teacher to continue adding data to the weather boards across the school year. I ask students to take the temperature of the outside air when they arrive, at lunch time, and during the last few minutes of the school day. I ask students if the sequence of taking the temperatures across the day makes a difference. They soon note that the temperatures are different at the three times the data are collected. I ask them if the order of the data collection matters, followed by, "What makes the order matter?" They quickly learn that they need each data point for each day. Next, I ask if there is a cause-and-effect pattern they can determine based on the data. The "If" question often follows up with, "How do you know?" I use this sequence because I want students to note that time of day makes a difference and that temperature changes over time. Some students even note that the position of the sun in the sky makes a difference, and others notice that cloudy days (or times of the day) result in cooler temperatures.

Because children are very aware of what is fair and what is not, I generally finish a session with questions like, "What happens if I did not conduct my test fairly?" "What happens if others gain different results (I promise that students using the same thermometer will read the results differently)?" Then I move on to other ladders to scaffold questions toward higher levels of thinking that include making sense of the data through application, analysis, evaluation, and creation. These steps are discussed in the following section.

Questions to Guide Scientific Inquiry. Scientific inquiry has specific practices. Science practices that students can develop and use include: asking questions, making either a prediction or a hypothesis, gathering materials needed to conduct an experiment, creating an experiment, making observations to collect data, using data tables in which data are written, interpreting the data, and finally, making meaning from the data and expressing the meaning to others. It is important to note that, in science, a scientist's job is to disprove the hypothesis and not to confirm it.

This notion of science practice is often in conflict with the notion that students are to remember and understand facts. Thus, the activity is often not an experiment, but rather a confirmation lab. In other words, science teachers typically ask students to complete experiences to confirm what is already known. Such practice does not disprove a hypothesis and thus is inconsistent with doing science. In addition, there are no aspects of surprise or autonomy to confirmation lab/activities. Such work often frustrates students. I often hear them say, "Just tell me the answer," or "This is dumb, everybody already knows. . . ." This frustration with confirming the known limits students' ability to deeply understand pattern formation or the concept being studied. Secondly, and invariably, something goes wrong and a group of students get the wrong answer. This outcome most frequently frustrates a student with a resultant, "See, I told you, I'm not good at science." When this happens the potential for talent development has ended.

Additional examples of questions I ask when students are conducting a hands-on experience include: "What information do you need to observe and record?" "How will you record your observations?" Once students have succeeded with these questions and have completed data collection, I often ask them to classify or form patterns by asking, "What groups of items from your recorded observations 'fit together'?" and "What patterns do you notice based on your recorded data?" "What is your evidence?" Finally, to get students to generalize, I query them with questions like, "Based on the patterns you identified, what questions can you ask now?" "How many of your new questions will require you to create a new test and collect new data?"

Students' questions are often implicit and need help to gain clarity. Some sentence starters that help students formulate questions include, "I wonder . . ." or "I am curious about . . ." or "What is happening . . . ?" In other cases, students may begin with an implicit hypothesis that then can be recreated into a question. Either way, providing opportunities for students to learn to ask questions is as important as a teacher asking questions to help guide an inquiry.

The KWHL Chart. A different way to think about questioning addresses students' ability to be the authority through autonomy. Traditionally, we, as teachers, ask students what they already know, which shows us their current authority with content. We also have practices that ask students what they want to know, which gives them some autonomy. Both the Clarion units and the U-STARS~PLUS materials use an expanded model of the Know, Want to know, and Learned (KWL) chart known as the KWHL chart (see Figure 6.2). The KWHL chart adds How students will learn what they Want to know. In science, the how is the starting point of setting up an experiment to test an idea or gather more information about an idea. Once students have chosen a way to discover answers to a question, we then ask questions until they describe a procedure.

There are overlapping opportunities within the use of the KWHL chart and the other features of successful science teaching. The W column gives me more opportunity to learn about students' interests and ideas. Students' passions encourage them to take the opportunity to thoroughly engage with the content. When students engage to this degree, they begin to show their talents. The W column also gives me the opportunity to use the Frayer Model of vocabulary development (Frayer et al., 1969) and Taba's (1962) concept development model, as they are useful in science as well as in English language arts and social studies. The H column provides me with insight into how students want to solve a problem and whether their thoughts are experiment-oriented or for language development. Finally, ensuring that students complete the final column provides a snapshot into the language and concept development on the given topic. Thus, students gain some authority over the content and autonomy through both stating what they want to learn and how they want to go about it.

An example activity about the unifying concept of change focused on the young student making decisions from the *Weather Reporter* unit (Center for Gifted Education, 2010b) is:

Figure 6.2
Example KWHL Chart

K What do I know?	W What do I want to know?	H How can I find out?	L What did I learn?

Note. This is one example of how to construct a KWHL chart.

Create small groups of three or four students. Give each group sticky notes, markers, and a chart with the Taba Concept Model graphic. Ask each group to think of examples of change and write one idea per sticky note. Circulate as the groups complete this task, making sure that all students understand the task. Have each group share its examples with the whole class. Write examples from each group on the whole class chart. After the groups have shared, they will place their sticky notes on their charts in the section labeled "Examples of Change." (p. 58)

Note the amount of autonomy each student has. Teachers' acceptance of student thinking helps students understand the authority they now possess about a concept. Student autonomy that encourages authority about a concept ultimately improves their ability to make decisions and develop conclusions. The students decided on how to think about and discover what the concept of change meant and then compared their own definitions to what the unifying theme means to scientists.

The Scientific Wheel of Reasoning. When developing talent, it is important to learn the skills of the discipline. This means that students need to know what scientists do and how they do it. The Clarion units focus on developing expertise to support an expert form of thinking in science. Students need to understand how scientists approach problems and then solve them. Scientists use investigations to test new ideas through examination of evidence (data). They ponder multiple perspectives through collaborative actions that include reading and gathering current science explanations. Then scientists communicate their findings. Each of these ideas are part of the Scientific Wheel of Reasoning. When students use the Scientific Wheel of Reasoning, they learn the practices of the field, which makes them better able to participate in a meaningful manner.

Different curricula help students focus on the discipline of science. The Clarion units use the Scientific Wheel of Reasoning to help students learn in an authentic manner. A major feature of the Scientific Wheel of Reasoning is the number of science practices it includes. For example, the practices include, but are not limited to, tell others what was found, learn more, make observations and so on. See Figure 6.3 for an example.

Kim et al. (2009) aimed for the development and use of the Scientific Wheel of Reasoning to introduce young learners to macroconcepts (e.g., systems or change), the scientific investigative process, and key science concepts. The science education community describes the integration of these practices as what scientists do. I used the Scientific Wheel of Reasoning to help students develop a systematic set of inquiry, analytical, and argumentation skills in science.

In the past, when I used the Scientific Method as represented in most elementary classrooms, students became very frustrated and learned to quickly say they were not good at science. They thought they were not good at science because as soon as something went wrong or they did not produce an expected or correct answer, they wanted to quit. The students thought the process was linear and that something was wrong with them when they encountered a challenge. Students also did not see the iterative nature of science testing and

Figure 6.3
Scientific Wheel of Reasoning

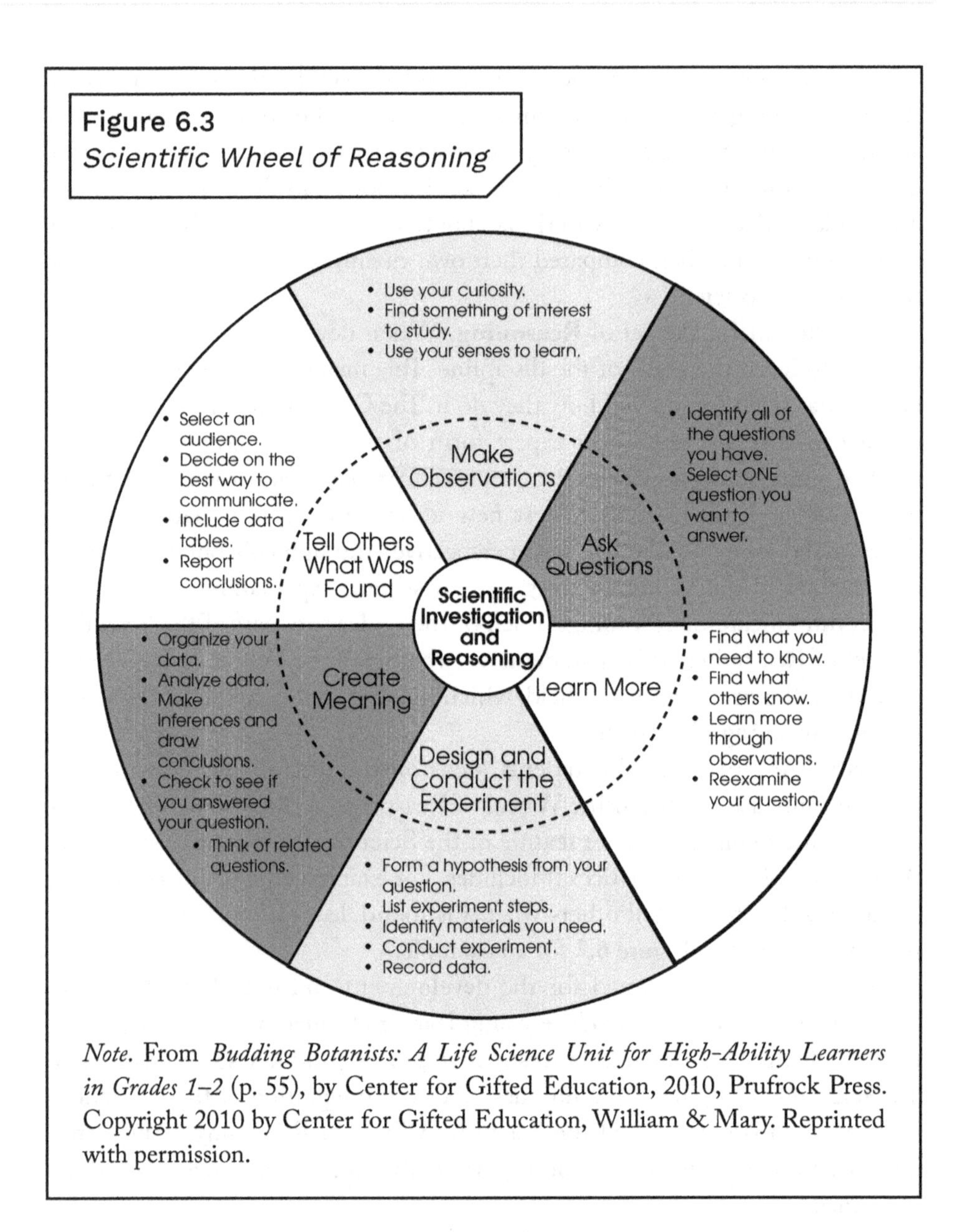

Note. From *Budding Botanists: A Life Science Unit for High-Ability Learners in Grades 1–2* (p. 55), by Center for Gifted Education, 2010, Prufrock Press. Copyright 2010 by Center for Gifted Education, William & Mary. Reprinted with permission.

that science is a process of deepening and refining answers. They thought it was a one-and-done model. Although adults know this is not true, my students did not.

In contrast, the Scientific Wheel of Reasoning is used as a nonlinear approach to understand the components of "doing" science. A key feature is autonomy—students are asked to find the component of science they are conducting (from observing to analyzing and reporting to others) and describe how they know that is what they are doing and then say the component they plan to do next. The components they choose from are on a wheel. Note that science practices have many components that students can develop and that are named on the wheel. Students then understand that they choose the starting point and the practice they will choose next. The students decide the order, including the decision to work on a science practice again. All of the science practices on the wheel are completed before the project is finished. Students are encouraged to improve a science practice instead of quitting or giving up. Using the wheel to encourage revisiting the components of doing science provides students the opportunity to make a mistake and fix it. They can complete any component on the wheel as many times as needed without reprisal or failing on the basis of one attempt on one component. Students now know the power of yet: "I get to work on this again because I am not there *yet*, but I can get there."

This ability to continue working on a problem helps young students tell their story and include the information they gained across the unit or activity. Thus, students again have autonomy to create the message they tell using the information they gained from many sources—including, but not limited to, the testing and activities they designed and completed, what the adults in their world told them, and the books and other resources they used in solving their problem(s).

One example from a Clarion unit asks students to look for patterns and then consider how their findings have an impact on other systems. Then, when students consider how their new ideas, in the form of a question or hypothesis, relate to a crosscutting theme in science such as stability or change, they are more able to think about and study more aspects of the problem. Scientists look for collaborators on a problem like students do in the classroom. Finally, the results need to be communicated to others.

I often begin questioning students before they conduct a hands-on activity. The sequence of questions generally includes information that will help students conduct a "fair" test. By fair test, I mean an experiment that others can repeat and get the same answer. Students know when something is fair. So, I would begin by asking sequence questions like, "Which order do you need to complete the steps of your plan to gain data that will help answer your question . . . or disprove your hypothesis?" "Does the order of the steps you complete matter?" "What makes the order matter?" (For an example of using Jacob's Ladder for questioning, see Figure 6.1.) Next, I ask about cause and effect: "Does my fair test allow me to determine a cause and an effect?" "How do you know?" Finally, I ask questions about consequences and implications about

Figure 6.4
Sample Concept Map

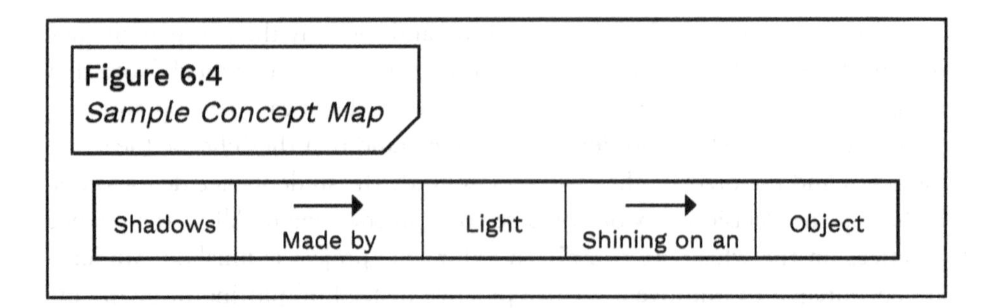

running my test: "What happens if I do not conduct the test fairly?" "What happens if others gain different results? "Did I set my test up in a way to help you disprove your hypothesis?" "What's your evidence?" Notice the thinking involved with each question.

The Clarion units each end with students expressing the data, the analyses of the data, and what the data mean to others. This teaching approach is consistent with scientific practices involving communication. The students learn to focus on the data and state what they mean. These lessons encourage students to ask questions of the presenter. This peer review is an essential component of science practice. By having students communicate what they understand is a great way to continue the concept development. In other words, a great assessment continues the learning.

Concept Mapping. To gain insight into students' concept development is equally important. Gaining a snapshot of their thinking is important because, as teachers, we need to know what they know, when they know it, and what is not yet understood or is a misconception. To gain this insight I often use a specific form of a mind map called the concept map. The language and concept development of each student is illustrated in the map they create. The vocabulary words are in a word wall. The students develop a series of hierarchies to describe their work. The vocabulary words are circled and then connected using lines with arrows on the ends to illustrate the direction of each student's thoughts. Connecting words are used between the vocabulary words to show how students relate one word to another. For example, a student discovers that it takes a light source and an object to block the light source to create a shadow. A segment of the concept map might look like Figure 6.4.

More hierarchies will be added as the student learns more about shadows. They can add more specific information, such as if the light is natural or human made, if the shadow changes position when the light source moves, if all objects are equally good at producing a shadow, and so on. I have seen students produce concept maps that are pages long due to their interests. When

I see examples like this, I know students are deeply engaged and finding a passion for the concept.

Lessons Learned

The teacher matters the most in determining the learning outcomes for the students in their classrooms. When teachers understand their own prejudices, biases, and bigotry, then they can begin to deeply discover the thoughts and ideas their students bring to the classroom. These sincere and acute observations make the difference in students' ability to discover and develop their talents in the sciences. Using an activity from a Project Clarion unit might encourage a young student to describe something about how the world works. Each of the practices described encourage students to become the authority on the concepts being taught, give autonomy to what and how the concepts are studied, and allow students to develop a passion for the sciences.

Encouraging Students to Become the Authority on the Concepts

An activity in a Project Clarion unit might encourage students to describe what happened, in what order, and which of the events they believe mattered the most. Then, being asked to provide examples, categorize their examples, show understanding, and use their examples in the explanation, students develop the concepts. These practices help young learners develop metaphors and logic chains as they learn to explain what they know, what they want to know, how they will learn it, and ultimately, what they learned. These practices allow students to observe, question, and investigate, moving them from reading science to doing science like scientists.

These units provide students with the opportunity to be involved in evidence-based argumentation in a civil or tactful manner as they learn the concepts. What matters most to the students becomes visible because the teacher is asking students to provide examples, categorize their examples, show understanding, and then use their examples in the explanation.

Giving Students Autonomy

All of the descriptions of the practices in this chapter give students autonomy. In the case of the practices described, the teacher can learn about the potential students can develop. Potential talent becomes perceptible when students are encouraged to explore their passions and are given opportunities to persist with their studies and think about ideas. Such experiences provide the teacher who has seriously developed their keen eyes and ears to discern the talents of each student in a class through the performances and products. These student behaviors and teacher practices are an important part of talent development.

Developing Passion

Both students and teachers can develop passion. In early science development, students are best served when teachers encourage them to pursue their natural curiosity. Using natural curiosity is a great starting point for students to grow their passion for science. Developing passion generally requires one to have the opportunity to gain authority through autonomous practices in the classroom. When we, as teachers, learn, we appreciate, and when we appreciate, we provide opportunities. It is our job to ensure that the wide variety of talents that present themselves in our classrooms can develop.

How Teachers Develop Talent

Teachers develop their talents over time. They want to develop their teaching talent so that students deeply engage, show curiosity, and grow happiness. One of the areas that provides interesting, relevant, and curiosity-driven passions for students is the use of science curricula. Thus, it becomes important to develop your own talent to teach science. This section uses Subotnik et al.'s (2018) model to frame talent development in teacher professional learning. Key components of the model are that: (a) abilities are specific and malleable, (b) domains have differing trajectories, (c) opportunities are essential, (d) opportunities must be taken, (e) mental skills are important, (f) social skills are important, and (g) long-range thinking and planning are necessary for development.

Specific and Malleable Abilities

Teachers are taught specific sets of competencies that include information about the learner, what and how to teach and assess, ways to create an environment conducive to learning, and how to grow and learn as a professional. The set of competencies includes learning how to function as a professional. A professional teacher wants to and knows how to collaborate, create, and learn and grow in knowledge and skills. When a teacher accepts these responsibilities, they also understand the need for professional learning.

Teachers, like students, have specific and malleable abilities that they can develop. When teachers choose to explore specific concepts and/or new teaching strategies within a content area, they are acting as a professional. When schools provide professional learning, they want teachers to develop new knowledge and skills. Science is best taught to young students when it is inquiry oriented and developmentally appropriate. Thus, teachers might seek a professional learning that provides both specific science concepts and ways in which to teach it so that young children learn. Some of my most memorable moments are working with teachers who want more—want to reach more students and gain better student science learning outcomes for all of their students.

Domain Trajectories

Teachers in the schools that promote a talent development model for teaching have a specific domain within which to work. These domains include enough content and teaching practices to seek and find the latent talents among the students they teach. Talents of people include the arts, sciences, writing, math, and humanities, as well as soft skills such inter- and intrapersonal relationships. I would add teaching to this list. Elementary teachers have traditionally focused on reading and math and not on science. Such a practice leaves out the potential for students to develop a deep passion for the sciences at an early age. Thus, domain-specific professional learning would include both the content and the teaching methods that are most effective with young children so that a teacher can gain talent in this area, too.

Finding and Taking Opportunities

In the Talent Development Instructional Model described in this book, teachers were provided with many opportunities to learn in many ways. They had choices in the content and skills they were going to learn and the way the professional learning was provided. I provided both workshop sessions and in-classroom observations and assistance. It is great fun to have teachers in a workshop extend their own learning. For example, in one workshop where we were learning about plants, especially flowers, a group of teachers decided it would be fun to press the flower petals onto the paper. Next, they called me over to look at the "mess they made" and wanted to see how I would reprimand them. Instead, I said something like, "I see that you discovered where many dyes come from. What do you know about dyes? How are they made? Do dyes interest you?" When they said yes, they were given the opportunity to use their tablets and find more details. They found an opportunity, albeit by accident, and they ended up learning something unexpected and that they enjoyed. As we debriefed the workshop this was a deep topic of interest showing talent development in science teaching. The teachers were able to apply this personal information to the way students might perform in their classes.

Personal Mental and Social Skills

Dispositions and attitudes toward children, such as patience, care, respect, and kindness, are central to students' performance. The ability to communicate well with diverse individuals and to engage constructively and effectively within groups is considered essential in teaching. Further, high expectations for all learners and the belief that all students can learn are dispositions valued in education. Preparing teachers to accept feedback and critique of their work contributes to development of grit, persistence, and a growth orientation to learning. A next step in the process is to learn to use tactful interactions that help forward the information (van Manen, 1991). The use of tact helps direct the students to new learning.

Planning for the Long Term

Thinking about professional growth is evident in schools that promote a Talent Development Instructional Model for student learning. The professional learning in this model was effective with highly talented teachers and those striving to become highly competent because it has a formal mentorship where professionals went into classrooms to assist and model. This model provided teacher/professional mentors for teachers. Research on the impacts that resulted on TDA teachers in this study (Swanson et al., 2019) indicate long-term gains on several measures (see Chapter 12 for more details).

Overall, when teachers decided to become more talented and professional, they chose domain-specific content and skills to learn. They persisted with the information until they could use it in their classrooms. Moreover, they invited the coaches in to help them gain clarity on what they were doing, how they were doing it, and ultimately, on why it works with so many children.

Conclusion

It takes planning and thoughtfulness on the part of teachers to execute lessons that help young learners gain the skills and knowledge that they are capable of because of the many actions and thoughts teachers need to be conscious of while in the classroom. Teachers who work this hard are wonderful and need all of the support possible so that they keep the opportunity doors open for students in their classroom. Talent development only happens when teachers choose to intentionally overcome their personal biases, prejudices, and bigotry and see the potential in each student. Science is an area where passion, curiosity, and creativity are able to be enjoyed. Teachers who are prepared to accept that many students will thrive in an environment that promotes this level of deep interest and work will notice the increase in the number of students exhibiting great talent. To me, that outcome is the purest form of joy.

End of Chapter Discussion/ Reflection Questions

1. For what reasons are Project Clarion science units, U-STARS~PLUS materials, and the Teacher's Observation of Potential in Students (TOPS) tool recommended for use in talent-focused schools?
2. What are some of the ways described in the chapter of knowing your students and letting them know you? How do you know your students and allow them to know you? Why is this instructional practice essential in talent development?
3. Examples of conceptual thinking in science teaching and the use of questions are described. What insights did you gain about conceptual thinking and questioning as related to growing student talent?
4. In what ways can you integrate instructional ideas and lessons from the chapter into your science teaching? Select a series of science lessons and revise them based on your understanding of how to make science teaching more talent focused.

References

Advanced Academic Programs Office. (2012). *Young Scholars handbook*. Instructional Services Department, Fairfax County Public Schools. http://www.casenex.com/casenet/frontPages/ysRC/resources/2012_YS_Handbook.pdf

Anderson, L., & Krathwohl, D. R. (Eds.). (2001). *A taxonomy for learning, teaching, and assessing: A revision of Bloom's taxonomy of educational objectives* (Complete ed.). Longman.

Atwater, M. M. (2010). Dr. Geneva Gay: Multicultural education for all disciplines. *Science Activities, 47*(4), 160–162. https://doi.org/10.1080/00368121003753902

Bland, L. C., Coxon, S., Chandler, K., & VanTassel-Baska, J. (2010). Science in the city: Meeting the needs of urban gifted students with Project Clarion. *Gifted Child Today, 33*(4), 48–57. https://doi.org/10.1177/107621751003300412

Center for Gifted Education. (2010a). *Budding botanists: A life science unit for high-ability learners in grades 1–2*. Prufrock Press.

Center for Gifted Education. (2010b). *Weather reporter: An earth and space science unit for high-ability learners in grade* 2. Prufrock Press.

Coleman, M. R., Coltrane, S. S., & Harradine, C. (2008, November). *Results of U-STARS~PLUS* [Paper presentation]. Annual meeting of the National Association for Gifted Children, Salt Lake City, UT, United States.

Coleman, M. R., Coltrane, S. S., Harradine, C., & Timmons, L. A. (2007). Impact of poverty on promising learners, their teachers, and their schools. *Journal of Urban Education: Focus on Enrichment, 6*, 59–67.

Coleman, M. R., Shah-Coltrane, S., & Harrison, A. (2010). *U-STARS~PLUS: Teacher's observation of potential in students (TOPS): Individual student observation form*. Council for Exceptional Children.

Frayer, D. A., Fredrick, W. C., & Kalusmeier, H. J. (1969). *A schema for testing the level of content mastery*. Wisconsin Research and Development Center for Cognitive Learning.

Harradine, C. C., Coleman, M. R. B., & Winn, D. M. C. (2014). Recognizing academic potential in students of color. *Gifted Child Quarterly, 58*(1), 24–34. https://doi.org/10.1177/0016986213506040

Kim, K. H., VanTassel-Baska, J., Bracken, B. A., Feng, A., Stambaugh, T., & Bland, L. (2011). Project Clarion: Three years of science instruction in Title I Schools among K–third grade students. *Research in Science Education, 42*(5), 813–829. https://doi.org/10.1007/s11165-011-9218-5

Kim, M., Bland, L. C., & Chandler, K. (2009). Reinventing the wheel. *Science and Children, 47*(3), 40–43.

NGSS Lead States. (2013). *Next generation science standards: For states, by states*. The National Academies Press.

Subotnik, R. F., Olszewski-Kubilius, P., & Worrell, F. C. (2018). The talent development framework: Overview of components and implications for policy and practice. In P. Olszewski-Kubilius, R. F. Subotnik, & F. C. Worrell (Eds.), *Talent development as a framework for gifted education: Implications for best practices and applications in schools* (pp. 7–24). Prufrock Press.

Swanson, J. D., Russell, L. W., & Anderson, L. (2019). A model for growing teacher talent scouts: Decreasing underrepresentation of gifted students. In S. R. Smith (Ed.), *Handbook of giftedness and talent development in the Asia-Pacific* (pp. 1–20). Springer. https://doi.org/10.1007/978-981-13-3021-6_55-1

Taba, H. (1962). *Curriculum development: Theory and practice*. Harcourt, Brace & World.

Ukpokodu, O. N. (2011). How do I teach mathematics in a culturally responsive way?: Identifying empowering teaching practices. *Multicultural Education, 18*(3), 47–56.

van Manen, M. (1991). *The tact of teaching: The meaning of pedagogical thoughtfulness*. State University of New York Press.

VanTassel-Baska, J., & Stambaugh, T. (2017). *Jacob's Ladder Reading Comprehension Program: Grades 1–2* (2nd ed.). Prufrock Press.

Part III

Teacher Talent Scouts and Culturally Responsive Teaching

7

Culturally Responsive Educators and Talent Development

Melanie J. Lichtenstein

Talent development as a districtwide approach to serving gifted students and students with potential is still an emergent practice. Implementation requires the alignment of a school district's cultural values, curricular approaches, change models, and leadership initiative to carry out the approach. The key to districts successfully implementing an aligned talent development model across schools is deliberate planning, coordination, and serendipity. Asking critical questions around systemic and common practices that create barriers for culturally, linguistically, and ethnically diverse (CLED) students is imperative to follow a talent development framework when considering access and equity issues within gifted and talented education. In examining the barriers, some questions could be:

- Why do CLED students who are schooled and work in places (such as gifted and talented classrooms or academic magnet schools) that have previously been predominantly occupied by only White faces experience additional scrutiny?

- Why, if CLED students struggle with the same challenges that White students struggle with, is their "struggle" attributed to their ethnicity or culture, rather than the challenge itself?
- Why are CLED students persistently underrepresented and underserved in advanced academics and gifted education, science and technology professions, and higher education institutions?
- In addition to the tenacious and underrecognized scholarly work around CLED students and underrepresentation in gifted and advanced coursework (Ford, 2015; Ford et al., 2008, 2016; Grantham et al., 2020), what else can be done?

Gifted education and advanced academics were designed through a dominant cultural lens, and this is why that lens needs to change to see the strengths in all students. If it does not, the access and opportunity to academic achievement and success will continue to be limited to those who historically have held those spaces.

In this chapter, I align the Talent Development Megamodel (Olszewski-Kubilius et al., 2018; Olszewski-Kubilius & Thomson, 2015; Subotnik et al., 2020) with the culturally responsive educator model by Villegas and Lucas (2002). The alignment of the two frameworks calls upon understanding the dispositions of educators and the pedagogical implications that would require an approach to talent development through a culturally responsive framework. Such understandings include (1) how deficit-based thinking presents itself in talent development and gifted education, (2) strategies to work toward an asset-based lens, and (3) classroom and schoolwide examples that demonstrate the implementation of talent development by culturally responsive educators.

Context

Between March 2020 and the publication of this book, American educators watched our systems adapt due to the COVID-19 pandemic. Alongside this virus, the American people grappled with and continue to grapple with a sickness of another kind—perpetual systemic racism. I write this at the start of this chapter because to consider culturally responsive teaching and talent development, the cultural context of the nation and world must be taken into consideration. The impact of a global pandemic and a cultural awakening of antiracist thoughts is not just a singular event, but one with lasting implications. The collective trauma of medical, economic, educational, and ethical crisis positions educators with an opportunity to change the broken systems.

As the saying goes, necessity is the mother of invention. American educators are positioned to create new pathways and address the ones that have led us to the current crisis within education of inequity, division, and inconsistent access. Now is the time to break free of the once-held values of the dominant few in gifted education and to embrace the opportunity that reinvention of education can lead to in talent development.

The Problem

When addressing the pervasive and historic underrepresentation of CLED students in gifted and talented education the focus is often on recruitment and retention. This focus on student engagement and commitment puts the onus on the students. This chapter addresses the role that educators play in underrepresentation and access to talent development services through a culturally responsive teaching model.

The cultural identities of teachers are as important as those of the students. Culture shapes values systems, frames worldviews, generates understanding of social codes, and provides beliefs to give meaning to the world around us as well as the lives of others. Culture influences how one behaves, thinks, and believes, and as a result, directly affects how one teaches and learns (Gay, 2018). Educators bring a specific set of cultural values and beliefs that impact how instruction is conducted and how expectations are set; at the same time, students bring their own cultural identity and lens to the classroom. Culturally responsive teaching (CRT) is recommended as an approach to address underrepresentation and retention of CLED students within gifted education (Ford, 2015). Teachers' understandings of their students' abilities have implications on student success in the classroom and future opportunities. According to Delpit (2006), teachers are trained to connect school failure with socioeconomic status, cultural diversity, and family structure. As a result, teachers focus instruction and classroom interaction on so-called deficits instead of finding dynamic strengths. Talent development requires teachers to follow a strength-based or asset-based view of their students. When teachers see the potential in students within a talent development framework, opportunities are opened to the children with potential.

Culturally Responsive Education

Classrooms in the United States are diverse, and educators should be prepared to support a variety of CLED learners. Scholars suggest that teachers need to become more culturally competent or responsive to work with CLED students (DeJaeghere & Zhang, 2008; Ford et al., 2008; Griner & Stewart, 2012; Harris et al., 2004; Lucas & Villegas, 2013). An operational definition of cultural responsiveness is a set of behaviors, attitudes, and policies that a system or individual in the system utilizes in a multicultural setting (Howard, 2010). When an educator is culturally responsive, they have developed a belief system and specific behaviors that value diversity and support the cultures of the student and their family in the school setting.

Geneva Gay Model

Gay (2018) defined culturally responsive teaching as "using the cultural knowledge, prior experiences, frames of reference, and performance styles of ethnically diverse students to make learning encounters more relevant to and effective for them" (p. 36). Culturally responsive teaching is teaching "to and through [students'] personal and cultural strengths, their intellectual capabilities, and their prior accomplishments" (p. 31). Gifted, high-ability, and high-potential characteristics present themselves differently for different students based on their identities, contexts, and the opportunities afforded to them. How the characteristics are viewed depends on who is defining the gifts, abilities, and potentials. This issue is why examining educators' mindsets and lenses is imperative when considering talent development and gifted services. The role the educator plays in who accesses advanced educational opportunities depends on how that educator perceives students' strengths and capabilities and understands the sociocultural influences that impact students' lives. Gay (2018) called for a different paradigm to address systems and practices that perpetuate ongoing equity issues surrounding the education of CLED students. This paradigm change can be applied to talent development and gifted services in order to be culturally responsive. Culturally responsive teaching validates and affirms students' identities, creates connections between the home and school contexts, is student centered, and integrates relevant content and materials to facilitate learning.

Deficit Thinking

Gay (2018) identified deficit thinking as a significant element of educational paradigms that prevent equity and access in education. The singular focus on achievement and student performance gaps has perpetuated attributing "failure to what students of color don't have and can't do" (Gay, 2018, p. 31). This singular focus has led to a collective approach of instruction being aimed at fixing or repairing what is considered missing, instead of considering what is present in a student's performance or potential. Deficit thinking continues to contribute to the underrepresentation and exclusion of CLED students from gifted and talented services. If an educator sees a child through a deficit lens, the focus is not on what the child can do, but what the educator perceives is not there. The perception of the educator becomes skewed, and instruction is focused on deficits instead of toward potential.

Historically, the field of gifted and talented education has been centered within the experiences and values around Whiteness, affluence, and those who have access and opportunity. This dominance has led to a perspective that there is a single way to be gifted or high ability, and anyone who is different does not fit into that category. The deficit perspective of student difference may be interpreted as a resistance to assimilating with the dominant culture values and becomes a justification for exclusion from advanced and gifted services. The expectation of adherence or assimilation to the dominant practices in school by CLED students has been connected to systemic practices that perpetuate barriers to access and equity (Kendi, 2019). Differences in CLED students that may be interpreted as deficits instead of assets include, but are not limited to, linguistic abilities, intellectual capability, motivation, and behavior. Educators who adhere to deficit thinking interpret their assumptions about CLED students as the students lacking the ability to conform to the dominant (White and middle class) educational and social order. Thus, they are not included in gifted and talented services (Gorski, 2009).

Deficit thinking, also referred to as deficit thinking model, deficit perspective, and cultural deficit model, is the belief system that blames the cultural or social status of an individual for school failure (Valencia, 2010). Valencia (2010) identified six characteristics of deficit ideology or deficit thinking that are found in the context of schools. Deficit thinking in relation to talent development can be directly linked to the underrepresentation and underserved CLED students in gifted education (see Table 7.1).

Table 7.1
Six Characteristics of Deficit Thinking in Talent Development and Gifted Education

Deficit Thinking Construct	Deficit Thinking Characteristic	Example of Deficit Thinking in Talent Development and Gifted Education
Blaming the Victim	The ideological base of deficit thinking is found in blaming the victim. Blaming the victim first identifies social problems, then points out how groups are different, and once the difference is identified, aligns the difference with the cause of the social problem.	In gifted education, when identification and nomination is dependent on either a single test score or families navigating the system, educators may blame underrepresentation on culturally, linguistically, and ethnically diverse (CLED) families for not properly preparing their children for the test or for not reaching out to the school to pursue gifted identification.
Oppression	Oppression is the use of power to restrict groups of people from having access to opportunities, awareness, or information.	Oppression in gifted education is present when access to educational and enrichment opportunities is limited by policies that perpetuate segregation. For instance, when services for talent development are limited to a specific time of day and access is not considered during planning. The persistent underrepresentation of CLED students in advanced and gifted programming is a form of oppression. For a statement about oppression in gifted education, see Grantham et al., 2020.
Pseudoscience	Pseudoscience is when researchers do not address or harness their biases around CLED individuals. On occasion, the use of scientific method or empirical research is used to justify racist and biased assertions. This may include assumptions, poorly designed instruments, no effort to control for variables, and limited consideration of alternate hypothesis.	Unfortunately, the foundation of intelligence tests by Lewis M. Terman (1877–1956) was grounded in racist beliefs about CLED individuals that led to generalization and assumptions about ability of people of color. This has been a persistent shadow cast across gifted education, and although research has repeatedly demonstrated the faults in Terman's research, the assertions in the original work continue to sustain deficit thinking around ability of CLED students.

Table 7.1, continued

Deficit Thinking Construct	Deficit Thinking Characteristic	Example of Deficit Thinking in Talent Development and Gifted Education
Temporal Changes	Temporal changes perpetuate the pervasiveness of pseudoscience in which CLED students are considered less capabale or less than compared to dominant White students.	Temporal changes in gifted education are demonstrated when educators display their deficit thinking by generalizing that an entire group of students are not able to achieve because of their CLED status. The assumption that diversity is weak or less than, or inadequate to prepare students for academic achievement, limits how educators see students, and thus prevents access to opportunities and experiences that are traditionally afforded to affluent White students.
Educability	Educability is where ability or behaviors of CLED students are described as dysfunctional or needing to be fixed. Valencia (2010) referred to the practice as "description-explanation-prediction-modification sequence" in education and how deficit thinking frames the perception of CLED students (p. 14).	In gifted education, educability is directly connected to the Terman work that led to the origins of the Stanford-Binet intelligence test. This original explanation of intelligence has remained within the policies and practices of gifted education through how ability is defined and identified, and potential is ignored. Terman established the low expectations and foundational beliefs around how CLED students are to be educated in a deficit paradigm, and unfortunately, the paradigm persists in the use of fixed test scores, limited understanding of gifts and talents, and barriers that prevent equitable access to engaging and challenging coursework.

Table 7.1, continued

Deficit Thinking Construct	Deficit Thinking Characteristic	Example of Deficit Thinking in Talent Development and Gifted Education
Heterodoxy	Heterodoxy is the challenge of the status quo of a single dominant narrative of a single way of presenting ability in school. Researchers aim to challenge this in all forms of research, but working toward this goal still has not completely changed the scholarly approach to discussing diversity and CLED students.	Heterodoxy is demonstrated in the work produced by Black scholars in gifted education, who have actively presented the counternarrative around ability, assets, and strengths for CLED students. The Consortium for Inclusion of Underrepresented Racial Groups in Gifted Education (Grantham et al., 2020) is an organization of these scholars, who continue to advocate and lead the charge to address deficit thinking around CLED students in gifted education. More White allies who are members of the scholarly community in gifted education need to engage in the research around access and equity in talent development and gifted services to change the dominant narrative of what is considered gifted and high ability.

Note. This is a summary of the six characteristics of deficit thinking adapted from *Dismantling Contemporary Deficit Thinking*, by R. R. Valencia, 2010, and aligned with examples of deficit thinking that exist within gifted and talented education policies and practices.

The six characteristics along with examples in gifted education are:

1. **Victim blaming:** As mentioned previously, deficit ideology holds the individual student and their families as the reason for school failure. Valencia (2010) stated that students' poor performance is often inaccurately linked to fictional cognitive and motivation deficits. This excuses the school system, teachers, or administrators from any accountability for the failure. Victim blaming can be found when lack of representation of CLED students in talent development and gifted services is inaccurately connected to underperformance or engagement in school. Additionally, overreliance on parental advocacy or participation may limit who is represented in talent development or gifted services. Victim blaming arises when families and parents are blamed for lack of engagement or interest when not participating in systems that depend on parental action to gain access to programming or services. For example, parent-driven nomination to gifted identification as a singular method to identify students with gifts and talents falls under the practice of victim blaming.
2. **Oppression:** Valencia (2010) included oppression as a way to identify the power conflict between deficit thinkers and the students they oppress. The mindset of low expectations and limiting any possibilities for success is a model that oppresses CLED students. Oppression in underrepresentation in gifted services can be found in policy practices that perpetuate inequity, such as relying on a single cognitive test to determine identification or access to gifted and talented services or limiting access to talent development or gifted services because of student behavior or academic challenges. Oppression is exemplified when talent development or gifted services are limited to a specific time of the day when academic intervention is provided simultaneously. Thus, this causes the students who may require intervention or who are marginalized to miss out on opportunities.
3. **Pseudoscience:** Deficit ideology has very little empirical research to support the embedded biases that pervade the field of education. Valencia (2010) applied pseudoscience to research used to create rationale and reform that continues the pattern of oppression. The perception that intelligence or ability is fixed and not malleable is a pseudoscience that contributes to access and equity issues in gifted education. Racist beliefs about ability and achievement of CLED students are grounded in pseudoscience dating back to the origins of intelligence tests. The rationale for segregation was based in pseudoscience and

perpetuates to current applications in which CLED students are persistently considered through a deficit lens.

4. **Temporal changes:** Deficit ideology often follows archaic beliefs that attribute racial and cultural identity with "low-grade genes, inferior culture and class, or inadequate familial socialization" (Valencia, 1997, p. 2). Racist beliefs often contribute to CLED students not being recommended or considered for talent development and gifted services. The lack of representation within advanced programming perpetuates this false narrative linking cultural identity with ability.
5. **Educability:** Valencia (2010) found that deficit ideology has a specific model that explains, predicts, and makes pedagogical suggestions based on "educability perceptions" of CLED students. This perception can be found when advanced curricular materials and pedagogical practices minimize or marginalize the experiences of CLED students. The originator of the intelligence testing movement, Lewis M. Terman, provided the foundational belief that CLED students were less intelligent or capable when compared to White students. Gifted education was born out of these beliefs that continue when practices and policies perpetuate low expectations of CLED students.
6. **Heterodoxy:** There is a history of researchers who have challenged the dominant deficit-thinking model. Valencia (2010) found that many anti-deficit researchers focused on environmental, methodological, and alternate explanations for academic gaps between students from different racial and socioeconomical groups. This process has led to litigation and attempts for systemic change. Historically gifted education and advanced learner programs have reflected the cultural norms, values, and policies of a White-dominated field. This is orthodoxy. The movement to increase representation, provide culturally responsive practices, and ensure that opportunities are accessible to all students regardless of the identities is the shift to heterodoxy.

Educators' deficit beliefs persistently undermine potential for addressing academic and systemic barriers that perpetuate underrepresentation in gifted and talented education. Nelson and Guerra (2013) found that in addition to a resistance to address their deficit ideology, teachers also are ill prepared to address culture clashes or apply cultural understanding in their practice. Gay (2018) believed that the current approach to address the achievement gap will fail because the practices are saturated in the idea that CLED students "don't have and can't do" (p. 12). García and Guerra (2004) found that because deficit ideology pervades the U.S. society at large, the result is reflected in the schools and educators that work there. García and Guerra also pointed out that deficit ideology often starts with assumptions about family identity and moves to more widespread inaccurate beliefs that negatively impact students. The tendency to place the blame with the student, cultural group, or family hinders efforts to raise achievement and change systems at perpetually poor performing schools (García & Guerra, 2004; Nelson & Guerra, 2013).

Sleeter (2013) asserted that in the current political context of teacher training and professional learning, the focus has moved away from democratic participatory education to focus on high-stakes testing and prescribed curriculum. This movement away from equity pedagogy to capitalistic-focused instruction is detrimental to the future of the nation and especially CLED students and families. The deficit thinking model has been used to explain academic gaps and school failure, as well as underrepresentation for CLED students in talent development and gifted services (Valencia, 2010, p. 6). Deficit ideology is pervasive, and even well-intentioned educators may hold incorrect perceptions and beliefs about CLED students.

Asset-Based Thinking

In order to change from the "can't do" to "can do" in talent development and gifted services, educators must learn to shift their preconceived ideas and beliefs to student difference as a strength instead of a deficit. Talent development is grounded in the concept that gifts and talents are a part of a developmental continuum, where potential may be tapped through opportunities, access, and deliberate instructional practice (Olszewski-Kubilius et al., 2018). There is very little training in strength- or asset-based thinking for educators, especially when working with diverse population of learners (Zacarian et al., 2017). Talent development depends on educators seeing potential and strengths in all students, regardless of a gifted label. Through recognizing potential in students, educators can support students through the domain-based trajectories that talent development calls for by aligning strengths with potential future endeavors (Subotnik et al., 2020). Seeing the potential in students as aligned with domain-specific trajectories and abilities has a more predictive value for future achievement and performance than an IQ test alone (Subotnik et al., 2020).

In order for educators to see the potential in students, they must address their own biases and deficit-based thinking regarding CLED students (Hammond, 2015). This work involves delving into how one understands culture. Then educators should consider how their cultural frames of reference influence how they recognize potential and what it looks like in the classroom setting. The Teacher's Observation of Potential in Students (TOPS) tool (Coleman et al., 2010) is helpful to consider specific behaviors in the classroom that may indicate potential. TOPS is the second module of U-STARS~PLUS, a curricular and procedural approach to support the recognition and support of potential in historically underrepresented students in grades K–3 (Coleman & Shah-Coltrane, 2013). TOPS uses nine overarching domains with a variety of specific behaviors that could be "teacher pleasing" and "non-teacher pleasing." The nine domains are: (1) learns easily, (2) shows advanced skills, (3) displays curiosity and creativity, (4) has strong interests, (5) shows advanced reasoning and problem solving, (6) displays spatial abilities, (7) shows motivation, (8) shows social perceptiveness, and (9) shows leadership (Coleman et al., 2010). The non-teacher-pleasing behaviors are valuable to consider. These behaviors are often considered deficits and may contribute to teachers using punishment or discipline to address behaviors instead of opportunities. Examples of non-teacher-pleasing behaviors that could be interpreted as assets are "challenging the teacher" or "questioning authority." Hammond (2015) recommended that teachers "widen their interpretation aperture" when considering how they understand or interpret students' behaviors (p. 57). Consider the following example when broadening a teacher's view of a child's behavior from deficit-based to asset-based:

> Tiffany is the only Black female student in a first-grade class of mostly White students. She is taller than her peers and very observant of what is happening in the class. The teacher addresses the whole class to transition from a talent development lesson around creative thinking; the teacher rings a bell, calls for the whole class to be quiet, and starts calling individual students to return to their regular seats. Tiffany sees the teacher's apparent struggle with getting the classes' attention. Tiffany stands up tall, changes her vocal register, and in a very clear and loud voice directs her peers, "Attention, class, it's time to return to your seats!" Eventually the class settles for their next activity. In later discussion about the class transition with the teacher, the teacher frustratedly points out that Tiffany tries to do that all of the time—the teacher rolls her eyes and continues—"too much."

In this example, the teacher perceives Tiffany's behavior as happening too often and as disruptive. Instead, the teacher could consider Tiffany's potential as a class leader. The teacher's reaction may indicate the teacher's perception of Tiffany's behavior as non-teacher-pleasing. Using TOPS, the non-teacher-pleasing behavior observed may be translated as "dominating of others" or "bossy." In order to shift the interpretation of the behavior from deficit to asset, the teacher could reframe the behavior as situated in the students' cultural reference (Hammond, 2015). Is Tiffany the oldest sibling of other children? Does Tiffany have strong female role models that demonstrate how to talk to groups? Perhaps Tiffany was copying behavior she observed in the teacher? Using TOPS, the behavior could be a characteristic of leadership and social perceptiveness when Tiffany recognized the teacher's challenge of getting the class to transition. The use of TOPS, an observable behavior scale, allows for educators to consider what students are doing, which aligns with the talent development model's approach to creative productivity (Subotnik et al., 2020). How could the teacher have shifted their perception of Tiffany's behavior to practices in the classroom where Tiffany could use her potential leadership skills with purpose?

Asset-based thinking in education begins with educators identifying students' strengths and enabling their use in the classroom to help students attain their own excellence (Lewis & Louis, 2009). Consider the following example:

> Adam is a White male in a second-grade class. He is observed sitting at a desk in the hallway with his chin resting on his folded arms. Eventually Adam enters the class and sits at one of the reading stations. Adam begins touching items that are within his reach: books on bookshelves, learning kit boxes, other children's tablets, and so on. His name is called out multiple times by the teacher, "No, Adam," and "Don't do that, Adam." Eventually the lesson is completed, and the teacher directs the students to return the tables back to the regular configuration. Adam is observed leading a group of his peers moving the tables back, remembering to lock the wheels, and returning the classroom to its original layout.

In this example, Adam started class outside of the space in a timeout location. When he is given the opportunity to move and contribute to the classroom, he leads a group of students. His peers follow him willingly, clearly seeing an admirable characteristic that they want to follow. The teacher saw what

Adam was not supposed to do and did not acknowledge his strengths when it came to Adam determining how to return the class furniture to the teacher's desired state. Using TOPS, from this vignette, one can see Adam demonstrating strengths in two domains: "displays spatial abilities" and "displays leadership." He was being reprimanded for non-teacher-pleasing behavior while touching and moving around when he was not directed to. However, he rose to the occasion when tasked with moving and manipulating items under direction. Additionally, his peers sought him out, illustrating his potential in leadership. How could the teacher provide opportunities to channel his need for movement and physical engagement so that he could spend his time in class being successful, instead of sitting in the hallway, away from instruction?

In the examples of Tiffany and Adam, imagine if the non-teacher-pleasing behaviors were considered through an asset-based lens. Consider what may have happened if the teachers had found and created productive and deliberate opportunities for the students to succeed, instead of focusing on what the children were not doing or were doing wrong. The TOPS creators recommended familiarizing teachers with the domains and reflecting on personally normed examples of children who may represent each behavior (Coleman et al., 2010). Asset-based thinking is more than considering how well students follow directions or align with the values established in the classroom. It allows teachers to consider what strengths students bring to the learning environment. Consider the following questions:

- How can educators leverage students' strengths in order to create opportunities and provide space for engagement that allows for talent development to reach all children?
- What happens when educators only see the deficits?
- What if educators saw students through an asset-based lens?
- What would instruction look like if educators created opportunities for students to demonstrate, practice, and develop their strengths?

Viewing students, especially those who are marginalized or historically underrepresented, through an asset-based lens can greatly impact students' educational experiences. Students like Adam may be able to spend time in school in the classroom instead of being punished in the hallway. Students like Tiffany could channel their natural abilities toward leadership by having purposeful responsibilities in the classroom instead of the teacher interpreting their behavior as disruptive. Educators influence students not only through acquisition of content and standards, but also in how students perceive themselves. If students are viewed as badly behaved or rule breakers, they may never see themselves as capable. However, if an educator recognizes a child's potential through behavior that is both compliant and not, the child may feel appreciated and recognized, and ultimately valued as a member of a learning community.

Culturally Responsive Educators

Aligning culturally responsive teaching with talent development starts with a theoretical foundation that frames the approach to nurturing culturally responsive teachers. Scholars have suggested numerous methods to address teachers' cultural responsiveness (Banks & Banks, 2013; DeJaeghere & Zhang, 2008; Delpit, 2006; García & Guerra, 2004; Gay, 2018; Gorski, 2009; Nieto & Bode, 2012; Sleeter, 2013). Examination of what constitutes a culturally responsive teacher will consider six characteristics of a culturally responsive educator (CRE) based on the model by Villegas and Lucas (2002) and endorsed by the National Center for Culturally Responsive Educational Systems. The CRE model identifies specific characteristics of the educator and ways to address those attitudes and dispositions. The six characteristics of a CRE are (a) sociocultural consciousness, (b) affirming attitude toward CLED students, (c) change agent, (d) constructivist pedagogy, (e) learns about students, and (f) utilizes culturally responsive teaching practices (Villegas & Lucas, 2002).

Sociocultural Consciousness

Sociocultural consciousness is the understanding that one's perceptions, thoughts, and behaviors are situated deep within the multiple identities that make up an individual. This includes but is not limited to an individual's racial, ethnic, class, and linguistic identities. Teachers must become familiar with their own sociocultural identities before understanding their CLED students and the social and cultural identities that they represent. Because demographic data show that White female teachers are the dominant population in classrooms, these teachers need to become aware of their identities as racialized beings and understand the unearned privileges that come with being a member of the dominant culture.

In implementation of a talent development framework, teachers need to determine their preconceived ideas about giftedness and talent. How do these ideas impact how they view, interact, and instruct their CLED students? How might these perceptions impact opportunities and access for CLED students?

Affirming Attitude Toward Students From CLED Backgrounds

Teachers who affirm their diverse students' backgrounds recognize the differences as assets. Instead of suppressing the experiences and skills that the students bring from a diverse background, they expand on and build new knowledge that is connected to the students' identities. Gay (2018) described caring teachers as having affirming attitudes about their students. Affirming or caring teachers create learning environments in which students feel "nourished, supported, protected, encouraged, and held accountable on personal, academic, and civic levels" (Gay, 2018, p. 63). Teachers who aim to have an affirming attitude toward students must develop a positive relationship with the students and families they serve (Gay, 2018; Hammond, 2015). According to Villegas and Lucas (2002), teachers who affirm diverse backgrounds are more likely to believe that CLED students are capable, even if their ability is demonstrated through behavior, communication, and thinking that may differ from the dominant culture.

Within the talent development framework, educators see the assets and strengths students bring that may not align with a school structure modeled by and for dominant cultures. Looking at behaviors as strengths instead of deficits is a significant mind shift, but tools and resources have been developed to address this shift. As mentioned earlier, TOPS (Coleman et al, 2010) specifically frames behaviors often seen as inappropriate when considering CLED students in a framework that interprets the behaviors as strengths. TOPS demonstrated an increase of teachers' ability to see potential in CLED students (Harradine et al., 2014). Using TOPS within a talent development framework demonstrates a teacher's commitment to see potential in all students.

Commitment and Skills to Act as Change Agents

Educators need to be committed to equity in education and increased access and opportunity for all students. Change agent educators see schools and society as interconnected (Villegas & Lucas, 2002). They recognize that the act of teaching is fundamentally political and ethical, and they work to reduce oppressive practices that exist within the educational institution. The commitment to act as a change agent is a dedication to advocate for access and equity for historically underserved students in talent development and to raise awareness and influence school and district level change (Roberts, 2017). Advocacy in a talent development framework translates into working to ensure students who have been historically underrepresented or have been disadvantaged by systems have access to opportunities to expand their potential. Methods to lead change toward equity and access in talent development include raising awareness around access issues, identifying policy and practices that privilege some students over others, and working with colleagues to collaborate around changing mindsets regarding potential in CLED students. These opportunities may present as conducting equity audits of gifted and talented programs or identifying the specific systemic models that perpetuate deficit-based thinking around CLED students (see Table 7.1 for examples of systemic models and deficit-based thinking).

The use of TOPS (Coleman et al., 2010) to introduce asset-based thinking about students is one way to be a change agent. An example of raising awareness at an elementary school was when the teacher of the gifted created a professional learning opportunity around asset-based thinking using the domains in TOPS. The teacher created forms where the class rosters were on one side of the form with the nine TOPS domains across the top. Participating teachers were to mark the student names where they had seen student examples of the different domains. The results showed that based on the classroom teachers' cultural lens and awareness of issues of equity, they saw more or less assets. For instance, the teacher who was the parent of a CLED student indicated more strengths observed in her class, whereas the teacher with a fixed understanding of giftedness and high potential indicated strengths for students who followed typical teacher-pleasing behaviors. Using these data, teachers discussed how to support each other by collaborating to create opportunities for the students to learn or demonstrate different areas of strength. Additionally, the teachers discussed specific students and planned to take turns observing each student in the class where the teacher saw the student's strengths and to reflect on their own practice.

Constructivist Pedagogy

Epistemological understanding of the theory of constructivism focuses on "the meaning-making activity of the individual mind" (Crotty, 1998, p. 58). Constructivist pedagogy refers to how an educator facilitates understanding in the classroom through deliberate instructional choices that are student-centered (Richardson, 2003). Constructivist pedagogy requires students' identities and life experiences to be a significant part of instructional planning.

To be an educator with a constructivist approach, one must believe that learning is a process through which students construct knowledge by connecting new inputs with prior learning. To be a constructivist educator with a culturally responsive lens, the teacher values and recognizes the importance of their students' prior knowledge and experiences. This perspective believes that the knowledge students bring from personal and cultural experiences is essential to their education. Constructivist teachers facilitate connection making between what learners already know to new ideas and experiences. So that the educator does not sustain a dominant narrative value system, the educator must have strong understanding of the content and of their students. Constructivist pedagogy can be problematic if educators do not value or recognize the prior experiences students have before coming to the classroom. Educators must understand that all students come to school with different experiences and knowledge, and educators must expect the construction process to look different for each child. Constructivist pedagogy requires teachers to approach instruction as student-centered and be flexible enough to adjust to varied student needs. At the same time, teachers work to build on their students' strengths while they construct knowledge. Constructivist pedagogy acknowledges that all students are capable of learning, promotes critical thinking, supports problem solving that reaches beyond the classroom walls, and as a result, prepares children to be active participants in a democracy (Villegas & Lucas, 2002). Constructivist pedagogy calls for the purposeful creation of learning opportunities that allow for students to connect, challenge, or construct new knowledge with their previous understandings. This deliberate creation of learning opportunities is why it is essential for the talent development framework.

Learning About Students

Constructivist pedagogy requires educators to know what prior knowledge their students have and to facilitate their construction of new knowledge. This pedagogy includes knowing about students' lives outside of schools, their interests and passions, and their strengths and struggles. Teachers use this knowledge and construct their lessons and approaches to engage and motivate the students. Learning about students should include the students' previous learning experiences, their views of school, and how those experiences have shaped their current opinions of learning. Gay (2018) referred to this effort as fostering a caring relationship with the students. To be culturally responsive, caring relationships between teachers and students are imperative for student achievement. Villegas and Lucas (2002) asserted that responsive educators learn as much as possible about their students to inform their approaches to teaching and learning.

Students need to know that their teachers see their potential and gifts and are able to provide opportunities for the students to demonstrate their strengths as a part of a healthy classroom environment. Often, educators give interest surveys or ask questions about students to start off the school year, but little is done with that information. Culturally responsive educators find ways to integrate the information students share in productive and relevant ways.

Culturally Responsive Teaching Practices

Culturally responsive teachers use the knowledge that they have gained from and about their students to construct opportunities for active learning. This knowledge may include using differentiated instructional strategies when planning lessons and creating opportunities for student interest and learning preferences by adapting methods for students to demonstrate their knowledge and potential (Tomlinson, 2003). However, Villegas and Lucas (2002) reminded educators that culturally responsive teaching practices are not merely instructional techniques; they are the integration of all of the previous mentioned characteristics to facilitate student learning. A culturally responsive classroom is an environment where all students can learn, make sense of information, and have a better understanding of the world and their potential in it.

Talent Development and Culturally Responsive Educators

In order to implement the talent development framework, it is helpful to consider the whole child's needs and the impact that context, experience, and opportunity have on that child's development. To illustrate this, the culturally responsive educator (CRE) model recommended by Villegas and Lucas (2002) has been aligned with the talent development (TD) framework as summarized by Olszewski-Kubilius and Thomson (2015) so that the connections are explicitly laid out for consideration. The Culturally Responsive Educator and Talent Development model (see Figure 7.1) is not a linear model in which each characteristic aligns with a talent development framework (Olszewski-Kubilius & Thomson, 2015). Instead, the CRE and TD frameworks are set on two segmented rings that are influenced by sociopolitical, cultural, and environmental contexts. Villegas and Lucas's (2002) framework allows for the CRE to consider the policies, practices, and systems that contribute to disparities and issues of inequity across the contexts. This nonlinear model means that

Figure 7.1
Culturally Responsive Educator and Talent Development Frameworks

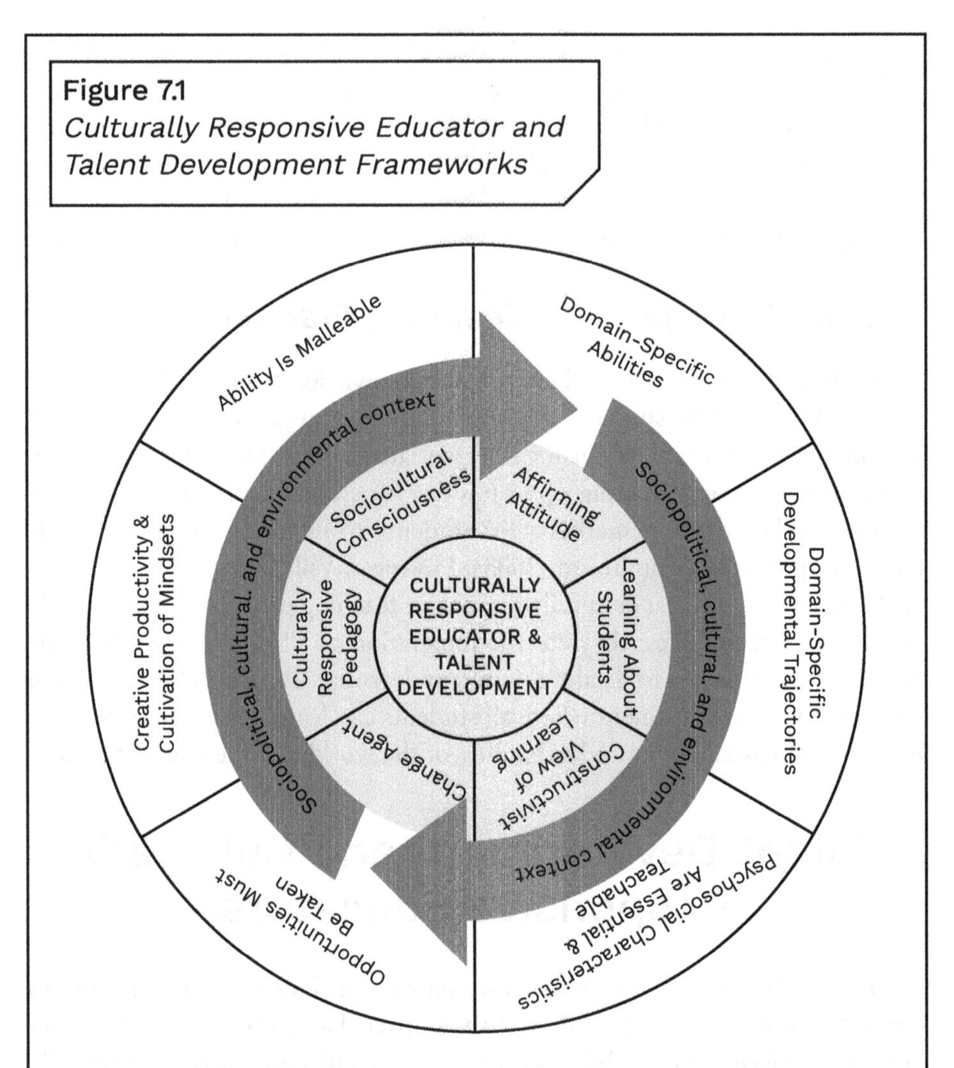

Note. This figure shows the domains of the six implications of practice for the Talent Development Megamodel (Olszewski-Kubilius & Thomson, 2015) and aligns them with the six characteristics of Culturally Responsive Educators (Villegas & Lucas, 2002). The two frameworks do not function in a linear manner; as a result, the rotating arrows titled "Sociopolitical, cultural, and environmental context" are included to illustrate the flexible nature of the framework.

within all approaches to TD, the CRE will understand that contexts influence everything through barriers, unequal opportunities, and an imbalance across cultural, linguistic, economic, and educational experiences. To illustrate the connections of the CRE model and TD, the remainder of the chapter focuses on examples of alignment between the two frameworks. The combined model is intended to be fluid and responsive, which means the following examples illustrate how the alignment could work.

Understanding That Ability Is Malleable and Sociocultural Consciousness

Understanding that ability is malleable requires an understanding of the sociocultural factors that contribute to students' lived experiences. CREs understand that values, behaviors, and practices of an individual are influenced by identity, social class, and linguistic diversity (Villegas & Lucas, 2002). A child's experiences prior to beginning school directly impact how the child views education, learns, and interacts with others. CREs understand the intersections of who the child is and where they come from. In order to achieve this understanding, CREs explore their own identities and experiences and consider how they correlate to their pedagogical practice. Once this exploration happens, educators are better able to recognize the sociocultural influence that creates policies, practices, and procedures that perpetuate access and equity issues in talent development and gifted services.

Olszewski-Kubilius and Thomson (2015) recommended that ongoing assessment throughout a student's academic career is one way to implement talent development. However, testing bias has been demonstrated as a factor that has prevented access for CLED students (Ford et al., 2016). Tests alone cannot be the access point to advanced coursework. Relying on a single measure ignores the fact that ability is malleable, and that people grow, change, and learn through experience. Creating opportunities for students to demonstrate strengths through multiple measures and student portfolios could change the impact of testing bias on representation and access. Additionally, using portfolios for students to document their talent development trajectory aligns with the other principles of TD. For instance, Kay (2019) asserted that a talent record or portfolio allows students to articulate what they are good at and their strengths. Many opportunities exist through using a portfolio or talent record system. For instance, portfolios can include student goal setting, longitudinal data to illustrate growth, and information on domain-specific skills to guide postsecondary decision making. A talent development portfolio that travels with the student throughout their academic career could inform choices around magnet programs, out-of-school opportunities, and school opportunities.

Opportunities Must Be Taken and Change Agents

The opportunities for children need to be created and accessible for all. The role of a change agent and the educator's responsibilities align here. Deliberate practice and planning are necessary to build strengths into talents (Kay, 2019). Educators as change agents include students in learning opportunities, regardless of identification status. Learning opportunities with multiple entry points and many possibilities should be available to all, not just students labeled gifted. Providing this service schoolwide or within a whole-class experience while partnering with homeroom teachers broadens access to students in the whole school, much like the Schoolwide Enrichment Model (SEM; Renzulli & Reis, 2014).

Opportunities do not need to be limited to the students alone. As explained earlier, supporting asset-based thinking requires professional learning opportunities for teachers. For instance, a schoolwide opportunity could be to choose two or three of the TOPS domains to focus teacher professional learning goals on creating instructional strategies to develop and explore students' strengths. Educators could use TOPS (Coleman et al., 2010) to discuss student achievement, using asset-based language focused on observable behaviors.

Psychosocial Characteristics Are Teachable and a Constructivist View of Education

Integrating asset-based thinking with professional learning opportunities aligns with Olszewski-Kubilius and Thomson's (2015) recommendation to explicitly teach psychosocial skills and characteristics in a TD framework. Professional learning communities provide for a space where the educators are trained in TOPS, work to view students through a strength-based lens, and consider the systems that create or perpetuate barriers to opportunities. In addition to shifting teacher mindsets around potential and talent, asset-based thinking instructional practices could significantly influence student performance and academic trajectories. Instruction that models metacognitive thinking and trains students to communicate their goals, accomplishments, and interests is essential to the TD framework.

Olszewski-Kubilius et al. (2019) identified psychosocial skills considered important in the stages of the Talent Development Megamodel:

> These included the four skills grouped under Emotional Self-Regulation: regulation of arousal/relaxation, coping for chal-

> lenge, coping for failure/resiliency, and anxiety management. Other skills identified as important at all stages were focusing attention and concentration control (under Cognitive Self-Regulation); goal setting, self-efficacy/self-confidence, and perseverance, commitment, and persistence (under Motivational Self-Regulation); time management and organizational skills (under Metacognitive Self-Regulation); and collegiality (under Social Skills). (p. 8)

Identifying needs and seizing the opportunity to create learning strategies that teach these skills has proven to be a challenge. For example, the online learning environment and at-home learning settings amplified the necessity of the skills students need to be successful. The COVID-19 pandemic shined a spotlight on why these skills are nonnegotiable and integral for all students.

Many behaviors exhibited by children interpreted as nonconforming—such as being deliberately defiant or presenting as underachievement, low self-concept, and lack of common peers—support that psychosocial characteristics need to be explicitly taught. Instead of dismissing the behavior as noncompliant, seeing the potential for strengths in the conflict is an opportunity to use constructivist pedagogy and build on the student's experiences. Constructivist pedagogy allows educators to connect with students' prior knowledge and align the behavior to strengths. Within the TD framework, tapping into prior knowledge includes determining ways to align with the psychosocial skills to ensure success, as well as prioritizing important skills within domains. Connecting what children do to relevant application of practices allows for a constructivist approach to teaching psychosocial skills for talent development.

Creative Productivity and Cultivation of Mindsets and Culturally Responsive Pedagogy

In the similar vein of explicitly teaching psychosocial skills, talent development calls for opportunities for students to apply their creative talents and strengths through creative production. As Erwin and Worrell (2012) noted, "Giftedness is not about who you are but what you do" (p. 75). Teaching with intentional opportunities for creative production (Dai, 2020) moves toward educability and away from the concept of ability (Valencia, 2010). Counter to many theories of high ability, the concept of a creative producer extends beyond a gifted trait to specific behaviors that show gifts (Dai, 2019, 2020).

Movement toward a TD framework is inherently culturally responsive because talent development is a process focused on growing potential to performance based on deliberate steps to teach and cultivate the psychosocial skills to perform.

Culturally responsive pedagogy calls for teacher awareness of their own identity and how it connects with instructional practice, including how teachers understand potential and ability (Gay, 2018; Hammond, 2015). If teachers are to cultivate mindsets and attitudes around creative production (e.g., perseverance and risk-taking), they need to understand their concepts of creativity and academic mindsets. Teachers are more likely to see strengths and guide children in the process of creative production if they have already done the work to fully develop their understanding of ability and the impact that instruction and opportunity has on student performance.

Domain-Specific, Affirming Attitude, and Learning About Students

Understanding that talent development requires performance rather than a single label also means that the production needs to be relevant and purposeful. Talent development's domain-specific focus in combination with creative production grows specific abilities and pathways for a student's continued trajectory toward expertise (Olszewski-Kubilius et al., 2018). In school districts moving toward a professional pathways model for secondary students, the TD framework allows for the skills and knowledge development before entering high school. Teaching the skills and providing opportunities for students to demonstrate them are dependent on the teacher's high expectations of students and a purposeful effort to learn about students and their families. Aligning student interests, strengths, and passions with domain-specific opportunities and trajectories allows educators to be responsive to the student-centered needs. This responsiveness is especially significant for the CLED student because the pedagogical choices will be focused on the student needs, rather than the dominant cultural understanding of the purpose of school. In Figure 7.1, domain-specific abilities and domain-trajectories are grouped differently, but they are connected. Their alignment is evident in the student-centered CRE affirming understanding of CLED students and deliberate practice in getting to know them.

Domain-Specific Abilities. Olszewski-Kubilius and Thomson (2015) explained that domain-specific abilities indicate that assessments are aligned to specific talents. Understanding the skills necessary to get on a pathway falls on the educator. The educator must know the student interests and experiences to understand what to assess and teach for a domain trajectory. Using the metaphor of a gate and a key, to get through the gate (the domain-specific pathway) the students must have the key (the skills). Appropriate assessments ensure that educators know what the students have mastered and where they need additional support.

For younger children, especially those from underresourced backgrounds, the creation of opportunities to introduce different potential domain-specific pathways is essential. Providing experiences for children to exercise their strengths with potential applications to opportunities allows emergent talent to develop. Cultivating relationships with students and families and valuing the skills and experiences they bring to the learning context requires a culturally responsive lens.

Domain-Specific Trajectories. Educators' knowledge of the domain-specific trajectories that students may go through in a TD framework relies on long-term understanding and implementation. This understanding brings together knowledge about students, assessment of their skills, and deliberate planning of opportunities for students to be on a path to expertise. This element of the TD framework connects many different roles and responsibilities together within a school system. Some examples of influential roles include school counselors, career and technical educators, content area experts, and teachers of the gifted. Educators must be knowledgeable of secondary school options, courses that are offered, and which pathway is appropriate for specific domains. Educators need to be aware of the systems and opportunities outside of their area of content or grade level (Olszewski-Kubilius & Thomson, 2015). Every step in the talent pathway must be through a culturally responsive educator lens because the plans should be supportive of student identity and prior experience, as well as understanding of the contextual situations that will influence the student's trajectory.

Connecting across these different entities, systems, and knowledge bases often makes implementing a TD framework difficult. Consider the example of a computer scientist trajectory (see Figure 7.2).

A district provides an enrichment program around computer education in which students learn coding using multiple applications and tools. The district planning committee would like to include an asset-based framework, TOPS, into the regular instructional lessons. The talent development specialist has been tasked to create a resource or tool for the enrichment teachers to use TOPS within a computer science domain. First, the specialist researches the dispositions and behaviors that a computer scientist must have to be successful.

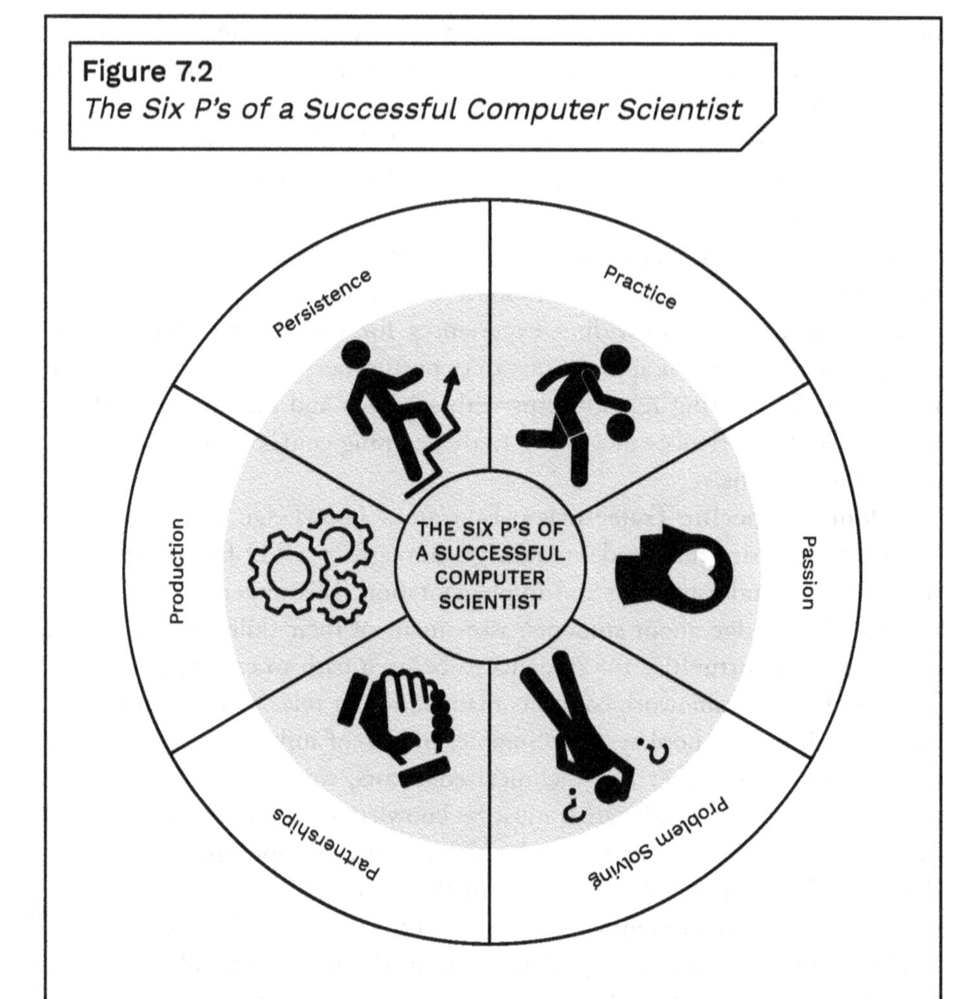

Figure 7.2
The Six P's of a Successful Computer Scientist

Note. This figure shows the six behaviors or skills necessary for a computer scientist trajectory. The figure was created by M. Jensen and M. J. Lichtenstein (2020) for a summer enrichment program around computers. Reprinted with permission of the author M. J. Lichtenstein.

Subotnik et al. (2019) brought together interviews and essential skills around domains in "The Psychology of High Performance." Using this text, the educator learns about what is expected of professionals in computer science and aligns it with student-specific language (Bedell, 2016; Knotek, 2019):

- **Persistence:** Computer scientists and coders keep trying and can debug their code to make it work.

- **Practice:** Computer scientists and coders learn new skills and will do them over and over again until they are memorized.
- **Passion:** Successful computer scientists and coders love learning new information, solving puzzles, and using what they learn to create new projects.
- **Problem solving:** Computer scientists and coders can put steps in order to finish a task or solve a puzzle.
- **Partnerships:** Computer scientists and coders can work by themselves, or with others. They ask for help when they need it.
- **Production:** Computer scientists and coders are willing to try new things and use what they learn to create or improve projects.

The effort's result was creation of "The Six P's of a Successful Computer Scientist" (see Figure 7.2). The educator aligned the P's with language from the TOPS so that the enrichment instructors had specific behaviors to look for when working with the children. Additionally, the team created conversation protocols and post-production frameworks for students in the enrichment program to complete as a reflection on their strengths, challenges, and next steps (Jensen & Lichtenstein, 2020).

The computer science example demonstrates one way of using culturally responsive teaching with the TD framework through research and creation. The partnerships among the educators with content expertise and understanding of students then take on the task of creating instructional lessons. The next steps would be to integrate the resulting student work into a talent development portfolio that students use to document their pathway progress, including evidence of growth, and to communicate progress toward a postsecondary computer scientist pathway with teachers.

Conclusion

This chapter started with a discussion of the impact of context. The COVID-19 pandemic revealed that there are areas of opportunity and change within how school systems, teaching, and learning happens. The recentering of race and equity in the public eye has increased a collective understanding of how intertwined culture, ability, and experience are. Integrating the talent development framework with a culturally responsive lens may be the paradigm shift to begin this change. The shift calls for educators to be intentional in understanding their own identity and experiences and how those may influence or impact students. The framework encourages educators to consider their understanding of ability and potential and employ protocols such as TOPS to guide a shift in mindsets and language. Consideration of the sociopolitical, cultural, and environmental context (see Figure 7.1) allows for educators to be responsive to situations impacting their students inside and outside of the classroom. Student experiences do not stop at the school door, so when CREs view student experiences as strengths to inform instructional planning, more students and families will experience school as a place with purpose, affirming beliefs, and relevancy. Through deliberate planning and collaboration, educators can create spaces that allow students to grow and experience opportunities made available for all children. This shift will not happen by chance but requires deliberate planning and practice to guide the decisions. Approaching talent development as a culturally responsive educator is a way to break through systems of inequity and rebuild through an understanding of strengths and potential for all students regardless of cultural, linguistic, socioeconomic, and ability label.

End-of-Chapter Discussion/ Reflection Questions

1. In what ways does the teacher's cultural identity contribute to underrepresentation and access to talent development services?
2. Define culturally responsive education. How do you employ culturally responsive practice in your teaching?
3. Compare and contrast deficit thinking and asset-based thinking. Relate each to talent development. How can educators leverage students' strengths in order to create opportunities and provide space for engagement that allows for talent development to reach all children?
4. In this chapter, the author states, "Educators need to be committed to equity in education and increased access and opportunity for all students. Change agent educators see schools and society as interconnected (Villegas & Lucas, 2002). They recognize that the act of teaching is fundamentally political and ethical, and they work to reduce oppressive practices that exist within the educational institution." How and why will you become a change agent in your school and classroom?

5. Examine the nonlinear model presented in Figure 7.1 that illustrates the relationship of the culturally responsive educator model and the talent development framework. Generate specific, real-world examples to show understanding of how aspects of these models intersect.

References

Banks, J. A., & Banks, C. A. M. (Eds.). (2013). *Multicultural education: Issues and perspectives* (8th ed.). Wiley.

Bedell, J. M. (2016). *So, you want to be a coder? The ultimate guide to a career in programming, video game creation, robotics, and more!* Beyond Words/Aladdin.

Coleman, M. R., & Shah-Coltrane, S. S. (2013). Recognizing and nurturing potential across the tiers: U-STARS~PLUS. In M. R. Coleman & S. K. Johnsen (Eds.), *Implementing RtI with gifted students: Service models, trends, and issues* (pp. 246–267). Prufrock Press.

Coleman, M. R., Shah-Coltrane, S., & Harrison, A. (2010). *U-STARS~PLUS: Teacher's observation of potential in students (TOPS): Individual student observation form.* Council for Exceptional Children.

Crotty, M. (1998). *The foundations of social research: Meaning and perspective in the research process.* SAGE.

Dai, D. Y. (2019). Toward a new era of gifted education: Principles, policies, and strategies. *Turkish Journal of Giftedness and Education, 9*(1), 2–15.

Dai, D. Y. (2020). Rethinking human potential from a talent development perspective. *Journal for the Education of the Gifted, 43*(1), 19–37. https://doi.org/10.1177/0162353219897850

DeJaeghere, J. G., & Zhang, Y. (2008). Development of intercultural responsiveness among US American teachers: Professional development factors that enhance responsiveness. *Intercultural Education, 19*(3), 255–268. https://doi.org/10.1080/14675980802078624

Delpit, L. (2006). *Other people's children: Cultural conflict in the classroom.* The New Press.

Erwin, J. O., & Worrell, F. C. (2012). Assessment practices and the underrepresentation of minority students in gifted and talented education. *Journal of Psychoeducational Assessment, 30*(1), 74–87. https://doi.org/10.1177/0734282911428197

Ford, D. Y. (2015). Culturally responsive gifted classrooms for culturally different students: A focus on invitational learning. *Gifted Child Today, 38*(1), 67–69. https://doi.org/10.1177/1076217514556697

Ford, D. Y., Grantham, T. C., & Whiting, G. W. (2008). Culturally and linguistically diverse students in gifted education: Recruitment and retention issues. *Exceptional Children, 74*(3), 289–306. https://doi.org/10.1177/001440290807400302

Ford, D. Y. Wright, B. L., Washington, A., & Henfield, M. S. (2016). Access and equity denied: Key theories for school psychologists to consider when assessing Black and Hispanic students for gifted education. *School Psychology Forum, 10*(3), 265–277.

García, S. B., & Guerra, P. L. (2004). Deconstructing deficit thinking: Working with educators to create more equitable learning environments. *Education and Urban Society, 36*(2), 150–168. https://doi.org/10.1177/0013124503261322

Gay, G. (2018). *Culturally responsive teaching: Theory, research, and practice* (3rd ed.). Teachers College Press.

Gorski, P. (2009). What we're teaching teachers: An analysis of multicultural teacher education coursework syllabi. *Teaching and Teacher Education, 25*(2), 309–318. https://doi.org/10.1016/j.tate.2008.07.008

Grantham, T. C., Ford, D. Y., Davis, J. L., Frazier Trotman Scott, M., Dickson, K., Taradash, G., Whiting, G. W., Cotton, C. B., Floyd, E. F., Collins, K. H., Anderson, B. N., Fox, S., & Roberson, J. J. (2020). *Get your knee off our necks: Black scholars speak out to confront racism against Black students in gifted and talented education.* The Consortium for Inclusion of Underrepresented Racial Groups in Gifted Education.

Griner, A., & Stewart, M. (2012). Addressing the achievement gap and disproportionality through the use of culturally responsive teaching practices. *Urban Education, 48*(4), 585–621. https://doi.org/10.1177/0042085912456847

Hammond, Z. (2015). *Culturally responsive teaching and the brain: Promoting authentic engagement and rigor among culturally and linguistically diverse students.* Corwin.

Harradine, C. C., Coleman, M. R. B., & Winn, D. M. C. (2014). Recognizing academic potential in students of color: Findings of U-STARS~PLUS. *Gifted Child Quarterly, 58*(1), 24–34. https://doi.org/10.1177/0016986213506040

Harris, J. J., III, Brown, E. L., Ford, D. Y., & Richardson, J. W. (2004). African Americans and multicultural education: A proposed remedy for dispro-

portionate special education placement and underinclusion in gifted education. *Education and Urban Society, 36*(3), 304–341. https://doi.org/10.1177/0013124504264444
Howard, T. C. (2010). *Why race and culture matter in schools: Closing the achievement gap in America's classrooms.* Teachers College Press.
Jensen, M., & Lichtenstein, M. J. (2020). *Talent development and CoderDojo* [Unpublished professional development curriculum]. Albemarle County Public Schools, VA.
Kay, S. I. (2019). *On human potential: Nurturing talents and cultivating expertise.* Rowman & Littlefield.
Kendi, I. X. (2019). *How to be an antiracist.* Random House.
Knotek, S. E. (2019). Gatekeeper interview: Michael Reed, Software engineer and site lead, Google Chapel Hill. In R. F. Subotnik, P. Olszewski-Kubilius, & F. C. Worrell (Eds.), *The psychology of high performance: Developing human potential into domain-specific talent* (pp. 135–140). American Psychological Association.
Lewis, S. J., & Louis, M. C. (2009). The principles of strengths-based education. *Journal of College and Character, 10*(4). https://doi.org/10.2202/1940-1639.1041
Lucas, T., & Villegas, A. M. (2013). Preparing linguistically responsive teachers: Laying the foundation in preservice teacher education. *Theory Into Practice, 52*(2), 98–109. https://doi.org/10.1080/00405841.2013.770327
Nelson, S. W., & Guerra, P. L. (2013). Educator beliefs and cultural knowledge: Implications for school improvement efforts. *Educational Administration Quarterly, 50*(1), 67–95. https://doi.org/10.1177/0013161X13488595
Nieto, S., & Bode, P. (Eds.) (2012). *Affirming diversity: The sociopolitical context of multicultural education* (6th ed.). Pearson.
Olszewski-Kubilius, P., Subotnik, R. F., Davis, L. C., & Worrell, F. C. (2019, November). Benchmarking psychosocial skills important for talent development. *New Directions for Child and Adolescent Development, 168,* 1–16. https://doi.org/10.1002/cad.20318
Olszewski-Kubilius, P., Subotnik, R. F., & Worrell, F. C. (Eds.). (2018). *Talent development as a framework for gifted education: Implications for best practices and applications in schools.* Prufrock Press.
Olszewski-Kubilius, P., & Thomson, D. (2015). Talent development as a framework for gifted education. *Gifted Child Today, 38*(1), 49–59. https://doi.org/10.1177/1076217514556531
Renzulli, J. S., & Reis, S. M. (2014). *The Schoolwide Enrichment Model: A how-to guide for talent development* (3rd ed.). Prufrock Press.

Richardson, V. (2003). Constructivist pedagogy. *Teachers College Record, 105*(9), 1623–1640.

Roberts, J. L. (2017). Planning for advocacy. In R. D. Eckert & J. H. Robins (Eds.), *Designing services and programs for high-ability learners: A guidebook for gifted education* (2nd ed.). Corwin.

Sleeter, C. E. (2013). *Power, teaching, and teacher education: Confronting injustice with critical research and action*. Lang.

Subotnik, R. F., Olszewski-Kubilius, P., & Worrell, F. C. (Eds.). (2019). *The psychology of high performance: Developing human potential into domain-specific talent*. American Psychological Association.

Subotnik, R. F., Olszewski-Kubilius, P., & Worrell, F. C. (2020). The talent development megamodel. In T. L. Cross & P. Olszewski-Kubilius (Eds.), *Conceptual frameworks for giftedness and talent development: Enduring theories and comprehensive models in gifted education* (pp. 29–54). Prufrock Press.

Tomlinson, C. A. (2003). *Fulfilling the promise of the differentiated classroom: Strategies and tools for responsive teaching*. ASCD.

Valencia, R. R. (Ed.). (1997). *The evolution of deficit thinking: Educational thought and practice*. Routledge.

Valencia, R. R. (2010). *Dismantling contemporary deficit thinking: Educational thought and practice*. Routledge.

Villegas, A. M., & Lucas, T. (2002). Preparing culturally responsive teachers: Rethinking the curriculum. *Journal of Teacher Education, 53*(1), 20–32.

Zacarian, D., Alvarez-Ortiz, L., & Haynes, J. (2017). *Teaching to strengths: Supporting students living with trauma, violence, and chronic stress*. ASCD.

8

Teacher Development

Culturally Responsive Teaching in the Context of Talent Spotting

Emma Tartt and Meta Van Sickle

When we, as educators, want to become culturally responsive, we need to become highly reflective. We first need to understand ourselves and then our students. We need to do so in a system that is filled with deficit thinking through research models that primarily view who can and who cannot do schooling through the lenses of race, class, and culture. These systemic models lead us to think that some students are less able and less capable than other students. To understand talent development, we must move beyond the identity structures of race, class, and culture used to create deficit thinking and instead think about the identity differences as exciting new ways to discover potential. What helps us see and hear potential?

Letting Our Keen Eyes and Ears See and Hear

This chapter features a review of students' life aspects and how teachers can use their keen eyes to see and listening ears to hear in order to notice talent in children from a variety of backgrounds. Life aspects traditionally studied in schooling research include students' race/ethnicity, gender, and socioeconomic backgrounds. However, in today's classrooms, these identities do not provide enough information to help a teacher understand students in the classroom. A useful idea for studying underlying life aspects is that differences matter but are not binary (Ramos-Garcia, 2004). Nonbinary means that identities are more complex and layered. Teachers who are able to address diversity in the many forms reflected in what they see in students' identities allow a positive image of students to form. Exploration about these varied notions of diversity leads the teacher to deeper levels of understanding the student and provides the teacher with the opportunity to see and promote talent development in each student they teach.

Diversity

Preservice and inservice teachers often have limited cultural experiences, making it difficult to envision themselves in a setting with students who represent a high level of diversity (Baker & Taylor, 1995; Butler et al., 2006; Merryfield, 2000; Morales, 2000). In one study, Butler et al. (2006) noted that a preservice student reflected about the notion that if teachers had a broad understanding of multicultural issues there might be better outcomes in the classroom. Further, that understanding would lead to a deeper support for the students they are teaching. Learning about the students in a class takes time because factors concerning family genealogy and background often require many narratives from multiple cultures, contextualized by historical events and timelines. Too frequently, we rely on family genealogies that are woven into a single story, such as Asian American, African American, German American, and so on. We need to think about the narrative or image each single story creates in our mind. Is the image overly optimistic or pessimistic about the group? Are we willing to recognize differences among those who were lumped together in an identity group? Reliance on a single narrative for a large group may miss more issues than it explains. Lee et al. (2015) explained this phenomenon as follows:

> We are told single stories that often neglect the sociocultural factors—the historical reality—of our past. Our family histories are constructed historically and are embedded in social, political, and economic processes and relationships. This article argues that we need to complicate what we know about our past and examine policies and cultural practices that lead to a racialized system of power and privilege, racialized policies, and racialized oppression and progression. (p. 28)

Recognizing the vast number of issues involved with the degree of diversity among our student populations is a time-consuming task. For example, understanding that different cultures express the same idea in different ways becomes important if a teacher is to be able to identify talent and work to develop it in students. The teacher needs to continuously ask of a lesson, "Is it worth it? Is it meaningful to the student?" Teaching with diversity in mind requires ongoing self-examination of personal biases, prejudices, and bigotry for each child's talent to become obvious. When a teacher reflects on their own implicit biases and slows down their thinking and assumptions, it allows them to learn more about students beyond the single-story perspective. Once this slower thinking and ongoing examination occurs as regular teaching practice, each child can be seen in the light of potential.

Perceptions of "Right"

In regard to the theme of keenly seeing and carefully listening as a means to deeply understand students, Aikenhead (2006) stated "Not only is cross-cultural science education founded on respect and inclusion of students' indigenous science, but also its humanistic ideology implies responsiveness to student heterogeneity" (p. 114). If a teacher is to be responsive, it requires a highly honed set of observations made by the teacher especially when they are from a dominant cultural background. Historic notions that Western ways of knowing are right/correct, and thus students' indigenous ways of knowing are wrong, must change if all students are to participate and make academic gains (Aikenhead, 2006). A keen observation about students' culture requires a teacher to see diversity in its many forms and to comprehend designations of other and what this designation means about perceptions of right (Howes, 2002). Learning the special knowledge your students bring from home can help you relate the content in the classroom to each student's life. A willingness on the teacher's part to see and hear what students know enables the building upon and extending of strengths and knowledge that already exists within the student. When a teacher sees and hears a student's examples and experiences, the student's passions, interests, and skills are evident.

When using keen eyes and ears, the reflective teacher notices that their perspectives are mostly from their own limited life experiences. Next, the teacher is wise to start the story from the others' perspectives. Thus, a student's story now holds multiple perspectives (at least two, that of teacher and student) in the teacher's mind and characterizes the other (the student) in more ways than either of the initial two single stories. This is an important step in moving beyond the initial stereotype and looking at multiple characterizations that can show students' strengths, rather than focusing on a stereotype, either positive or negative.

Teachers let their use of keen eyes and ears guide their understanding as they learn the ethnic, gendered, linguistic, racial, and socioeconomic backgrounds of their students. The more competent they become, the more they understand the importance of educating in an equitable and socially just manner. Although most teachers may arrive in classrooms with little or no intercultural experiences, it is necessary for them to learn about themselves and their students so that they are able to create instruction that is as effective, equitable, and as socially just as possible.

When reviewing results of the William & Mary language arts units (e.g., Center for Gifted Education, 2011), the Project Clarion units (e.g., Kim et al., 2012), the Project M^3 and M^2 units (e.g., Gavin et al., 2009, 2010), and U-STARS~PLUS (Coleman et al., 2007) materials, it became apparent that the teaching practices encouraged teachers to deeply invest in learning about their students. Teachers must want to know their students. Knowing your students can help you find examples, authentic problems, and interesting ideas to explore. Teachers who are vested in learning about their students to this depth want to ensure their learning. With use of interesting and challenging inquiry-based curriculum, such as the M^3 and M^2 units, the Clarion units, and U-STARS~PLUS lessons, students begin to reveal their knowledge, skills, and abilities. As the strengths become evident, talent is identified.

Another way to find talents is through the use of the Teacher's Observation of Potential in Students (TOPS; Coleman et al., 2010) as a tool for talent spotting. TOPS gives teachers a framework for observing and noting evidence of ability and strength that includes typical behaviors that come to mind when you think of high ability in students (i.e., learns easily or shows advanced skills) as well as atypical behaviors indicative of high potential (i.e., has strong interests, displays spatial skills; Coleman et al., 2010). The combination of powerful curriculum and instructional strategies (i.e., use of engaging curriculum and instructional strategies in combination with the use of TOPS to look for potential as it emerges) allows teachers to further identify the form of the strengths expressed by students. This combination yields a strength-based approach advocated by talent development models of teaching. The combination allows teachers to see students "at-potential" rather than "at-risk" (Coleman et al., 2007).

Teachers are ultimately the ones who need to identify talent among the students they teach. When teachers make sincere and acute observations, they discover students' talents and begin teaching in a manner to develop those talents. Thus, teachers make the most difference in the outcomes for the students in their classrooms.

Example From Practice

The goals of the William & Mary language arts units (e.g., Center for Gifted Education, 2011) are to develop students' skills in literary analysis and interpretation, persuasive writing, linguistic competency, and oral communication. This curriculum also strengthens students' reasoning skills and understanding of the concept of change. It requires complex reasoning, planning, developing, and thinking, such as comparing multiple works by the same author or from the same time period. This curriculum shifts from students working individually with feedback from the teacher toward students learning in a community in which students seek feedback from their peers.

The William & Mary language arts curriculum focuses on developing students' deep understanding of literary concepts. The anchor texts are multicultural as well as challenging for the students to read, but they provide great opportunities to teach literacy strategies, such as rereading, symbolism, text structures, text features, word study, and text connections to promote comprehension. These resources provide practical ways to use the literacy strategies that allow teachers to teach language arts in a more conceptual way. This curriculum also provides instruction using explicit vocabulary and a graphic organizer called a Vocabulary Web (Center for Gifted Education, n.d.), which helps expand students' knowledge of words, their meanings, and their origins. The units include embedded formative assessments and questions, and these aid teachers in identifying student strengths.

While teaching lessons included in the William & Mary language arts unit *Autobiographies and Memoirs* (Center for Gifted Education, 2011), advanced and deep-thinking students began to stand out to the teacher, as the literary analysis questions encouraged students to share their unique thoughts. Many of the questions were advanced and high level. For example, in one of the lessons in which students analyze a photograph from photobiographies, students were asked to describe the photograph in detail, to share what was noticed first, to decide what the reason was for taking the photograph, and to conjecture about the placement of people or objects in the photograph and if the placement adds meaning. The questions extended thinking, asking students to solve complex and authentic problems with unpredictable outcomes. The students were required to analyze, investigate, and reflect. The questions required creative thinking because most of the questions were open-ended.

The teacher adapted the photobiography lesson by asking students to view the painting titled *Soap Bubbles* by Thomas Couture (c. 1859). The painting shows a young person sitting at a table or desk. Unexpectedly, students who were perceived as lower performing were able to answer advanced and high-level questions. One female African American student, Janetta, stood out because of the explicit and thoughtful answers given during the study of *Autobiographies and Memoirs* (Center for Gifted Education, 2011). Janetta was not the typical student one would expect to be labeled gifted and talented because she presented as extremely defiant and disorganized. Her desk and the surrounding area were often covered in papers of unassigned art and writings. She rarely turned in her homework. Her maternal grandmother was her only adult family support. Janetta took longer than her peers to complete her assignments, yet her completed work was always correctly and uniquely finished. This set of characteristics highlighted some of the influences shaping teacher expectations of her academically and also revealed biases based on ethnicity, family structure, and observed behaviors.

After time was given to students for observation of the work of art *Soap Bubbles*, the students were asked to describe what was seen. Some students gave responses such, "I see as a boy" or "I see a girl." Deeper thinkers responded by describing the contrast in light and dark in the painting. Janetta said she thought the bubbles symbolized the possibilities in the child's life. Follow-up questions provided more insight into her thinking. When asked to explain with more details, she said, "The child will learn, grow, and change with education." Janetta pointed out the books on the table in the painting as evidence supporting the idea of education, learning, and growth. Her observations of details in the painting, the inferences she made about the artist's intention in composition, and the articulation of the symbolic link between the painting and its title, *Soap Bubbles*, gave evidence of this student's analytical thinking abilities. For the teacher, pushing beyond biases and preconceived ideas about Janetta, allowing wait time, asking planned higher order and advanced questions, and listening to students' thoughts helped the teacher to identify a talented student who had been overlooked. The questioning, waiting, and listening are important components in culturally responsive teaching.

Using TOPS (Coleman et al., 2010), a tool described earlier and used as part of the Talent Development Instructional Model, the teacher completed a talent scouting checklist on each student during the series of lessons. Designed to be used during learning that elicited high-level thinking, TOPS allowed the teacher to look beyond the "typical" at-potential student to look for other behaviors that were indicative of high potential. Using TOPS during the discussion of *Soap Bubbles* caused the teacher to realize that Janetta was exhibiting the majority of the gifted and talented behaviors. As a result of the teacher "seeing" her potential during this lesson, Janetta was recommended and screened for the gifted and talented program. Janetta qualified for gifted and talented services, and she began participation in the district's gifted and talented program. After she was identified as gifted and talented, her self-esteem improved drastically. She had more confidence and became less defiant. As an African American female, she was part of an underrepresented group often not identified as talented. Without use of interesting and stimulating materials, advanced and purposeful questions, and use of TOPS to notice student strengths during learning, her talent may never have been noticed.

Authenticity and Relevance

According to Cherng and Davis (2019), preservice teachers' attitudes persist with deficit thinking about students unlike themselves. To change the deficit teaching, starting lessons with information from the students' everyday lives allows the teachers to ask questions and pay attention to the students' answers about the concept being studied. Such an approach that uses personal inquiry highly relates to finding relevant content for the students. By using the students' answers, new avenues of inquiry are developed and generally interest each student. A possibility would be to have a spokesperson from a local culture describe what is a current, authentic tradition. This approach allows the teacher and the student to see that the culture is current and possesses authentic ways of knowing (Aikenhead, 2006). Aikenhead (2006) stated that such practice "values the diversity of student identities formed in part from local knowledge and social interaction patterns in the community. A cross-cultural (humanistic) perspective nurtures students' self-identities as savvy citizens capable of critically interacting with science-related events and issues in their everyday world"

(p. 118). Lessons that start with the students' everyday lives allow the teacher to ask questions and pay attention to students' answers.

Because of the broad diversity in this country, educators must encourage curriculum and practice that address the needs of students from diverse groups in the classroom every day. These students are negotiating multiple and complex identities, and they need cultural recognition and for the adults in their world to recognize that their citizenship identities are important (Abu El-Haj & Bonet, 2011). Teachers must address the needs of the diverse student body that they teach as well as notice the intersection points between school content, such as language arts, mathematics, and science, and the way students "know" or practice the specific discipline in their culture (Grimberg & Gummer, 2013).

Example From Practice

While observing in a classroom, I, Meta, noticed a young girl who was making fabulous drawings that were expressing the concepts beautifully. This girl had arrived in the United States about 9 months earlier than my visit to the school. The school had placed her in second grade because of her age even though she spoke no English. By the end of the school year she was still not proficient in speaking, reading, or writing English, and had been retained in second grade due to her lack of progress in these areas. She was a very gentle and soft-spoken girl who mostly interacted with only her drawing pencils and paper.

Even though she spoke no English, she was able to illustrate a plant growing, from a seed, to a seedling, to growing fruit, and finally dying in the fall. Thus, she not only knew the sequence, or changes the plant when through, but also, over time, was able to draw the plant in an anatomically correct manner from frame to frame in her depiction. The level of storyboarding she was able to complete with excellent representation of both plant parts and phases of the plant's life was extraordinary. Her life as the child of a migrant farm worker showed the knowledge with which she arrived at school.

The ways in which this student exhibited talent included (1) showing advanced skills, (2) displaying curiosity and creativity, (3) having strong interests, (4) showing advanced reasoning and problem solving, and (5) displaying spatial abilities. She continued with her meticulous work long after the other students had finished. During this time, she rarely spoke. So, I asked her a few questions, "What are the names of the plant parts you are drawing?" "Do you have the same parts in each frame you have drawn?" She barely whispered any answers, but she was able to say words that matched her drawings.

The disappointing part of this story is that even after presenting the evidence to the teacher, the teacher could not see talent in the student because (1) the student did not speak English and (2) she had been retained the prior year. This is a case in which a teacher needed more work on identifying talent and ending their prejudices. Missed opportunities are harmful to the academic life of a students. Teachers being trained to use TOPS and remaining open to the possibility of talent being expressed are features of a talent development model that is working.

Home and School Link

According to Ferlazzo (2011), engaging parents and guardians in the work of the school and through the community influences student performance and achievement. Responsible adults caring for ethnically diverse students may not feel comfortable or welcomed in their child's school. Thinking carefully about parent engagement and involvement, and how to extend respect and courtesy to all parents is important. For example, the parent/guardian of a child who is learning English should be invited to school functions in both English and native languages. To improve parent involvement, teachers contact parents from the beginning, often and in positive communication about their student. Teachers engage parents in volunteering to share their time, talents, and expertise, and, for example, sponsor family science nights and share meals together during family nights.

Example From Practice

In one TDA school, a system for parental involvement was created for parents to volunteer to help teachers to prepare the resources for talent-focused curriculum lessons. An area in the school office was designated for teachers to leave materials needed for the lessons. Parents volunteering signed in and spent the time preparing materials the teachers provided. This mutually beneficial effort improved parent involvement in furthering the goal of talent development in the school because parents were supporting the classes. They were allowed to bring their younger children with them as they helped to prepare materials. This parent volunteer system maximized the parents' ability to help teachers without interrupting classes, and teachers appreciated this assistance because it cut down on the time they had to stay after school to prepare materials. This volunteer system strengthened relationships, developed mutual respect, and reduced intimidation parents felt when entering the school. The expectation for success the Talent Development Instructional Model brought to the TDA school made parents proud to attend science nights and other events. Parents were important partners in the learning process.

Conclusion

For teachers who are learning to use a talent development lens, moving toward a strength-based approach in the classroom is possible through reflection and learning. In summary, key considerations as you grow your culturally responsive practice include:

1. Move beyond the identity structures of race, class, and culture toward identity differences as ways to discover potential that exists in your students. Use nonbinary thinking about your student's life aspects, meaning that identities are more complex and layered and not a single-story perspective.
2. Rely on ongoing self-examination of personal biases, prejudices, and bigotry as you seek to teach for diversity and to see each student's talent. With time, slowing down your thinking in the effort to see implicit biases will become a part of your teaching practice.
3. Draw on authenticity and relevance by starting with students' experiences, using questioning to draw out those experiences. See and hear your students' examples and experiences, as this extends the knowledge that students already have and shines a light on the interests and passions of each student. These strengths become a bridge to nurture and grow potential into talent.
4. Use TOPS in combination with powerful curriculum as a tool for uncovering learners' talents.
5. Draw on authenticity and relevance by starting with students' experiences, using questioning to draw out those experiences.
6. Recognize that parents are partners, so engage with them in authentic ways to build trust and relationships supportive of your students.

Culturally responsive practice is an essential pillar in teaching with a talent development philosophy. It takes work and time to refine practice that values strengths and diversity.

End-of-Chapter Discussion/ Reflection Questions

1. What is the "single-story perspective"? In what ways might such a perspective shape a person's view of talent? How do you as a teacher overcome the "single-story" narrative and "teach with diversity in mind?"
2. Review the example from practice describing use of TOPS in combination with a lesson from the William & Mary curriculum and reflect on your own practice. What are your personal blocks in seeing the potential in students? How did the teacher begin to see Janetta differently? Why?
3. What is the role of relationships in the teacher's ability to see and grow student potential?
4. What are actions you can take to deepen authenticity and relevance in your teaching?

References

Abu El-Haj, T. R., & Bonet, S. W. (2011). Education, citizenship, and the politics of belonging: Youth from Muslim transnational communities and the "war on terror." *Review of Research in Education, 35*(1), 29–59. https://doi.org/10.3102/0091732X10383209

Aikenhead, G. S. (2006). *Science education for everyday life: Evidence-based practice.* Teachers College Press.

Baker, D., & Taylor, P. C. S. (1995). The effect of culture on the learning of science in non-western countries: The results of an integrated research review. *International Journal of Science Education, 17*(6), 695–704. https://doi.org/10.1080/0950069950170602

Butler, M., Lee, S., & Tippins, D. J. (2006). Case-based methodology as an instructional strategy for understanding diversity: Preservice teachers' perceptions. *Multicultural Education, 13*(3), 20–26.

Center for Gifted Education. (n.d.). *Vocabulary web.* https://education.wm.edu/centers/cfge/_documents/curriculum/teachingmodels/vocabularyweb.pdf

Center for Gifted Education. (2011). *Autobiographies and memoirs* (2nd ed.). Kendall Hunt.

Cherng, H.-Y. S., & Davis, L. A. (2019). Multicultural matters: An investigation of key assumptions of multicultural education reform in teacher education. *Journal of Teacher Education, 70*(3), 219–236. https://doi.org/10.1177/0022487117742884

Coleman, M. R., Coltrane, S. S., Harradine, C., & Timmons, L. A. (2007). Impact of poverty on promising learners, their teachers, and their schools. *Journal of Urban Education: Focus on Enrichment, 6*, 59–67.

Coleman, M. R., Shah-Coltrane, S., & Harrison, A. (2010). *U-STARS~PLUS: Teacher's observation of potential in students (TOPS): Individual student observation form*. Council for Exceptional Children.

Ferlazzo, J. (2011). Involvement or engagement? *Educational Leadership, 68*(8), 10–14.

Gavin, M. K., Casa, T. M., Carroll, S. R., & Sheffield, L. J. (2009). The impact of advanced curriculum on the achievement of mathematically promising elementary students. *Gifted Child Quarterly, 53*(3), 188–202. https://doi.org/10.1177/0016986209334964

Gavin, M. K., Casa, T. M., Chapin, S. H., & Sheffield, L. J. (2010). *Project M^2: Level 2: Designing a shape gallery: Geometry with the meerkats, teacher guide*. Kendall Hunt.

Grimberg, B. I., & Gummer, E. (2013). Teaching science from cultural points of intersection. *Journal of Research in Science Teaching, 50*(1), 12–32. https://doi.org/10.1002/tea.21066

Howes, E. V. (2002). Learning to teach science for all in the elementary grades: What do preservice teachers bring? *Journal of Research in Science Teaching, 39*(9), 845–869. https://doi.org/10.1002/tea.10049

Kim, K. H., VanTassel-Baska, J., Bracken, B. A., Feng, A. X., Stambaugh, T., & Bland, L. (2012). Project Clarion: Three years of science instruction in Title I schools among K-third grade students. *Research in Science Education, 42*, 813–829. https://doi.org/10.1007/s11165-011-9218-5

Lee. J., Sleeter, C. E., & Kumashiro, K. (2015). Interrogating identity and social contexts through "critical family history." *Multicultural Perspectives, 17*(1), 28–32. https://doi.org/10.1080/15210960.2015.994426

Merryfield, M. M. (2000). Why aren't teachers being prepared to teach for diversity, equity, and global interconnectedness? A study of lived experiences in the making of multicultural and global educators. *Teaching and Teacher Education, 16*(4), 429–443. https://doi.org/10.1016/S0742-051X(00)00004-4

Morales, R. (2000). Effects of teacher preparation experiences and students' perceptions related to developmentally and culturally appropriate practices. *Action in Teacher Education, 22*(2), 67–75. https://doi.org/10.1080/01626620.2000.10463006

Ramos-Garcia, M. (2004). *Avoiding binary thinking: Using multiperspectivism as a classroom tool.* South Dakota State University.

Part IV

Psychology of Learning: Noncognitive Influences

9

Noncognitive Influences on Talent Development

C. Anne Gutshall and Cara L. Kelly

More than 15 years ago, I (Anne) entered my first graduate teacher education class as the instructor. The class was intended for practicing teachers to learn advanced information about human learning, motivation, and cognition. As a practicing school psychologist for more than a decade, I was unprepared for the lack of understanding my students, graduate-level learners and practicing teachers, had regarding the basics about the human brain and how it works. The students looked at me inquisitively when I described the rudimentary concepts of neuroplasticity and told them, "Classroom teachers are literally brain changers!" This insight led me on a journey not only to craft improvements in the graduate course, but also to conceptualize a series of professional learning sessions that include components of the psychology of learning and noncognitive factors that influence student motivation. For the past 5 years, I have been adopting whole schools and teaching practicing teachers these important concepts through a project called BrainBuilders (Gutshall, 2020; Gutshall & Attafi, 2020) in order to understand more about how teacher beliefs and learning might impact student beliefs and motivation.

Components of the BrainBuilders project were customized to become the third pillar for Talent Development Academies (TDA), a multiyear project that seeks to grow talent in students from traditionally poor-performing elementary schools by helping teachers to view all students as "at potential" even when they are learning in "at-risk" schools. It turns out that, in order to grow talent in students, you need to support teachers' growth and development as well. Alongside powerful curriculum and instruction and cultural influences, teaching teachers how their students learn, how the brain works, and how concepts related to the psychology of learning connect to growth mindset beliefs and academic persistence, or grit, is the third component of growing talent (Swanson et al., 2019).

Why Neuroscience and Noncognitive Factors?

When considering the vast amounts of information regarding neuroscience and motivation theory that teachers need to know, it can be difficult to narrow it down into a few hours' worth of essential professional learning for busy teachers, especially those already committed to the time-intensive yearlong projects using a talent development model. After teaching the graduate course for many years, I began to notice the content that, year after year, teachers did not appear to be familiar with, as well as key motivational constructs that resonated with experienced teachers about how their students learn and respond to both failure and mistakes. Eventually, this led to BrainBuilders and the custom pillar of the Talent Development Instructional Model called the psychology of learning. This pillar grew from essential content harvested from two key educational research areas: neuroscience and noncognitive factors.

When teachers learn about the malleability of the human brain directly linked to the concepts of neuroplasticity, including the responsiveness of the brain to classroom learning and experiences and the science of learning on the cellular level, this knowledge impacts teacher's mindset beliefs in a positive trajectory (Gutshall, 2020; Gutshall & Attafi, 2020). Teachers who understand neuroplasticity are more likely to hold growth mindset beliefs about students. Growth mindset beliefs, in turn, influence a teachers' approach to student failure and impact the type of feedback a teacher is likely to give a student who makes mistakes. Growth mindset beliefs, in conjunction with understanding the science of learning and neuroplasticity, make it more likely that teachers will not only reframe learner mistakes and errors, but also design their class-

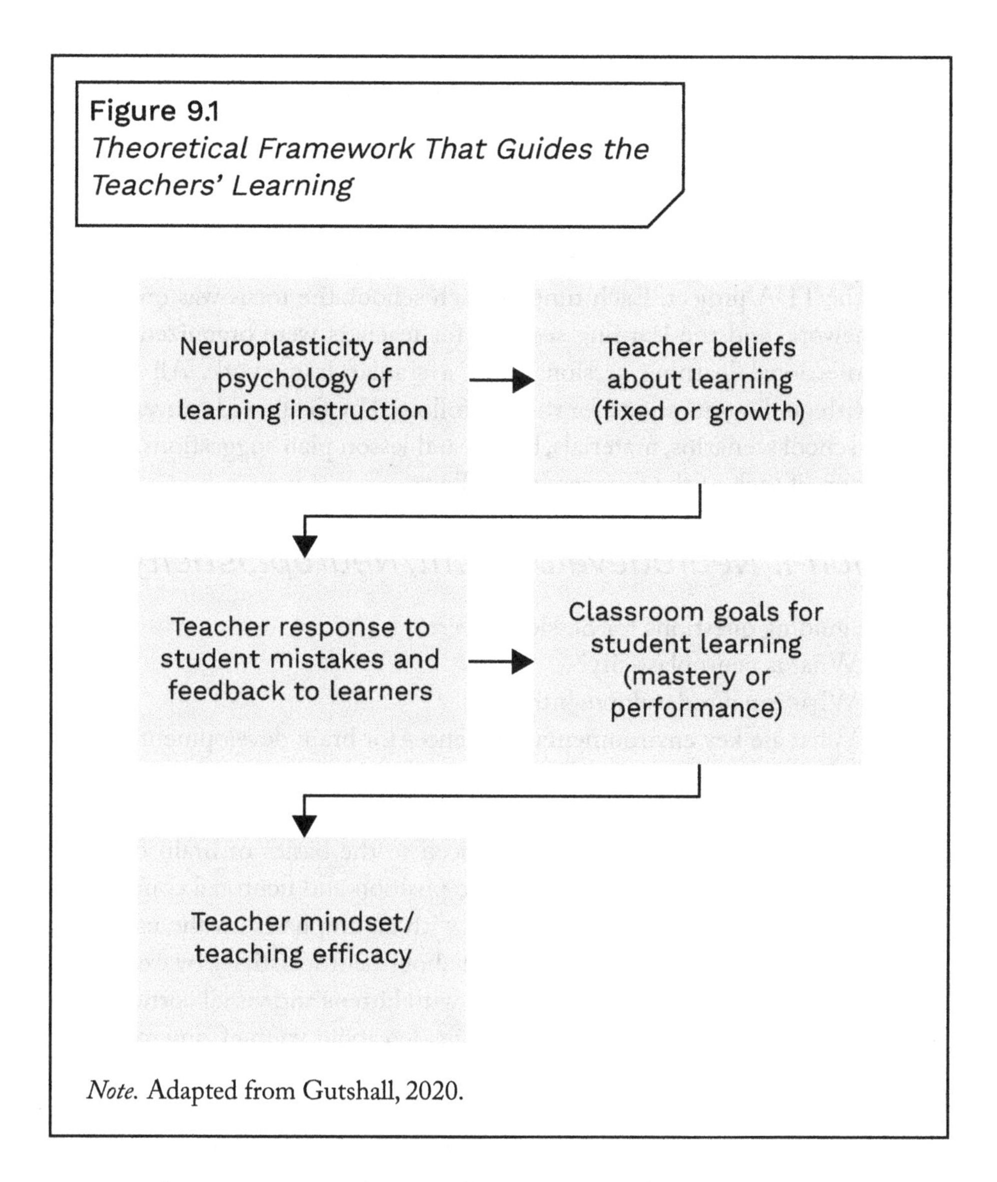

Figure 9.1
Theoretical Framework That Guides the Teachers' Learning

Note. Adapted from Gutshall, 2020.

room goal structures away from performance goals (like top score, or being the best) to mastery goals (like improving skills and personal growth over time). Improving teachers' understanding of neuroplasticity and the science of how the brain learns not only improves mindset beliefs for teachers, but also influences their teaching efficacy, which has been shown to be a key determinant in teacher effectiveness (Donohoo, 2017; Hattie & Zierer, 2018). A probable theoretical framework that guides the teachers' learning is depicted in Figure 9.1.

How Did the Professional Learning Sessions Work?

This section outlines and describes how the professional learning sessions were designed for teachers in the talent development intervention schools during the TDA project. Each time, in each school, the focus was on a similar framework, and the learning sessions for teachers were organized around four professional learning sessions with a similar framework. All sessions began with guiding questions for the day followed by facilitated conversations, applied school scenarios, materials, books, and lesson plan suggestions. A brief description of each of the four sessions follows.

Session 1: Neurodevelopment/Neuroplasticity

The guiding questions for Session 1 were:

1. What is neuroplasticity?
2. What is neurodevelopment?
3. What are key environmental influences for brain development?
4. What does it all have to do with scouting for talent?

In this session, teachers were introduced to the basics of brain development, including how neurons migrate into position and neuronal connections are established during neurodevelopment with an emphasis on the use-it-or-lose-it principle. The teachers were taught about neuroplasticity by examining the early Greenough et al. (1987) research with kittens and visual cortex development, as well as by viewing a compelling video about young Cameron Mott, who underwent a hemispherectomy but recovered extremely well. The positive potential of the malleability of the human brain and the cautions of neuroplasticity were revealed and discussed with special focus on educational settings and topics. In addition, the focus on the malleability of the human brain was consistent within the Talent Development Megamodel put forth by Subotnik and colleagues (2011). The basics of how learning takes place at a cellular level were explained with a demonstration of neuronal synaptic processes and neural pruning.

Teachers began to explore how classroom environments may positively impact not only learning, but also brain development itself. In an exploration of experience-expectant versus experience-dependent neurodevelopmental impacts, the effects of screens, physical activity, and, importantly, sleep on child development were also shared with the teachers. Typically, the importance of high-quality and sufficient sleep for memory and learning was very well received, and teachers began to get excited about the ways they could teach their learners about the importance of sleep. Teachers were also excited to share the concepts of neuroplasticity with their students when they were shown examples of even very young children writing about, drawing, and understanding neuroplasticity. As closure, teachers brainstormed how the concepts of neurodevelopment and neuroplasticity might impact their scouting for talent in classrooms as well as how these new understandings might challenge their own well-established notions regarding children with Individualized Education Programs (IEPs), English language learners (ELLs), or those who have been identified as gifted and talented.

Session 2: Motivation Theory and Mindset

The guiding questions for Session 2 were:

1. What are the theoretical perspectives on motivation to learn?
2. What is mindset theory? What is growth mindset?
3. How does growth mindset connect to neuroplasticity?
4. How and why should I teach students about noncognitive factors, like academic mindset?

In this session, teachers were reminded of past learning regarding neuroplasticity and neurodevelopment with the goal of linking these previously introduced concepts to mindset theory. Briefly, the concept of motivation to learn was outlined, as teachers were asked to describe their own perceptions of motivated versus unmotivated learners in their classrooms. Next, teachers were guided to understand the ways in which schools traditionally have an overreliance on behavioral motivation strategies, including the use of "carrots" and "sticks." By sharing Ryan and Deci's (2000a, 2000b) research, as well as additional work on the shortcomings of rewarding children in order for them to learn (Brophy, 1988; Fryer, 2013; Guryan et al., 2016; Kohn, 2018; Tough; 2016), teachers were guided to realize that when students are given a reward for learning, they have no choice but to attribute their learning to the reward and not to their own internal desire to learn or grow. Next, teachers were taught briefly about Dweck's (2006/2016, 2008) work to understand learned helplessness versus resilience and the notion of implicit beliefs about intelligence or ability. Dweck and colleagues' (Blackwell et al., 2007) seminal research regarding learning about neuroscience versus study skills/organization at the middle school transition was shared. Teachers were guided to comprehend that student understanding of neuroplasticity can facilitate effort, persistence, and resilience in the face of failure.

Teachers then took the mindset belief three-question quiz (see Figure 9.2) and began to examine their own beliefs about learning and intelligence. The seeds of questioning were sown as teachers grappled with the idea that a student's intelligence or ability can be known, quantified, labeled, or decided in the context of constant change, learning, neurogenesis, and neural consolidation and pruning. Although most teachers hold growth mindset beliefs, examination of labeling practices in schools creates a certain amount of dissonance for teachers, especially when they are encouraged to teach their students about how learning takes place at a cellular level and how infinite the capacity for change and growth in every brain is. Teachers wrestle with the idea that telling a learner they are "gifted or talented," while positive in nature, is still a fixed mindset belief, akin to telling a learner they have Attention Deficit/Hyperactivity Disorder (ADHD) or a learning disability. Time permitting, teachers were shown Boalers's "Rethinking Giftedness" video (Phillips Brook School, 2018) to further examine the idea of "gifted" education and its impact.

Next, Dweck's (2007) work on praise for effort versus intelligence was explained, and Ragan's (2014) excellent video depiction of this research was shown. Teachers learned how students who hold growth mindset beliefs about ability versus traits consistent with fixed mindset beliefs respond to failure or mistakes. This session ended with teachers being reminded that growth mindset is not just another way to shame learners (i.e., if students just try harder, they can learn), but it is a fundamental perspective about learning, potential, effort, and persistence after failure that is positive because it is based on the knowledge and understanding of neuroplasticity. That is, the brain is like a muscle and the more one works it, the more connections and pathways it grows. The session closed with teachers being asked to consider how teaching their students about the brain and the concept of growth mindset beliefs might change student motivation and behavior. Typically, teachers were very excited by this approach. Teachers were tasked with continuing to work on nurturing and fostering student beliefs that brains can learn and grow through effort more than merely rewarding fast, quick, perfect work with stickers and other rewards.

Session 3: Growth Mindset Feedback Strategies

The guiding questions for Session 3 were:

1. What is the mentor's dilemma?

Figure 9.2
Mindset Belief Quiz

	Strongly Disagree	Disagree	Somewhat Disagree	Somewhat Agree	Agree	Strongly Agree
You have a certain amount of intelligence, and you really cannot do much to change it.	1	2	3	4	5	6
You can learn new things, but you cannot really change your basic intelligence.	1	2	3	4	5	6
Your intelligence is something about you that you cannot change very much.	1	2	3	4	5	6

Note. Adapted from Gutshall, 2014.

2. What does research say about effective teacher feedback to build a growth mindset?
3. What is the wise feedback strategy?
4. How can we teach students about feedback and encourage a growth mindset?

This session began with a presentation slide depicting a hamburger and the acknowledgement that many teachers have been taught the following model of providing feedback: bun (say something nice), burger (say some sort of critique), bun (say something nice again). Next, teachers began to explore the concept of the mentor's dilemma—that people who work to mentor and support kids often have difficulty honestly telling kids that they have made mistakes or need improvement.

Then, teachers were shown Hattie and Timperley's (2007) research on effective feedback. Teachers explored what it is like for learners to consistently receive positive or neutral feedback after failure. Typically, teachers are taught that feedback is always critical and that praise is positive. In this session, teachers learned that when a student receives positive or even neutral feedback after failure or mistakes, the student adopts the belief that their teacher has low expectations for them. Teachers generally experienced some discomfort during this part of the session. They asked questions about praise, student esteem, and how effective and supportive feedback can really be delivered.

Teachers further explored the concept of effective feedback through several demonstrations. First, a video (EL Education, 2012) about critique and feedback was shown to the teachers. This video depicts an excellent example of someone modeling how feedback is a wonderful way to improve and grow skills (see Chapter 10 for further discussion about teaching using this video). Next, research outlining the wise feedback strategy was detailed, and teachers came to understand that the process of having high expectations that learners can meet is essential for growing authentic mastery and competence (Aronson et al., 2002). Two lesson plan ideas for students were shared with the teachers. One involved use of the book *Thanks for the Feedback . . . I Think?* (Cook, 2014), and the second was a slide presentation, adapted for elementary students, of fictitious students who learn the value of feedback for learning and growing. An example is shown in Figure 9.3.

At the end of this session, teachers were encouraged to praise students and to give feedback, but not at the same time, in order to strengthen growth mindset beliefs. Teachers learned that their own perceptions of failure were equally as important as student growth mindset beliefs when promoting moti-

Figure 9.3
Example of Presentation Highlighting the Value of Feedback for Learning and Growing

Jordan, age 8

"Teachers who give me feedback that corrects my mistakes are the ones who really care. They take you seriously, like a good coach does. You might not get good criticism all the time in school but when you do get it, it's like gold."

Note. Adapted from Gutshall, 2019.

vation and resilience in young children. Teachers who are trained to spot talent are encouraged to help their learners and themselves embrace struggle and get curious about mistakes (Dweck, 2006/2016) as a natural and welcome part of the learning process.

Session 4: Grit and Self-Control

The guiding questions for Session 4 were:

1. What is self-control?
2. What is grit?
3. How are self-control and grit connected to each other and to other noncognitive factors, including growth mindset?
4. What is the relationship with inquiry and autonomy?

In this final session, teachers learned about the basics of self-control and the underlying neurological components of developing self-control and grit. They learned the basic definition of self-control as: "the voluntary regulation of attentional, emotional, and behavioral impulses when immediate temptations conflict with more enduringly valued goals" (Duckworth et al., 2014, p. 200). Through guided conversations, teachers explored how self-control is connected first to a child's neurological developmental trajectory. Additionally, language development, goal setting, free time, and choice were highlighted as helpful influences on a child's ability to develop self-control. In addition to learning about autonomy and supportive teaching practices, teachers spent time thinking about the proportion of teacher-controlled time to self-controlled time their students experience during the school day. Teachers often came to interesting realizations about overly structured school settings and the possible deleterious impacts on children's self-control development. Teachers learned that self-control grows out of directing oneself, not by adult-directed time. This notion often proves to be dissonant for many classroom teachers who often struggle to maintain control of students in a school climate that plans every minute of students' experience in the classroom with "bell-to-bell" instruction and "time-on-task" initiatives.

Next, the concept of grit, or academic perseverance, was introduced to the teachers through Duckworth's (2013) TED Talk. Duckworth's talk was always well-received, and teachers also enjoyed a reminder from her about the merits of fostering a growth mindset, thereby reinforcing the psychology of learning concepts that are essential to the talent development model. Grit is defined as "having passion and perseverance for long term goals" (Duckworth, 2016, p. 233). In the TED Talk, as Duckworth (2013) summarized her years of research that stem from being a curious classroom teacher, she helped teachers by explaining that talent does not predict grit, nor does IQ. Rather, growth mindset and self-control are connected to and facilitate the development of grit, which is highly predictive of positive outcomes for kids. She emphasized that students who know about and understand the malleability of their own brains and adopt a growth mindset are much more likely to persevere in the face of failure or adversity, which is essential for long-term success in life. Likewise, self-control can be likened to short-term grit, which can be scaffolded and nurtured in schools. Using Willingham's (2016) work, teachers learned how self-control is an important component of grit. The following quote about self-control was presented to teachers:

> So the conscientious teen practices piano because he knows he is supposed to. The teen with self-control practices even when he is tempted to play Xbox instead. But the gritty teen practices because he is passionate about his dream of playing in a jazz trio. (Willingham, 2016, p. 30)

Teachers were given lesson plans for three books that can be used to teach the concepts of self-control and grit to their students as part of developing talent. The books are *What Were You Thinking?: A Story About Learning to Control Your Impulses* (Smith, 2016), *Stuck* (Jeffers, 2011), and *Just Make a Path* (Gutshall, 2017), an unpublished book I that wrote to illustrate the concept and that I shared with teachers. Lesson plans included heavy use of cognitive reattribution strategies to promote student understanding of the concepts. Rooted in educational research evidence, teacher resources about the importance of the teacher's role in supporting their students to persist and demonstrate grit when they make mistakes, struggle, and exert effort are essential components of the third pillar, psychology of learning, in talent development interventions.

In breakout sessions, the following questions were posed for discussion (adapted from Gutshall, 2019):

- Is your classroom setting a sprint or a marathon?
- Do your learners have opportunities to regulate themselves and their emotion/behavior, or is their school day highly structured with no opportunity to direct themselves?

Ultimately, at the end of this session, teachers were guided to reconsider the pacing of their lessons, the structure of their classrooms, and the ways in which inquiry and autonomy can be more infused in classrooms that are dedicated to spotting and developing talent. In the talent development model, "quick" and "easy" learning was deemphasized, and deeper, self- and slower paced, active learning by the student, coupled with reflection and sharing of student learning, was emphasized (Mackenzie & Bathurst-Hunt, 2018).

Conclusion

Teachers are brain changers. Teachers in schools that adopt a talent development model need to be aware of this fact and be mindful of the positive impacts that the classroom teacher has on students' understanding of their brains' power to learn. Although the idea of IQ is important, it takes less prominence in a talent development model in which all learners are growing their capacity, improving their skills, stretching their abilities, and making mistakes. Likewise, teachers in talent development schools are also actively looking to grow each student's capacities by nurturing their strengths and supporting their weaknesses. A focus on the science of learning helps teachers to abandon some of the outdated ideas regarding whether giftedness is easily determined forever at a young age. Instead, understanding neuroplasticity and malleability permits teachers to understand that any child can emerge with identifiable strengths at any point in their development when they are given proper opportunities, appropriate feedback, and autonomy-supportive learning environments. Teachers who are able to understand that they change brains with the learning opportunities they structure and prepare in their classrooms are better able to understand effort and struggle and normalize mistakes in learning. These understandings on the part of TDA teachers in the Talent Development Instructional Model intervention underscore the essential mindset for fostering student growth and improved efficacy. Focus on noncognitive factors, such as growth mindset, academic perseverance, or grit, encourages teachers to promote mastery goal orientation structures in their classrooms, thereby creating a positive, recursive loop that promotes individual learners' motivation and talent development.

End-of-Chapter Discussion/ Reflection Questions

1. In what ways are neuroscience and noncognitive factors related to talent development?
2. How does a student's motivation and mindset toward effort and challenge impact learning?
3. Self-direction and self-regulation are important aspects of talent development. What opportunities do you provide for students to become stronger in self-direction and regulation?
4. How are you a "brain changer"?

References

Aronson, J., Fried, C. B., & Good, C. (2002). Reducing the effects of stereotype threat on African American college students by shaping theories of intelligence. *Journal of Experimental Social Psychology, 38*(2), 113–125. https://doi.org/10.1006/jesp.2001.1491

Blackwell, L. S., Trzesniewski, K. H., & Dweck, C. S. (2007). Implicit theories of intelligence predict achievement across an adolescent transition: A longitudinal study and an intervention. *Child Development, 78*(1), 246–263. https://doi.org/10.1111/j.1467-8624.2007.00995.x

Brophy, J. (1988). Research linking teacher behavior to student achievement: Potential implications for instruction of Chapter 1 students. *Educational Psychologist, 23*(3), 235–286. https://doi.org/10.1207/s15326985ep2303_3

Cook, J. (2014). *Thanks for the feedback . . . I think?* (K. De Weerd, Illus.). Boys Town Press.
Donohoo, J. (2017). *Collective efficacy: How educators' beliefs impact student learning*. Corwin.
Duckworth, A. (2013, April). *Grit: The power of passion and perseverance* [Video]. TED Conferences. https://www.ted.com/talks/angela_lee_duckworth_grit_the_power_of_passion_and_perseverance
Duckworth, A. (2016). *Grit: The power and passion of perseverance*. Scribner.
Duckworth, A. L., Gendler, T. S., & Gross, J. J. (2014). Self-control in school-age children. *Educational Psychologist, 49*(3), 199–217. https://doi.org/10.1080/00461520.2014.926225
Dweck, C. S. (2016). *Mindset: The new psychology of success*. Ballantine Books. (Original work published 2006)
Dweck, C. S. (2007). The perils and promises of praise. *Educational Leadership, 65*(2), 34–39.
Dweck, C. S. (2008). Brainology: Transforming students' motivation to learn. *Independent School, 67*(2), 110–119.
EL Education. (2012). *Austin's butterfly: Building excellence in student work* [Video]. https://modelsofexcellence.eleducation.org/resources/austins-butterfly
Fryer, R. G. (2013). Teacher incentives and student achievement: Evidence from New York City public schools. *Journal of Labor Economics, 31*(2), 373–407. https://doi.org/10.1086/667757
Greenough, W. T., Black, J. E., & Wallace, C. S. (1987). Effects of experience on brain development. *Child Development, 58*(3), 540–559. https://doi.org/10.2307/1130197
Guryan, J., Kim, J. S., & Park, K. H. (2016). Motivation and incentives in education: Evidence from a summer reading experiment. *Economics of Education Review, 55,* 1–20. https://doi.org/10.1016/j.econedurev.2016.08.002
Gutshall, C. A. (2014). Pre-service teachers' mindset beliefs about student ability. *Electronic Journal of Research in Educational Psychology, 12*(3), 785–802.
Gutshall, C. A. (2017). *Just make a path* (C. Gutshall, Illus.). https://sites.google.com/view/brainbuilderschssecondary/neuroplasticity
Gutshall, C. A. (2019, November). *The value of feedback for learning and growing* [Professional development for teachers]. Berkeley County School District Targeted Intervention Schools, Berkeley County, SC, United States.
Gutshall, C. A. (2020). When teachers become students: Impacts of neuroscience learning on elementary teachers' mindset beliefs, approach to learning,

teaching efficacy, and grit. *European Journal of Psychology and Educational Research, 3*(1), 39–48. https://doi.org/10.12973/ejper.3.1.39

Gutshall C. A., & Attafi, H. (2020). *BrainBuilders: Teachers and students learning neuroscience together in the elementary school setting* [Unpublished manuscript].

Hattie, J., & Timperley, H. (2007). The power of feedback. *Review of Educational Research, 77*(1), 81–112. https://doi.org/10.3102/003465430298487

Hattie, J., & Zierer, K. (2018). *10 mindframes for visible learning: Teaching for success*. Routledge. https://doi.org/10.4324/9781315206387

Jeffers, O. (2011). *Stuck*. HarperCollins Children's Books.

Kohn, A. (2018). *Punished by rewards: The trouble with gold stars, incentive plans, A's, praise, and other bribes* (25th Anniversary ed.). Houghton Mifflin Harcourt.

Mackenzie, T., & Bathurst-Hunt, R. (2018). *Inquiry mindset: Nurturing the dreams, wonders, and curiosities of our youngest learners*. EdTechTeam.

Phillips Brooks School. (2018). *"Rethinking giftedness" video premiere • GATHER talk by Prof. Jo Boaler* [Video]. YouTube. https://www.youtube.com/watch?v=0JJF3AP1PNM

Ragan, T. (2014). *Carol Dweck - A study on praise and mindsets* [Video]. YouTube. https://www.youtube.com/watch?v=NWv1VdDeoRY

Ryan, R. M., & Deci, E. L. (2000a). Intrinsic and extrinsic motivations: Classic definitions and new directions. *Contemporary Educational Psychology, 25*(1), 54–67. https://doi.org/10.1006/ceps.1999.1020

Ryan, R. M., & Deci, E. L.(2000b). Self-determination theory and the facilitation of intrinsic motivation, social development, and well-being. *American Psychologist, 55*(1), 68–78. https://doi.org/10.1037/0003-066x.55.1.68

Smith, B. (2016). *What were you thinking?: A story about learning to control your impulses* (L. M. Griffin, Illus.). Boys Town Press.

Subotnik, R. F., Olszewski-Kubilius, P., & Worrell, F. C. (2011). Rethinking giftedness and gifted education: A proposed direction forward based on psychological science. *Psychological Science in the Public Interest, 12*(1), 3–54. https://doi.org/10.1177/1529100611418056

Swanson, J. D., Russell, L. W., & Anderson, L. (2019). A model for growing teacher talent scouts: Decreasing underrepresentation of gifted students. In S. R. Smith (Ed.), *Handbook of giftedness and talent development in the Asia-Pacific* (pp. 1–20). Springer. https://doi.org/10.1007/978-981-13-3021-6_55-1

Tough, P. (2016). *Helping children succeed: What works and* why. Random House.

Willingham, D. T. (2016). Ask the cognitive scientist: "Grit" is trendy, but can it be taught? *American Educator, 40*(2), 28–32.

10

Linking Psychology of Learning to Classroom Instruction

Margaret M. Lee

In order to grow and develop their strengths and talents, students must be carefully guided and coached. A student who understands what is correct and how to improve is empowered. Feedback is a tool that seeks to inform students where they are on their learning path—directing them toward improvement, growth, and development. Within the context of a classroom, various dynamics, such as teacher instruction, environment, and student motivation, combine to set the stage for learning. Feedback is also a component of instruction that brings value to and improves student learning and potential. It is a constructive intervention that provides clarity and direction, thereby deepening student understanding of an assignment or task, while developing their self-confidence in their ability to successfully accomplish a task. Additionally, as students' understanding of content and skills improves along with the psychological aspects of learning, such as self-efficacy, confidence, and the willingness to persist, a formula for student success and talent development is created.

This chapter explores the essential role feedback plays in student learning and its fundamental connection to talent development. The chapter begins with an overview of the levels and types of feedback and how varying feedback responses impact student learning. The chapter also includes discussion on the use of feedback in the development of student talent through an exploration of one school's powerful and adaptable series of lessons utilizing peer feedback to foster student growth. The lesson discussion demonstrates how direct, focused feedback impacts student growth and provides an illustration of students as both the creators and the recipients of feedback, ultimately leading them to become advocates for their own learning.

Feedback

The goal of feedback is to close the gap between current understanding and a desired level of understanding. Quality feedback moves students toward learning goals and leads to improvement in both cognitive and affective domains. Strategic feedback increases students' cognitive domains through growth in knowledge and understanding. Feedback impacts students' affective domains by enhancing students' feelings of personal control over their learning (Brookhart, 2017).

Simply stated, feedback answers three basic questions: (1) Where am I going?, (2) How am I doing?, and (3) Where to next? (Brookhart, 2017; Hattie, 2011; Hattie & Timperley, 2007). Hattie (2011) contended that goals are needed to answer the first question. Learning goals are important because they provide targets for students. The use of models and exemplars helps guide students' development toward their learning goals. When students understand where they are going (the goal)—or as is often asked in the classroom, "Why is this important?"—feedback becomes a powerful learning tool (Brookhart, 2017; Hattie, 2011).

The second question (How am I doing?) informs students as to their level of progress or understanding toward the goal, or where they are on their learning continuum. It answers the question: How close am I to the desired outcome? In addition to informing students of their progress toward their goal, this type of feedback can guide students on how to proceed forward (Hattie & Timperley, 2007). It may relate to a required standard or level of task performance (Brookhart, 2017; Hattie, 2011). Feedback at this level is most effective when it is formative in nature, as the purpose is to advise students with the intent to improve the learning journey.

The third question (Where to next?) interjects a level of self-regulation for students. Feedback related to this question gives learners the opportunity to consider alternative paths or strategies. It may encourage students to seek more in-depth learning about the goal or task (Hattie, 2011). Hattie and Timperley

(2007) cautioned teachers to deliver feedback at this level carefully, as students can mistakenly relate this feedback to more work or extra work instead of connecting it to an opportunity for learning possibilities. Feedback addressing this question can provide enhanced challenge, opportunity for self-regulated learning, increased awareness of strategies and task processes, deeper content understanding, and information about what is and is not understood (Hattie & Timperley, 2007).

The most common type of classroom feedback occurs after initial instruction. Feedback is often information focused or corrective. It is primarily delivered through teacher questions and comments on assignments. It is specific, often correctional, and may be information- or task-focused. It can be effectively delivered individually but is also effective in group settings. Feedback at this level is important in the development of foundational understandings (Brookhart, 2017; Hattie, 2011).

After foundational learning has been addressed, a deeper level of conceptual or process learning begins to take place. Feedback directed at this level may be more thought provoking. It often informs students of alternative processes or research opportunities. It may encourage more in-depth learning or perhaps assist students in evaluating learning strategies they have used or inform them of potential learning strategies that could be used. When formative, rather than summative, in nature, feedback increases student confidence and self-efficacy, particularly at the conceptual level (Hattie, 2011). Providing students with the opportunity to take advantage of the feedback, revise work, and see improvements to their work is a critical component of viewing feedback as a means of improvement rather than a criticism of work (Brookhart, 2017). As students experience skill development through the guidance of feedback, personal self-efficacy, confidence, and persistence grow, further enhancing talent development.

As learners become more reflective and self-evaluative, a third level of feedback becomes beneficial. Feedback at this level assists students in learning self-regulation. Learning becomes a motivator for future skill and talent development (Brookhart, 2017). This level of feedback encourages students to seek and accept feedback as a tool for personal improvement. As students move in this direction, understanding gaps diminish and a sense of control over learning is created. Strengthening the psychological components of learning empowers students. Increasing levels of student motivation and persistence create an upward spiral of growth, advancing knowledge, confidence, and development of students' talents.

Students' personal attitude toward their ability to accomplish a task will influence the amount of effort they put toward task achievement. When feedback is received as a mechanism for improving work, when it is received as a tool for personal improvement and not seen as a criticism of work, motivation occurs (Brookhart, 2017). A mastery-oriented mindset will improve performance leading to strengthening students' growth mindset. Further, the belief that traits, abilities, and talents are malleable and not fixed entities can be taught to students (Dweck, 2017). This personal belief that one's abilities, talents, and intelligence can be developed creates a foundation for a psychological framework for achievement (Dweck, 2017). Believing that one's efforts lead to achievement encourages students to connect their work to learning and talent development (Dweck, 2017; Swanson et al., 2020). Effective feedback is capable of altering a fixed mindset and contributing to a growth mindset. When students use feedback as a means for improvement, a sense of personal control is created, and growth mindsets are strengthened. Building these psychological skills is foundational in the development of student talents (Moon, 2014).

Feedback directed toward a student, with terms such as "great student" or "smart girl," although positive in intent, rarely enhances student learning (Brookhart, 2017; Hattie & Timperley, 2007). Although students may like to hear the affirmative words, research confirms that these vague accolades harm learning and performance (Dweck, 2017). This type of student-focused feedback may dilute other types of feedback and ultimately detract from or diminish learning (Hattie, 2011) and contribute to a fixed mindset (Brookhart, 2017; Dweck, 2017). Feedback directed toward misconceptions, strategies, and learning processes is more effective than personal comments about students (Brookhart, 2017). This type of feedback provides concrete steps toward improvement. Feedback directed toward the process of learning helps students connect their efforts to a positive outcome, reinforcing students' beliefs that their efforts lead to success (Mofield & Parker Peters, 2018). The focus of the feedback matters. Hattie (2011) suggested six variables to consider when providing student feedback:

1. Feedback may be given, but this does not mean it is received or understood by the student. Pay attention to how the student responds to the feedback. Do they understand the purpose and goal of the feedback?
2. A student's background and culture can impact how the feedback is received and how feedback is best delivered. Students from some cultures respond to group-focused feedback, while others prefer more individually-focused feedback. Having awareness of and being respect-

ful of cultural feedback preferences will incur more positive student responses from the feedback.

3. Per Hattie (2011), "Disconfirmation is more powerful than confirmation" (p. 8). When students' erroneous understandings are corrected, a more impactful change occurs than when confirming student understanding. Error correction is key, and therefore, creating a classroom environment that allows students to safely share their thinking, correct and incorrect, will benefit student growth.
4. Feedback is most effective during the process of learning new content, tasks, or understandings.
5. Peer influence is powerful. Students must be taught how to give appropriate feedback.
6. Teachers should use feedback from assessments to adjust their teaching to better serve student learning. Feedback is a two-way street; both the giver and the receiver need to respond to the feedback.

Related to Hattie's (2011) suggestions, and to further enhance effectiveness, Brookhart (2017) recommended asking the following questions about feedback:

> Is it descriptive? Is it timely? Does it contain the right amount of information? Does it compare the work to criteria? Does it focus on the work? Does it focus on the process? Is it positive? Is it clear (to the student)? Is it specific (but not too specific)? Does its tone imply the student is an active learner? (p. 5)

Peer Feedback

Peer feedback, or feedback given between classmates, allows feedback to occur in a greater volume and timeliness than when it is the sole responsibility of the teacher (Topping, 2009). When students participate in peer feedback, both the giver and the receiver become thoughtful participants in the evaluation process. The student assuming the role of the assessor must carefully review the work to be evaluated in light of the evaluation criteria. The student evaluator must study the work, the exemplar, and the evaluation criteria. Frequently, students assume the roles of evaluators and recipients of feedback, requiring consideration of dual perspectives and more time immersed in the experience, which further enhances learning (Topping, 2009).

To be successfully implemented, peer feedback should adhere to the same criteria as effective teacher feedback. The feedback should be specific or tangible, goal-referenced, actionable, and user friendly (Wiggins, 2012). Teaching explicit protocols will guide students in the process of feedback giving and receiving (Berger et al., 2016; Topping, 2009; van Zundert et al., 2010). Berger et al. (2016) suggested that students should observe a teacher modeling the critiquing process using student work before engaging in the process. Such modeling will help students understand the role of the assessor, as well as the benefits of the feedback. Demonstration of the recipient's application of the feedback is also beneficial to the total peer review process (Berger et al., 2016).

Peer assessment can initially be awkward for students (Topping, 2009; van Zundert et al., 2010). Modeling, practice, and a predetermined list of evaluation questions to use during the protocol review will help students generate more specific, focused, and descriptive feedback (Berger et al., 2016). Ultimately, as students participate in peer feedback sessions, they will become more comfortable with the process, more reflective about their own work, and more receptive to suggestions from their peers (Topping, 2009).

When participating in the peer feedback process, a greater volume of feedback may be obtained by the recipient and often with a shorter wait time than when feedback is provided by only the teacher. Topping (2009) stated that although students may not have the assessment skills of their teacher, the extra time spent participating in the process increases the evaluation reliability and validity levels to those of the teacher. When evaluation occurs in teams of three, each student receives feedback from two classmates and gives feedback to two classmates, leading to an increased rate of validity (Topping, 2009). Evaluation reliability can be further increased with the use of training, checklists, exemplars, and teacher monitoring. According to Topping, peer feedback occurring during formative learning stages increases a student's sense of accountability and promotes metacognitive self-awareness. The following list outlines peer feedback steps recommended by Topping:

1. If possible, teachers should collaborate with students when planning the student peer evaluation process.
2. Predetermine the purpose, rationale, and expectations.
3. Involve the students in the development of the evaluation criteria. Student participation will increase ownership and understanding of the criteria and decrease anxiety during the evaluation process.
4. Student groups should consist of students with similar ability levels.

5. Provide examples, training, and practice. Students should know what is expected of them in the role of assessor and assessee. Model the process for both roles.
6. Provide scaffolding guidelines and simple checklists.
7. Specify what is to be done and the time expected to complete the process.
8. Monitor and coach.
9. Review the quality of the feedback and provide guidance as needed, especially early in the process.
10. Review the reliability and validity of the feedback. When reviewing the feedback, inform the students as to how it is similar or different from your own assessment of the work.
11. Evaluate and provide feedback on the peer assessments. The exercise in peer feedback is a learning process for students, and feedback will inform students for future peer assessments.

Feedback Lessons

The feedback lessons discussed in this chapter provide examples of the utilization of peer feedback to improve student work. The lessons were created as part of the Talent Development Academies (TDA; Swanson et al., 2020) project and the Talent Development Instructional Model (TDIM), a teacher professional learning model with the goal to inform and equip teachers to identify and develop student talents. More specifically, the lessons were used in TDA schools to help teachers understand how to grow student potential through the use of feedback. The Models of Excellence video "Austin's Butterfly: Building Excellence in Student Work" (EL Education, 2012) was both the lessons' starting point and the feedback exemplar for the participating teachers and their students. The effectiveness of feedback in encouraging and creating outstanding student work is demonstrated in the video through repeated sessions of peer feedback and work revisions, leading ultimately to a final student exemplar.

"Austin's Butterfly" (EL Education, 2012) is powerful in its clarity and simplicity and in the fact that the transformative feedback is given by elementary students. In the video, educator Ron Berger works with a class of elementary students and introduces them to a real-world scenario. Berger then guides student critiques of a butterfly drawing created by Austin, a former first-grade student from Boise, ID. In the scenario, Austin's first drawing of a Western Tiger Swallowtail butterfly was missing details and definition. It was a child's elementary drawing of a butterfly, basic and unembellished, but based on feedback from students in his class, he worked through several drafts to improve his work.

In the video, Berger encourages the students he is instructing to critique Austin's drawing through the lens of a scientist, as the students in Austin's class would have done. Using an exemplar drawing as the model and under Berger's guidance, the students provide thoughtful, explicit descriptions of what should be changed or what was not quite right with Austin's drawing. After each critique, Berger reveals Austin's revised work for further review. With each revision, the students can see the improvements made to the drawing as a result of the feedback. Following a series of directed feedback critiques and drawing revisions, Austin's butterfly is transformed into a remarkable lifelike scientific drawing of a Western Tiger Swallowtail butterfly.

Lesson Development and Implementation

This discussion of the lesson development and implementation is largely based on interview and email correspondence with a TDA teacher coach who was instrumental in the development and delivery of the feedback lessons. The TDIM is a teacher-focused instructional model, in that it seeks to train teachers in the use of curriculum and instruction as a means to increase talent spotting and talent development (Swanson et al., 2020). The TDIM and the teacher development conducted with the TDIM emphasize the use of powerful curriculum and instruction, inclusion and recognition of cultural influences, and utilization of the psychology of learning (Swanson et al., 2019, 2020). Through the use of strategies and curriculum instruction, an outcome of the teacher development seeks to target student populations who have traditionally been underrepresented in gifted programs, specifically culturally, linguistically, and ethnically diverse students. A critical psychosocial factor influencing talent development, and strongly embraced by the TDA, was the need for growth mindsets (Swanson et al., 2019). The TDIM provides teacher education and ongoing follow-up support in order to build teachers' conceptual understanding of talent development and increase the use of strategies and curricular approaches to grow teachers' capabilities as talent spotters and talent developers (Swanson et al., 2019, 2020).

The instruction that teachers received through the TDA project clarified the connection between feedback experiences and the promotion of students' growth mindsets. During the TDIM training, teachers watched the "Austin's Butterfly" video. For the teachers, the video clearly illustrated the significant role of feedback in fostering student growth and improvement.

Subsequent to the TDIM training and inspired by what they had learned about the brain's malleability, two TDA instructional coaches developed a series of lessons based on the psychology of learning and its connections to talent development. More specifically, the lessons used peer feedback to enhance students' academic growth and development, increase students' understanding of the positive influence of a growth mindset, and enhance students' social and emotional growth. As stated by one coach, the "Austin's Butterfly" video was a "game changer, as it provided a concrete example of how teachers could assist students in understanding the role of critical feedback, how to give and receive such feedback, and the effects specific feedback can have on growth" (L. Russell, personal communication, January 13, 2020). After the lessons' creators viewed the video, their question became how to apply Berger's approach to more advanced content:

> It is fairly easy for kids to look at the butterfly photograph (the goal) and give recommendations for improved drawings based on the exemplar. How could we help teachers and students do something comparable with much more rigorous, advanced curricula like that used in the TDA schools? (L. Russell, personal communication, January 13, 2020)

Using Berger's approach as a springboard, the TDIM feedback lessons emerged. The instructional coaches, in collaboration with the TDA second-grade teachers, began the lesson development process with an analysis of students' work. The teachers reviewed unit pretest results and writing samples from the William & Mary English language arts (ELA) curriculum unit *Beyond Words* (Center for Gifted Education, 2011b), and the Project M² curriculum unit *Designing a Shape Gallery: Geometry With the Meerkats* (Gavin et al., 2010). Through the analysis, areas for student improvement were determined. Collaboratively, it was determined that interpretation of metaphor and personification were the areas needing the most improvement. Shaping a broad plan, the teachers decided that comparisons of beginning-of-the-year pretest results and current test results would determine student starting points. Students would be given opportunities to provide one another feedback on how to improve their work using a rubric, an exemplar, and William & Mary and Project M² curricular scaffolds. The lessons would use the advanced research-based second-grade ELA curriculum unit *Beyond Words* (Center for Gifted Education, 2011b), the fifth-grade ELA curriculum unit *Autobiographies and Memoirs* (Center for Gifted Education, 2011a), and the Project M² unit

Designing a Shape Gallery: Geometry With the Meerkats (Gavin et al., 2010). The lesson development goals were to "(1) increase students' growth mindset orientation, (2) develop students' understandings that success comes with effort, while (3) strengthening students' metacognition and (4) boosting student achievement" (L. Russell, personal communication, January 13, 2020).

After an overall vision of the lessons was outlined, more detailed development occurred. First, in order to provide a midyear comparison for growth, teachers either readministered a pretest assessment question or pulled a recent student writing sample. The original pretest results and student writing samples, and midyear test results and student writing samples, were placed side by side for a review of student growth. The analysis of the comparison samples informed teachers as to the target areas where students would most benefit from additional feedback.

After selecting the content focus for the feedback lessons, and before teaching the actual lessons to the students, the teachers chose the criteria or benchmarks (rubrics) and the scaffolds (graphic organizers, thinking models, analysis models) to be used during the feedback discussions. For example, for the questions that addressed inferencing with metaphors and personification, the William & Mary Metaphor Analysis Model (see Center for Gifted Education, 2011b) was used to provide scaffolding. For the writing samples, the William & Mary Hamburger Model (see Center for Gifted Education, 2011a) was used to provide student scaffolding. The use of the models assisted students in the discussion and exploration of the shared characteristics upon which the metaphor was based. When reflecting on the process, one coach stated, "We didn't know at the time, but this was us creating a shared language for feedback that would allow for greater specificity of our recommendations" (L. Russell, personal communication, January 13, 2020).

In order to model the feedback process, teachers selected two students who would share their work with the class. The second-grade teachers chose students who were relatively confident, who would respond positively to the feedback, and who would be comfortable with receiving feedback in front of their classmates. This selection process matched suggested recommendations in peer feedback research (Hattie, 2011; Hattie & Timperley, 2007). Also, before proceeding with the protocol feedback lesson, the lesson creators received permission from the students to have their work critiqued by their classmates.

The lesson began with a class viewing the "Austin's Butterfly" video. The video served as the exemplar model for the peer feedback process. Students were able to view the protocols involved in giving peer feedback, and they were able to see the power of the feedback through the improvements made

Figure 10.1
Discussion Prompt and Visual Representation of Austin's Butterfly Drawings

How did Austin's classmates help him get better at drawing the butterfly?

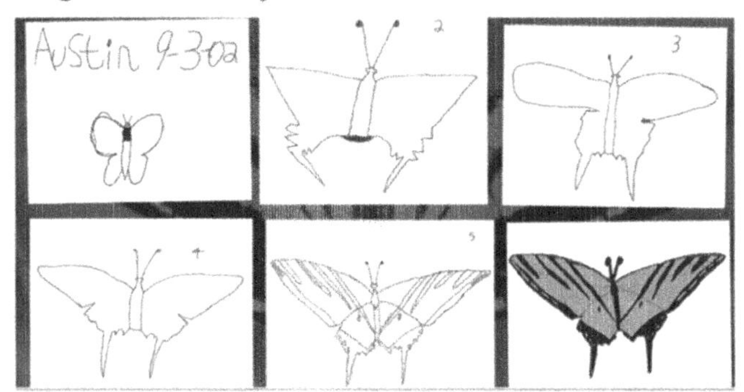

Note. This is a presentation slide used with students to visually teach how peer feedback can lead to exemplary work. Students viewed the progression of Austin's butterfly drawing and used the slide's prompt to guide their discussion of the feedback Austin received from his classmates (EL Education, 2012; Gutshall, 2014; Brock & Hundley, 2016; as cited in Russell et al., 2018). The images are reprinted from *Austin's Butterfly: Building Excellence in Student Work* [Video], by EL Education, 2012, https://modelsofexcellence.eleducation.org/resources/austins-butterfly. Reprinted with permission.

to Austin's drawing. After viewing the video, the teachers used the progression of Austin's butterfly drawing to facilitate the discussion of peer feedback protocols. Figure 10.1 depicts the slide used to assist the lessons' discussion of Austin's Butterfly and student feedback (EL Education, 2012; Russell et al., 2018).

After the video, the teachers led a student discussion on the importance and benefits of a growth mindset orientation. During the discussion, students reviewed peer feedback guidelines. Discussions emphasized the need to share kind, specific, and helpful feedback, as stated by Berger in the video (EL Education, 2012). Teachers and students discussed examples from the video of how Austin's classmates were kind, specific, and helpful. The video also gave the students a visual depiction of how the feedback comments improved

Figure 10.2
Chart Depicting Desired Feedback Characteristics

Giving strong feedback

Protocol	Sounds like:	Looks Like:
1) Be Kind		
2) Be **Specific**		
3) Be Helpful		

Note. Representation of presentation slide used to facilitate student discussion on the traits of effective feedback (Russell et al., 2018). Reprinted with permission of the author.

Austin's drawing. Figure 10.2 is a representation of the visual used to facilitate the discussion of the traits of helpful feedback.

After viewing the "Austin's Butterfly" video and after the follow-up discussion on feedback protocols, the students, as a group, critiqued a classmate's writing sample. The student's preassessment sample was compared to the most current sample. The class used the rubric to explore the growth in their classmate's work. Using the exemplar, students were encouraged to consider how the current writing or response could be improved upon. Figure 10.3 shows the Center for Gifted Education Hamburger Model scaffold and the discussion prompt used in the evaluative discussion. The shared language of the rubrics and the scaffolds—the Hamburger Model (Center for Gifted Education, n.d.), the Analysis Model (Center for Gifted Education, 2011b), and the Talk Frame (Gavin et al., 2010)—guided students as they delivered specific feedback on how the student work could be improved.

The experience of giving feedback as a class created a vision of what giving effective feedback would look like and sound like. Using the skills learned from the group experience, the lessons learned from watching the "Austin's Butterfly" video, and the follow-up feedback discussion, the students began

Figure 10.3
Presentation Slide of Center for Gifted Education's Hamburger Model and Discussion Prompt

Hamburger Model/Rubric discussion prompt: How could we use a rubric to guide our feedback and help the writer improve his/her persuasive piece? Let's start by looking at the rubric components.

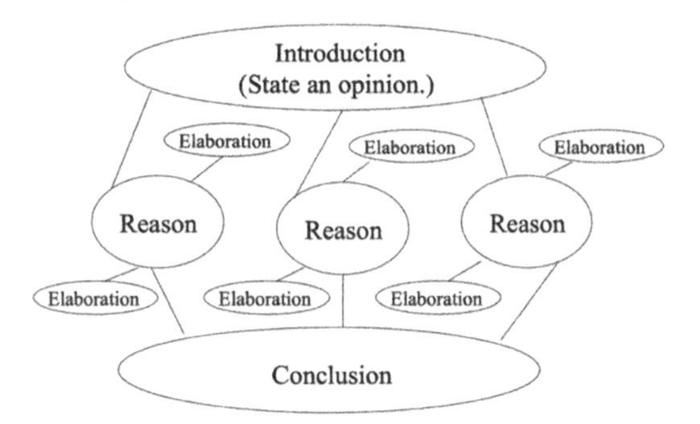

Note. This is a presentation slide (Russell et al., 2018) with discussion prompt for feedback lessons based on writing using the Hamburger Model. The model is from *Hamburger Model for Persuasive Writing*, by Center for Gifted Education, n.d., https://education.wm.edu/centers/cfge/_documents/curriculum/teaching models/hamburgermodelregular.pdf. Copyright by Center for Gifted Education. Reprinted with permission.

working in pairs to evaluate each other's work. Figure 10.4 provides a sample of one student's feedback to a classmate. In the sample response, the peer assessor is responding to their partner's answer to a question about the meaning of the word *fog* from a Carl Sandburg poem. After receiving the peer feedback and critical to their learning process, students made revisions to their original work.

Following the peer feedback and revision sessions, students were asked to complete a final reflection on the feedback process they had experienced. Students responded to the following questions:

1. What was your experience with this task like? (How did it feel? What were your thoughts?)
2. How did you grow as a writer or thinker?
3. How might it help you in the future?

Figure 10.4
Sample Peer Feedback

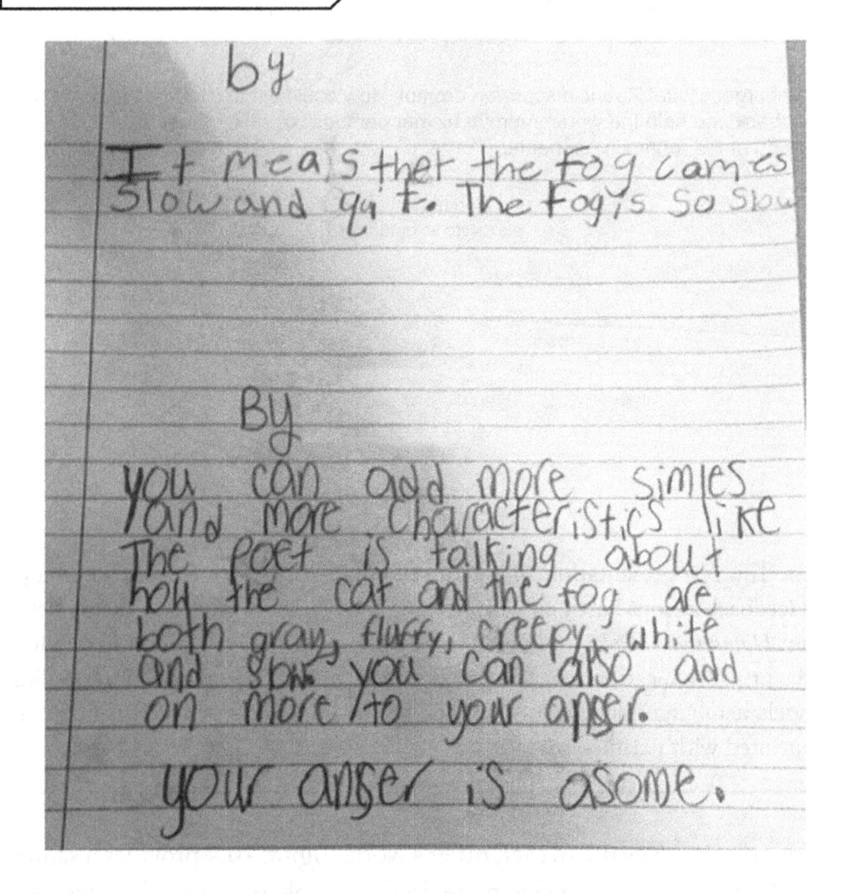

Note. Using a rubric to guide their responses, students provided feedback to their partner's work. This is a copy of one student's peer feedback response (Russell et al., 2018). The student responses are included with permission of the author.

Overall, and consistent with research findings (Topping, 2009), the student responses indicated that the initial experience of peer feedback was uncomfortable, but comfort levels increased as students participated in a back and forth process. Figure 10.5 provides sample second-grade student responses. Figure 10.6 provides a sample fifth-grade response to the feedback process.

Figure 10.5
Second-Grade Student Responses to the Feedback Lesson

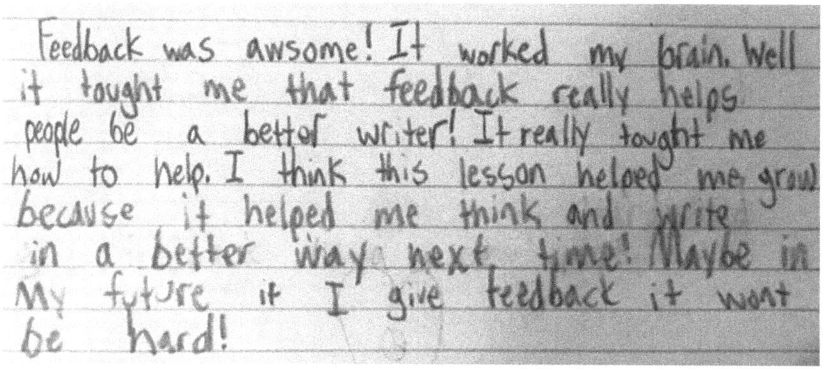

Feedback was awsome! It worked my brain. Well it tought me that feedback really helps people be a bettor writer! It really tought me how to help. I think this lesson helped me grow because it helped me think and write in a better way next time! Maybe in My future if I give feedback it wont be hard!

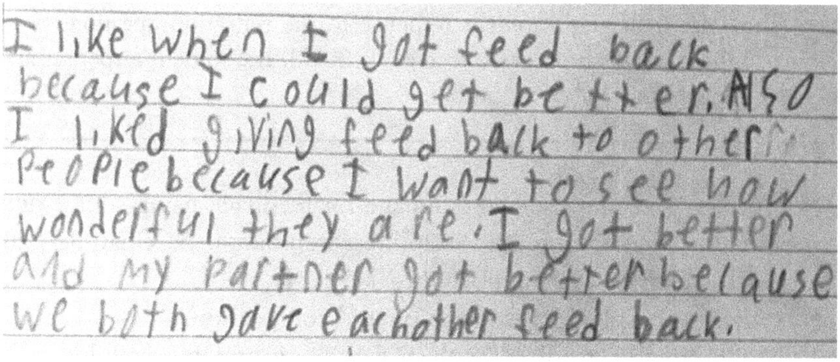

I like when I got feed back because I could get better. Also I liked giving feed back to other People because I want to see how wonderful they are. I got better and my partner got better belause we both gave eachother feed back.

Note. Second-grade student responses to the reflection questions pertaining to the feedback process (Russell et al., 2018). The student responses are included with permission of the author.

Reflecting on the feedback lessons, the TDA coaches created a list of "Aha's and Recommendations" for guidance in future lessons. Recommendations included the following:

- Emphasize that our brains are malleable, and feedback is an act of "growing your brain" (Gutshall, 2014).
- Explore growth via the revisiting of initial preassessment work.

Figure 10.6
Fifth-Grade Student Responses to the Feedback Lesson

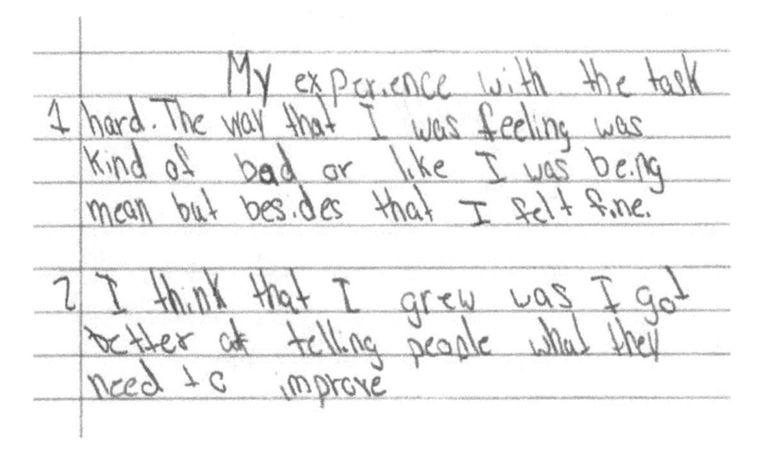

Note. These are fifth-grade student response to the reflection questions pertaining to the feedback process (Russell et al., 2018). The student responses are included with permission of the author.

- Develop and use a shared language for feedback using sound rubrics and the language of the discipline (Stambaugh & Chandler, 2012; VanTassel-Baska & Stambaugh, 2006).
- Provide exemplars for exploration and comparison.
- Model effective feedback with student work, and use scaffolds to facilitate greater access and opportunity (Stambaugh & Chandler, 2012).
- Base feedback on the overarching goals of the assessment (e.g., well-reasoned arguments vs. proper spelling or grammar; Center for Gifted Education, 2010a).

The lessons' authors found students' responses to the lessons to be the single most inspiring outcome associated with the lessons. Students with underachieving tendencies began seeking guidance on how to make their work better: "Just tell me. I know it's not my best. What can I do to make it better?" (L. Russell, personal communication, January 13, 2020). According to one coach, the teachers also "observed their students practicing more metacognition relative to the thinking skills required for each task. They also noted that students left the feedback sessions with a deeper understanding of the task" (L. Russell, personal communication, January 13, 2020). Students had increased levels of engagement. Even traditionally hesitant participants engaged in the lessons. When beginning the lessons, students were somewhat hesitant to give peer feedback. In keeping with Topping's (2009) findings, teachers observed that with practice, comfort levels increased, students were able to provide more effective peer feedback, students appreciated the feedback, and students utilized the feedback in their revisions. The student reflections reiterated that feedback practice created growth in comfort levels. Additionally, teachers found that students' communication and writing skills improved, and the use of metacognition in relation to student learning increased. When referring to the process the lesson developers reflected:

> The work appeared to increase their (students) ownership and responsibility for their work. In the words of one teacher, students seemed to have the burgeoning awareness that "Ooohhhh, this is MY work. I CAN make it better." (L. Russell, personal communication, January 13, 2020)

As the lessons were being developed, the TDA coaches grounded their work in three key TDIM instructional pillars: (1) Powerful curriculum and instruction can help unmask student potential; (2) consideration of a student's background and culture should guide instruction, and knowing that background and culture influences how talent is revealed; and (3) brains are malleable, and understanding that leads students to connect effort and motivation to growth. An objective of the lessons was that through participation in the feedback and revision process, students would grow in their understanding that feedback can help move one toward their goals. The student responses to the peer feedback experience confirmed the positive connections made between feedback, growth, and talent development.

Conclusion

When students are given the opportunity to be the change initiators in their learning process, they experience being self-directed learners. As students exercise control of their learning, they develop a sense of personal empowerment and strengthen their growth mindsets. This dynamic demonstrates that the psychological tools of self-efficacy pave a path toward talent development. Through the experience of the feedback lessons, students at the TDA elementary school experienced the power of their own feedback on their classmates' work and the power of their classmates' feedback on their own work. Students' growth mindsets were strengthened when they saw the tangible improvements in their writing and problem-solving skills. Teachers witnessed and students experienced the progress incurred as a result of the feedback. For students, the experience of giving and receiving feedback, coupled with the understanding that feedback yields achievement, created enhanced growth mindsets and meaningful steps toward talent development.

End-of-Chapter Discussion/ Reflection Questions

1. What are types and levels of feedback? How is each type relevant and useful?
2. How do the ways in which teachers provide feedback impact student learning? Be specific and explain with details.
3. Discuss the example of teaching students how to give each other feedback using "Austin's Butterfly." How could you adapt this approach in your classroom?
4. Why is focused feedback essential to one's talent development? Illustrate with an example.

References

Berger, R., Woodfin, L., & Vilen, A. (2016). *Learning that lasts: Challenging, engaging, and empowering students with deeper instruction.* Jossey-Bass.

Brock, A., & Hundley, H. (2016). *The growth mindset coach: A teacher's month-by-month handbook of empowering students to achieve.* Ulysses Press.

Brookhart, S. M. (2017). *How to give effective feedback to your students* (2nd ed.). ASCD.

Center for Gifted Education. (n.d.). *Hamburger model for persuasive writing.* https://education.wm.edu/centers/cfge/_documents/curriculum/teachingmodels/hamburgermodelregular.pdf

Center for Gifted Education. (2011a). *Autobiographies and memoirs* (2nd ed.). Kendall Hunt.

Center for Gifted Education. (2011b). *Beyond words.* Kendall Hunt.

Dweck, C. S. (2017). The journey to children's mindsets—and beyond. *Child Development Perspectives, 11*(2), 139–144. https://doi.org/10.1111/cdep.12225

EL Education. (2012). *Austin's butterfly: Building excellence in student work* [Video]. https://modelsofexcellence.eleducation.org/resources/austins-butterfly

Gavin, M. K., Casa, T. M., Chapin, S. H., & Sheffield, L. J. (2010). *Project M²: Level 2: Designing a shape gallery: Geometry with the meerkats, teacher guide.* Kendall Hunt.

Gutshall, C. A. (2014). Pre-service teachers' mindset beliefs about student ability. Electronic *Journal of Research in Educational Psychology, 12*(3), 785–802.

Hattie, J. (2011). Feedback in schools. In R. M. Sutton, M. J. Hornsey, & K. M. Douglas (Eds.), *Feedback: The communication of praise, criticism, and advice* (pp. 265–278). Lang.

Hattie, J., & Timperley, H. (2007). The power of feedback. *Review of Educational Research, 77*(1), 81–112. https://doi.org/10.3102/003465430298487

Mofield, E., & Parker Peters, M. (2018). *Teaching tenacity, resilience, and a drive for excellence: Lessons for social-emotional learning for grades 4–8*. Prufrock Press.

Moon, S. M. (2014). Personal talent theory and high-ability students. In J. A. Plucker & C. M. Callahan (Eds.), *Critical issues and practices in gifted education: What the research says* (2nd ed., pp. 493–504). Prufrock Press.

Russell, L., Anderson, L., & Swanson, J. (2018, November 15). *Teaching effective feedback to culturally and linguistically diverse GTS for academic and social-emotional growth* [Conference session]. Annual convention of the National Association for Gifted Children, Minneapolis, MN, United States.

Stambaugh, T., & Chandler, K. L. (2012). *Effective curriculum for underserved gifted students*. Prufrock Press.

Swanson, J. D., Brock, L., Van Sickle, M., Gutshall, C. A., Russell, L., & Anderson, L. (2020). A basis for talent development: The integrated curriculum model and evidence-based strategies. *Roeper Review, 42*(3), 165–178. https://doi.org/10.1080/02783193.2020.1765920

Swanson, J. D., Russell, L. W., & Anderson, L. (2019). A model for growing teacher talent scouts: Decreasing underrepresentation of gifted students. In S. R. Smith (Ed.), *Handbook of giftedness and talent development in the Asia-Pacific* (pp. 1–20). Springer. https://doi.org/10.1007/978-981-13-3021-6_55-1

Topping, K. J. (2009). Peer assessment. *Theory Into Practice, 48*(1), 20–27. https://doi.org/10.1080/00405840802577569

van Zundert, M., Sluijsmans, D., & van Merriënboer, J. (2010). Effective peer assessment processes: Research findings and future directions. *Learning and Instruction, 20*(4), 270–279. https://doi.org/10.1016/j.learninstruc.2009.08.004

VanTassel-Baska, J., & Stambaugh, T. (2006). *Comprehensive curriculum for gifted learners* (3rd ed). Pearson.

Wiggins, G. (2012). Seven keys to effective feedback. *Educational Leadership, 70*(1), 10–16.

11

One Teacher's Story

Noncognitive Influences on Talent Development

Jessica Ross

I always admired teachers, but I never wanted to be one. Growing up as a White middle-class child in rural Charleston, WV, I was always an average student. I never did particularly well in school, and I often felt that teachers did not understand me. I was *that* student. In terms of academics, I was the type of student that flies under the teacher's radar because I was not the lowest achieving student, but not the highest achieving, either. Teachers were never particularly concerned with my progress, but my report cards always had similar comments stating that I was not giving my best effort. For most of my educational career, starting in elementary school and through college, I was a mediocre student, mostly earning B's and a few C's. Although I did have some wonderful teachers, I was never interested in learning and could not find the motivation behind why I was learning all of these concepts. I never fully understood why I was so unenthused about my education until my time in graduate school, followed by my experience teaching with the Talent Development Academies (TDA) project (Swanson et al., 2019).

After graduating from West Virginia University in 2012 with a B.S. in public relations, I realized that I did not want to be working in a field within the scope of my degree. Upon visiting a friend's sister (who was a teacher), I took notice of her general demeanor and excitement about her profession and her students. I decided to look into teaching as a possible career, so I volunteered in a local kindergarten class and fell in love with educating children. This was a seemingly life-shattering realization because I had never enjoyed school. In light of this realization, I was determined to figure out my "why." Why did I not like school throughout my upbringing? Why did I fall in love with teaching? These were questions that I needed answered. During the next few months I continued to volunteer daily in the kindergarten class. I applied to and was accepted in the Graduate School at the College of Charleston, with the goal of obtaining my master's degree in early childhood education. I moved from Charleston, WV, to Charleston, SC, to continue my inquiry into my why.

After starting graduate school, I was immersed in a culture of learning that was very different from all of my previous experiences with education. I was eager to absorb every bit of information, and for the first time in my life, I felt deeply connected to my education coursework. I felt smart in ways I had never felt before. In learning about learning, I realized the fundamental importance of engaging students as equal partners in their education, especially in the primary grades. I finally understood why I never was quite interested in my education—I never felt that it was truly *my* education. It always felt like learning was an expectation, not a choice. I decided then that I never wanted children to feel that way. Throughout my teaching career, my why has always been to inspire children to be independent thinkers who feel that they are equal partners in their education in order to create a strong foundation of future learning.

Empowering My "Why" Through Neurodevelopment

My entire teaching career to date has been spent in Title I schools. I am incredibly passionate about ensuring that all children have access to an equitable and rigorous education, no matter their socioeconomic background. Prior to my third year of teaching, I was hired as the kindergarten teacher for the "Advanced Studies Program," which is housed within a rural Title I school nestled in the tight-knit community that is a quick 30-minute drive from a midsize city in the Southeast. This program aims to recognize and grow the talents of students in our community who may have been previously unrecognized. According to the 2018–2019 school report card, our school had 386 students with a poverty index of 89.6. Of those students, 63% were African

American, 15.1% were Hispanic, 10.8% were European American, and 3.8% were considered "other." Of all 386 students at our school in 2018–2019, 1.2% qualified as gifted and talented (Charleston County School District, 2019). I believe in the Advanced Studies Program, as I want to help create a pathway to success for gifted students who are typically underrepresented in gifted programs. My work with the Talent Development Instructional Model (TDIM) served as the catalyst in my work to accomplish this goal.

Before the school year started, the school staff attended a summer training seminar introducing our school to the TDIM. We were in the first year of being a TDA school, and I was eager to learn what that entailed. Throughout the seminar, I had many moments of clarity, but the most resounding was during a presentation led by a clinical school psychologist. Her presentation, titled "Neuroscience for Talent Scouts" (Gutshall, 2017), spoke to the direct impact that teachers' beliefs about learning have on student motivation and achievement. She empowered teachers to be talent scouts and ensure our mindsets are never fixed about educating our students because, physically, the brain is never finished learning. Upon hearing this information, my interest piqued. I had never fully understood how the brain acquires and reacts to new knowledge. This information seemed like something that all teachers should be aware of, yet I had never been exposed to the concepts before. Throughout the presentation, we discovered how learning occurs in the brains of our students and what that physically looked like. In her book *Transforming Your Teaching: Practical Strategies Informed by Cognitive Neuroscience*, Carraway (2014) described the process of learning as follows:

> Learning occurs when the receiving neuron fires faster and more readily in response to the sending neuron. Each time a sequence of neurons is fired together, connections are formed. Repetition and practice (repeated neuron firings) are the fundamental processes involved in learning. Learning involves the active construction of neural networks and recall involves the partial reactivation of previously created neural networks. (p. 71)

By the end of the TDIM seminar presentation, the teachers in the room were abuzz with excitement. Most of us had never thought to frame elementary education through a neuroscience lens.

Throughout the remainder of the breakout sessions during the TDIM training seminar, I recognized that the founding principles of the TDIM aligned directly with my personal teaching philosophies. In my opinion, the primary function of the TDA's partnership with public schools was to support educators to recognize the strengths in each student and provide each student with varied opportunities to build upon these strengths in a way that promotes autonomy and higher order thinking. This particular pillar of the TDIM really resonated with me. Many have heard the popular notion taking the education world by storm—growth mindset (Dweck, 2006/2016). The TDIM tackled the concept of growth mindset through educating teachers about neurodevelopment, how the brain develops, and neuroplasticity, or how the brain physically reacts during the learning process. An essential pillar of the TDIM is obtaining a complete understanding of the physical makeup of the brain and how the learning process takes place within it (Swanson et al., 2019).

Planning the Paradigm Shift

I was immediately drawn to the idea of teaching the concept of growth mindset in an early childhood setting. After doing some research, I decided to begin the year teaching students about having a growth mindset through the framework of learning about the physical attributes and functions of their brains. Duckworth (2016) stated:

> A fixed mindset about ability leads to pessimistic explanations of adversity, and that, in turn, leads to both giving up on challenges and avoiding them in the first place. In contrast, a growth mindset leads to optimistic ways of explaining adversity, and that, in turn, leads to perseverance and seeking out new challenges that will ultimately make you even stronger. (p. 192)

I could not help but wonder, if my students really understood what was taking place in their brains when they acquired new concepts, could that motivate them to take ownership of their learning and work harder? What impact would this knowledge have on their achievement? Could this framework positively impact the foundation of education from which my students would build all future experiences?

With these guiding questions in mind, I started to think about how utilizing neurodevelopment and neuroscience information with my students would affect their reactions to the developmental challenges that typical kindergarteners have during the year. One of the biggest challenges as a kindergarten teacher is instructing students in the semantics of reading. During the course of a year, students are expected to go from barely understanding the concept of what a letter is, to decoding words, to making meaning from words and reading entire stories. Achieving phonemic awareness is a tedious process, and students often get discouraged and begin to doubt themselves and their abilities. I began to wonder if teaching students about the innate neuroplasticity of the brain would alleviate some of these hardships and promote rigor and grit within my 5-year-old students.

When students try to do something and fail, they dwell on the failure. Instead, I wanted to move the emphasis of thinking from failing to trying. When we try and fail, we learn what we need to do differently. This is an essential lesson that students need to learn (Duckworth, 2013). This was my ultimate goal. I wanted my students to approach challenges differently. I wanted to create a classroom culture where mistakes are celebrated and difficult work is the norm. The first step in flipping the script for my students was to create a rough outline of the teaching progression of learning about the concepts during the course of the school year. The outline was as follows:

1. Introduce students to the idea of growth mindset:
   - Introduce key vocabulary (such as growth mindset, fixed mindset, mistakes, grit, persistence, self-talk, reflection, etc.).
   - Introduce the concept of "yet."

2. Relate growth mindset back to the anatomy of students' brains:
   - What do our brains look like when we learn and practice new things?
   - What do our brains look like when we are doing work we know how to do?
   - What happens in our brains when we do easy work?
   - What happens in our brains when we do harder work?
   - What happens in our brains when we make mistakes?

3. Teach students about neurons and what happens when they acquire a new concept.
4. Learn about how neural connections are made.
5. Discover the parts of a neuron.
6. Learn the functions of the parts of a neuron.
7. Learn what happens neurologically when a new skill is practiced and cemented.
8. How can we affect our brain growth over time?

Using this fluid framework, I began to research and develop lessons and activities to promote the acquisition of these guiding concepts. My primary goal was to shift the typical student paradigm about difficult work and create a classroom culture that celebrates students taking control of their learning through grit and rigor. I wanted students to understand that it is only when we do more challenging work that our brains grow, and we make neurological connections to cement our learning. When the school year began, I was armed and ready with a plan.

The "Big Brain Lesson"

The first day of school I introduced students to what I now call the "Big Brain Lesson." Gathered in a circle, we took turns going around and sharing what excited us about kindergarten and what made us nervous. During this activity, many students shared that they were nervous about homework or nervous that the work would be too hard. I used this concern as a starting point to discuss that hard work really is honing a skill that our brain has not mastered yet. Then we looked at an interactive presentation I created about the progression of learning and how it impacts our brains.

The activity started with having the students think about when they were babies. I led the discussion with: "Were we born with the ability to walk or talk? No!" I posed another question for the students: "How did we get these skills?" Students had "Think Tank Time" in which they paired with a student near them to explore and talk about the question. After some class discussion, we landed on the idea that as babies we had to practice hard things (like walking and talking) a great deal before we mastered them. After an abundance of trying and practicing, the skill became easy for us. I elaborated that the brain works in the same way. It is only when we try to do things that we consider hard, that our brains grow. I further explained that if we only did things we considered easy, our brains would not grow at all. The brain actually falls asleep. The students were enthralled with the idea of our brains growing versus falling asleep. To bring the content into familiar terms, I proposed a scenario to the class:

> There is a little boy named Calvin. Calvin is your age. He just started kindergarten, like you, and he is having some trouble. Calvin has decided that learning to read is too hard and that he doesn't want to do it. Calvin wants to quit. Use some "Think Tank Time" and discuss what you think Calvin should

> do. What advice would you give to him? What would happen if Calvin quits learning how to read?

We explored the different ramifications of both decisions and realized that Calvin needed to be persistent and have a growth mindset. It was a good introduction into neuroscience, and I was hopeful that it would begin to shift the mindsets of my students from a fixed orientation to one of growth. Over the following weeks I built upon that foundation, introducing many new concepts through a variety of activities and investigations. The students started to exhibit signs of taking ownership of their learning. For example, during our sight-word testing on Fridays, students normally would complain beforehand and get upset if the test was too difficult. Instead, I noticed that the students would motivate each other. If a student would start to get upset, other students would rally and remind the student about how their brain was growing. Approaching challenges began to look different. I was elated to see the change in mindset taking place in the classroom.

Mistakes Are . . . Good?

Another challenge that I found myself facing was teaching my students how to handle disappointment and mistakes. After the "Big Brain Lesson," my students were so excited about growing their brains that when they made a mistake, they would become discouraged. One day, about a month into school, a student made two mistakes on our math assessment. When I called him over to go over the mistakes with him, he broke down into hysterics saying things like, "My brain is shrinking because I messed up!" and "I must be stupid and have a broken brain!" It was in that moment that I realized I had to figure out a creative way to address the stigma surrounding mistakes with the entire class.

After doing research and conferring with the TDA teacher coaches, I devised a plan of attack. Throughout an entire day at school, I constantly made mistakes: I dropped everything, I spelled words wrong, I forgot what I was teaching, or I did math problems incorrectly. Each time, when I realized (or the students helped me realize) my mistake, I modeled for them, using self-talk, telling myself that it was okay and that mistakes are normal and actually a good thing. Over the course of the day, the students started to get inquisitive. They started to make comments like, "Ms. Ross, you sure are acting silly today" and "Why are you messing up so much?" Eventually, one particular student asked the question I was waiting for, "Ms. Ross, how can mistakes be a good thing?" At that moment I called everyone to the carpet for our "My Mind Makes Mistakes Lesson." Without any introduction, I read them the book *The*

Girl Who Never Made Mistakes (Pett & Rubinstein, 2011). The main character in the story is a girl named Beatrice who has never made a mistake and always wins the town's talent show. People around town even know her as "the girl who never makes mistakes." Throughout the book we witness the pressure that Beatrice is under to be perfect and her pervasive fear of making mistakes. At the talent show, the unthinkable happens, and Beatrice makes a mistake in front of the entire town! At this point of the story, I stopped and asked the students to discuss what they think her reaction would be. All of the students answered in similar ways, that she was going to be embarrassed, cry, and quit the talent show. I continued reading, revealing that in the end Beatrice started to giggle and eventually had the entire crowd laughing with her. From then on Beatrice felt relieved of the pressures of being perfect and learned that mistakes were good.

The students were shocked. They struggled to understand such a big concept. I led our discussion back to the brain. I asked them, "What do you think happens to our brain if we know all the answers all the time? Would that be the hard work that our brains need to grow?" The students started to catch on. They realized that if we never made mistakes, it would mean that our work was too easy, and what happens to our brain when work is easy? It falls asleep! Through more conversation about the nature of mistakes, the class came to the conclusion that mistakes are an important part of learning.

We discovered that when we make a mistake and figure out how to fix it, our brains grow the most. This was a huge paradigm shift within my classroom that had a resounding effect on my students' levels of motivation and achievement for the remainder of the year. My students suddenly were excited when they made and corrected their mistakes. They were no longer afraid of messing up. In fact, the process of fixing their mistakes turned into a celebration. When students mastered a skill with which they made mistakes and had difficulty in mastering, we celebrated! A student favorite was mastering books in guided reading groups. The students would work for weeks to master challenging books with me during groups. During these weeks, they struggled through first-grade leveled readers, making numerous mistakes. I noticed a shift. Throughout the struggles and mistakes, they never gave up, not a single student. Self-talk was commonly used during groups by the students as intrinsic motivation. When they mastered the books, what a celebration we had! But no extrinsic celebration could compete with how proud they were of themselves. This change in thought made my students even more empowered to succeed and achieve for the remainder of the year.

The Power of "Yet"

In shifting the mindset of students, I utilized a variety of activities surrounding individual goal setting with my students. Together, we learned that there is nothing that we cannot learn how to do. Our brains are completely malleable and ready for a challenge. One of my favorite activities to do with primary students introduces the power of "yet" through a children's picture book, *Giraffes Can't Dance* (Andreae & Parker-Rees, 2001). In the story, a giraffe named Gerald desperately wants to learn how to dance but is often discouraged by the other jungle animals who tell him that "giraffes can't dance." But Gerald is determined, and through perseverance and some encouraging words from a friend, Gerald ends up being the hit of the great Jungle Dance. After reading the story, the class discussed Gerald's grit and determination. We concluded that there is nothing we can't do, but there are things we can't do *yet*. We explored alternate endings and their ramifications, for example: What would have happened if Gerald had quit dancing after he was discouraged? What if Gerald thought that learning how to dance was too hard?

Throughout the remainder of the week and the following week the students performed reader's theaters with this story, reenacting all endings and discussing how they would impact Gerald's life. As a closing activity, each student thought of something that they could not do yet that they really wanted to work toward achieving this year, and we made a class poster that we displayed for motivation (see Figure 11.1). We continually referred back to that poster throughout the year, doing weekly check-ins, discussing how we could work harder to achieve our goals, and empowering each other to keep working hard.

The first year after implementing this lesson, I noticed a visible shift in the mindset of all of my students. Rarely did a student say that they could not do something without following it up with "yet." On the rare occasion that a student did say that they could not do something, another student would quickly follow it up with, "Don't forget the yet!" The children became each other's biggest cheerleaders. If someone was feeling down or discouraged, other students would cheer them on, reminding them to, "Be like Gerald and work hard to grow your brain!" or "Use your grit! That's what helped Gerald make his brain grow!" Phrases like these became commonplace in my classroom.

Lessons and activities like this one also served as the introduction to student goal setting. Throughout the remainder of the year, students were in charge of their educational goals. For example, I challenged the students to come up with a SMART goal (i.e., Specific, Measurable, Achievable, Relevant, and Time bound; Mind Tools Content Team, n.d.) each Monday with regard

Figure 11.1
All of the Things We Can't Do Yet Anchor Chart

Note. Reprinted with permission of the author.

to their mastery books, or the books they were working on in guided reading. The students continued to impress with the scope of their understanding. Examples of student goals included the following:

- "Learning the meaning of four new words in my book."
- "Using my reading finger without forgetting on every page."

- "Using my stretchy snake reading strategy to sound out words more than five times."
- "Knowing all the sight words in my book."

This method of student-led goal setting afforded students the opportunity to take real ownership of their progress. I have not seen children work so hard as when they worked to achieve their individual goals. I began to see levels of intrinsic motivation not previously witnessed in my teaching career. The TDIM provided a framework through which I could truly shift students' mindset around hard work within my classroom. Students took ownership of their learning, reflected on their goals, and strove to make progress. The power of yet, persisting to meet goals, showed my students that giving up was not an option. Anything was within their grasp.

Teaching Neuroscience to 5-Year-Olds

In early spring of the school year, when my students had a strong grasp on the big picture of the brain and had a growth mindset regarding their education, it was time to introduce them to the concept of neuroscience. Students knew the abstract functioning of the brain, but could their ownership of their learning deepen by helping them discover the physical neuroscience behind the learning process? I began with a lesson about the human body. We discovered that the human body is made up of cells. The students learned that the cells in our brains are called neurons and that their job is to transmit electrical signals (our learning) throughout our brain.

Through a number of lessons, research, and activities, the class studied the basic anatomy of a neuron and what role each part of the neuron played in the process of acquiring new knowledge. We discovered that when we learn something new or practice a new skill, the dendrites in our neurons connect with the dendrites of other neurons, sending electrical signals that travel along the neuron's axon to the axon terminal connecting to the dendrites of more neurons. This electrical signal creates a learning pathway. The more we practice the skill, the more we cement and strengthen our learning pathways. Learning the neuron's structure and function was revolutionary in my classroom. Within the weeks that followed, students demonstrated their learning through various projects including building neurons out of playdough (see Figures 11.2, 11.3, and 11.4) and out of paper (see Figures 11.5 and 11.6).

Figure 11.2
Learning Neural Anatomy With Playdough

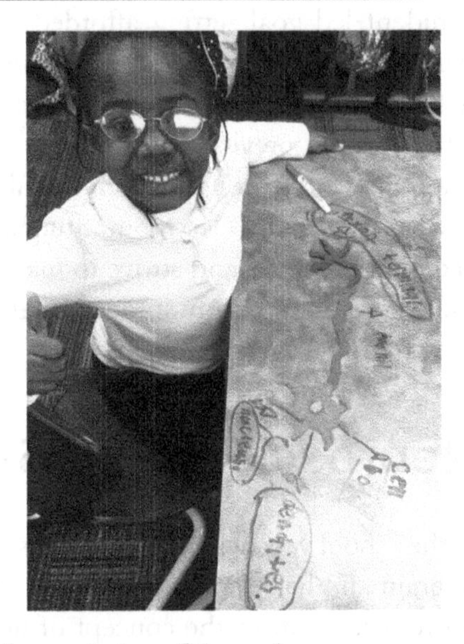

Note. Reprinted with permission of the author.

Figure 11.3
Learning Neural Anatomy With Playdough

Note. Reprinted with permission of the author.

Figure 11.4
Learning Neural Anatomy With Playdough

Note. Reprinted with permission of the author.

Figure 11.5
Creating Neurons With Construction Paper

Note. Reprinted with permission of the author.

Figure 11.6
Creating Neurons with Construction Paper

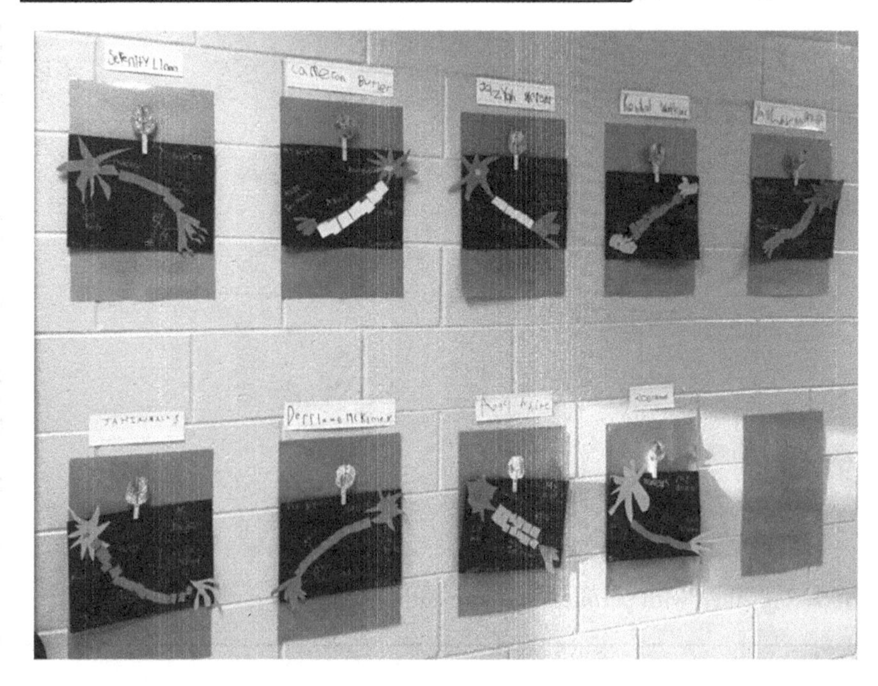

Note. Reprinted with permission of the author.

My students were obsessed with neuroscience, and for the remainder of the school year, we deeply studied the brain. We watched all of the videos we could about neuroscience, even if the students and I did not fully understand them. Recognizing that each student has individual talents, I used the TDIM to create individualized ways that the students could show their learning about the brain. We studied numerous books and used thinking models (e.g., the Literature Web, the Vocabulary Web) to break down thinking and show our knowledge. We challenged our brains and took every opportunity to create new learning pathways and cement existing ones.

Our exploration of neuroscience started to gain outside attention. Our class received numerous visitors from the district, the county, and even the State Department of Education. Each visitor had the same reaction. Everyone was in awe of how articulate students were when explaining the neurological process of acquiring and sustaining knowledge. In late winter of that year, our school was named a "Cool School" by a local news channel that features local schools that are participating in innovative initiatives around the region. Our classroom was featured because of our work with neuroscience. A couple of students were interviewed and given an opportunity to show their knowledge about the topic on the news show. The students were so proud, and the community had a wonderful reaction. The attention we received further confirmed my hypothesis that using the TDIM as a framework to teach students about the physical components of their brains and the process in which learning happens within their brains would lead to greater levels of student engagement, achievement, and ownership. The wonderful things happening in our classroom mirrored the purpose of the TDIM. Through hard work, grit, and ownership, the students started to take control of their education.

Reflecting on a Year of Learning for *All* of Us

After the year was over, I spent a large portion of the summer reflecting on the changes observed in students and my personal pedagogy. I believe that because students were engaged in learning about neuroscience and promoting a growth mindset consistently throughout the entirety of the school year, they benefited in numerous ways. As a result of the content and skills taught throughout the year, my students scored higher on state standardized tests than any kindergarten class at my school ever had. All of the students left kindergarten reading above a first-grade level. They could complete double- and triple-digit addition problems with carrying with ease. The students became more creative writers and would often craft such intricate stories that I had to dictate the ends because their brains moved faster than their fingers (see Figures 11.7 and 11.8).

Perhaps most importantly, my students became much more inquisitive and engaged learners. They would often ask such deep questions that I would not know how to answer. One particular story exemplifies this point. One day in late fall during our daily creative free time, one of my students approached me with a small book-like creation in her hands (see Figure 11.9). She informed me that, "This is a mystery book for every mystery I want to discover." I immediately pulled out my cell phone to record the announcement of her important creation (as I did frequently to document my students' aha moments). She opened the first page to show lined blank pages and proceeded to say:

Figure 11.7
The Rainforest Adventure

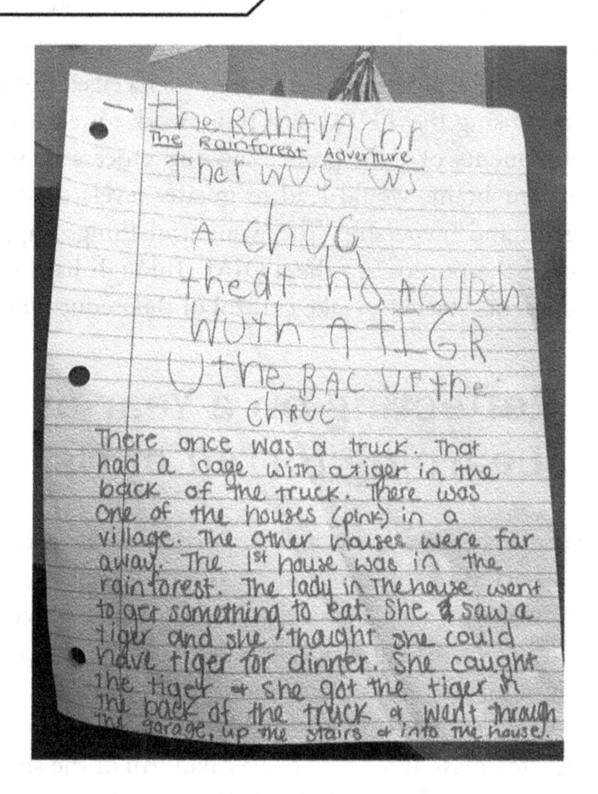

Note. The student responses are included with permission of the author.

> Each mystery I get, I write the title here and write all about that mystery that I think will happen. Once I get a new mystery, I will start all over again on this side (the next blank page), and when I get finished with the mystery on that side and the next side and the next side, I will write a new book!

I could not wait to see what mysteries she was going to unearth. The next day, the student approached me again with more to say. She told me:

> I have a mystery book and so far, I have a lot of mysteries . . . like how does the moon shine? And what makes iPads and tablets work? And how do toys work? I saw this toy that was

Figure 11.8
The Rainforest Adventure Continues

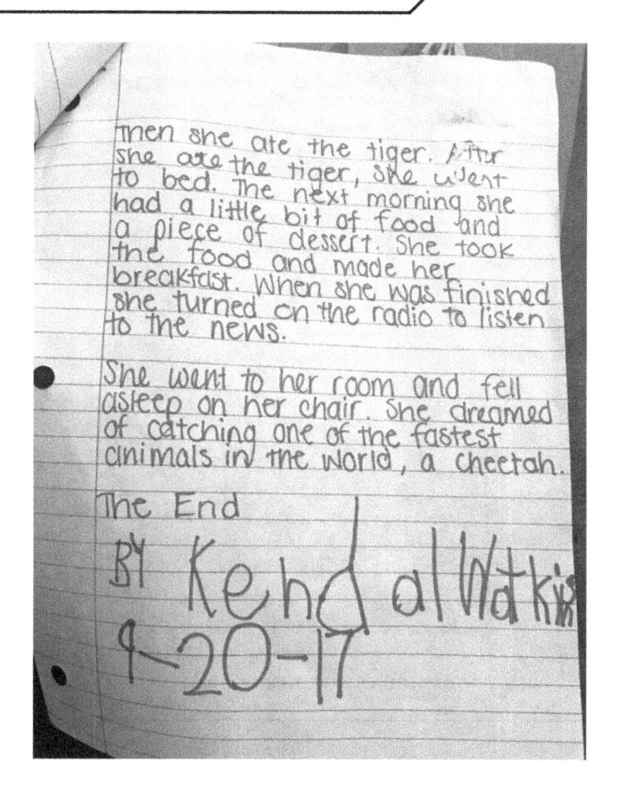

Then she ate the tiger. After
she ate the tiger, she went
to bed. The next morning she
had a little bit of food and
a piece of dessert. She took
the food and made her
breakfast. When she was finished
she turned on the radio to listen
to the news.

She went to her room and fell
asleep on her chair. She dreamed
of catching one of the fastest
animals in the world, a cheetah.

The End
By Kendal Watkin
9-20-17

Note. The student responses are included with permission of the author.

> a bucket and it shooted [sic] out balls. I wonder how it shoots out the balls? It doesn't have a battery, or maybe it does run on batteries or wires. Who knows? It could work on both!

It was an incredible moment for me as a teacher. I was able to really see the inner working of her brain. Her thought process was so deep and filled with higher order thinking skills. It was at that moment I knew that the TDIM had provided me with the support and framework from which I was able to positively impact my students' ownership of their own education and, through that, encourage a true love of deeper learning.

Figure 11.9
The Book of Mysteries

Note. Reprinted with permission of the author.

Encouraging a Growth Mindset and Teaching Neuroscience in Your Classroom

One of my biggest pieces of advice for teachers wanting to encourage a growth mindset and teach neuroscience in your classroom is to get to know your students as individuals and see where their real talents lie. Being a true talent scout means paying attention to the child as a whole, not just one facet of giftedness. As teachers, it is our job to uncover students' strengths, which may not look like the classic case of academic giftedness, but, under the right care, can be honed to promote academic learning. Use those strengths and talents to extend content learning and give students ownership of their education. If you notice one of your students is particularly skilled with creative writing, find assignments that use that skill to show subject mastery or ask the student to assist with teaching writing. Do you have a student who enjoys working with their hands and building things? Encourage that student to complete projects that show off and hone that skill. For example, assign the student to research and build a replica of a famous landmark, and then measure it with standard units of measurement. If the student is younger, you could encourage sight-word acquisition through building sight words with LEGO bricks. There is no limit to the creativity that we can use when we know the talents of our students!

Do not be afraid to take risks. This is relatively new territory in teaching, so do not be apprehensive about tackling a concept as big as the brain. I found that breaking a concept down into the simplest of terms helped my students internalize a big idea. Use picture books as introductions to teaching large and seemingly daunting concepts, such as growth mindset, mistakes, neuroplasticity, and neuroscience. In Table 11.1, I list books that I highly recommend. I use all of these books throughout the school year to assist with teaching such dynamic content. These books have helped guide my approach in teaching the concepts of neuroscience and the TDIM, and have taught me new knowledge as well.

When it comes to promoting and implementing a growth mindset within your classroom, walk the walk and talk the talk. Use every opportunity to model perseverance and grit. Show your students how to work through the hard times and to understand they come out on the other side better for it. Make specific vocabulary an integral part of your daily language (see Table 11.2). Exposure is everything. Nothing is too challenging for students who are ready to take ownership of their own educational experiences. As a teacher, make sure you take risks and show students that mistakes are an awesome part of the learning process. It is imperative that our students understand that the learning process never stops, even for teachers.

Talent Development: The Future Is Bright

My work with the Talent Development Instructional Model provided me with lessons that have completely shaped my current pedagogy. As a facilitator of learning, it is my job to provide students with content and skills to empower them to take control as partners in their education. The students take the concepts I present to them and mold them to fit their individual intelligences. In my role as an educator, my job is not simply to teach kindergarten content to

Table 11.1
Children's Books to Teach Growth Mindset and Neuroscience

Title and Author
▪ *The Girl Who Never Made Mistakes* by Mark Pett and Gary Rubinstein
▪ *Giraffes Can't Dance* by Giles Andreae
▪ *The Book of Mistakes* by Corinna Luyken
▪ *After the Fall* by Dan Santat
▪ *Jabari Jumps* by Gaia Cornwall
▪ *What Do You Do With a Chance?* by Kobi Yamada
▪ *What Do You Do With a Problem?* by Kobi Yamada
▪ *What Do You Do With an Idea?* by Kobi Yamada
▪ *The Dot* by Peter H. Reynolds
▪ *Ish* by Peter H. Reynolds
▪ *The Most Magnificent Thing* by Ashley Spires
▪ *Your Fantastic Elastic Brain: Stretch It, Shape It* by JoAnn Deak
▪ *Beautiful Oops!* by Barney Saltzberg
▪ *Bubble Gum Brain* by Julia Cook
▪ *Not Yet* by Lisa Cox and Lori Hockema
▪ *Salt in His Shoes: Michael Jordan in Pursuit of a Dream* by Deloris Jordan
▪ *I Can't Do That, YET: Growth Mindset* by Esther Pia Cordova
▪ *Thanks for the Feedback . . . I Think?* by Juila Cook
▪ *How Does Your Brain Work?* by Don L. Curry
▪ *My Little Brain!: Explaining the Human Brain for Kids* by Baby Professor
▪ *Think Tank! The Human Brain and How It Works* by Baby iQ Builder Books

Note. This is a list of children's books in my personal library that I have found extremely beneficial in my teaching of growth mindset and neuroscience.

students for one year. My real purpose entails scouting, nurturing, and encouraging individual student talent within my classroom. Using the tools provided to me by the TDIM, I feel confident that my students will succeed and leave kindergarten with a set of honed higher order thinking skills and neurological knowledge that will continue to benefit them in future endeavors.

The effects of teaching my students about neuroscience and how it relates to having a growth mindset are completely remarkable. I watched in awe as my students grew into confident, motivated learners who took ownership and directed the pathway of their education. Knowing the inner workings of their brains armed students with the power of intrinsic motivation, shifting their outlook of school and hard work. As an educator, this revelation has changed my career. I no longer struggle with the pervasive problem of figuring out creative ways to motivate my students—my students are their own motivators. Difficult and challenging work is seen as normal, and students approach

Table 11.2
Vocabulary Words to Teach Growth Mindset and Neuroscience

▪ Grit ▪ Rigor ▪ Perseverance ▪ Growth mindset ▪ Fixed mindset ▪ Yet ▪ Persistence ▪ Determination ▪ Mistakes ▪ Self-talk ▪ SMART goal	▪ Intrinsic motivation ▪ Neuroscience ▪ Neuroplasticity ▪ Neuron ▪ Dendrites ▪ Axon ▪ Axon terminal ▪ Cells ▪ Learning pathway ▪ Synapses ▪ Malleability

Note. These are important vocabulary words to explicitly teach and use daily to promote a growth mindset and a complete understanding of neuroscience within the classroom.

the work with fervor and excitement. When students make a mistake, they are eager to reteach their brains a correct way to approach the task. Student engagement and achievement are no longer a problem, as my students are constantly coming up with creative ways to approach their learning. By relinquishing control of their learning back to my students, even 5-year-old students are able to show that intelligence comes in all shapes and sizes and can be shown in a variety of ways. As educators, we simply have to know how to pay attention, provide guidance, and support growth, grit, and persistence. Then, we can step back and watch our students soar.

End-of-Chapter Discussion/ Reflection Questions

1. Discuss teaching your students about the brain, its malleability, and how they can "grow" their brains. What do you see as pros and cons of teaching your students about the brain? How do you believe that knowledge would impact their effort and embrace of challenge?
2. How do you use mistakes in the teaching and learning process? Why is failure an important part of talent development?
3. The author describes the power of "yet" and how she used it with her students in this chapter. How might you use the power of yet in your own talent development and with your students?

References

Andreae, G., & Parker-Rees, G. (2001). *Giraffes can't dance* (G. Parker-Rees, Illus.). Orchard Books.

Carraway, K. (2014). *Transforming your teaching: Practical strategies informed by cognitive neuroscience*. Norton.

Charleston County School District. (2019). *E. B. Ellington Elementary fall 2019 data dashboard*. https://www.ccsdschools.com/cms/lib/SC50000504/Centricity/Domain/121/059%20EB%20ELLINGTON%20F19%20DASHBOARD-.pdf

Duckworth, A. (2016). *Grit: The power of passion and perseverance*. Scribner.

Duckworth, A. (2013, April). *Grit: The power of passion and perseverance* [Video]. TED Conferences. https://www.ted.com/talks/angela_lee_duckworth_grit_the_power_of_passion_and_perseverance

Dweck, C. S. (2016). *Mindset: The new psychology of success*. Ballantine Books. (Original work published 2006)

Gutshall, C. A. (2017). *Neuroscience for talent scouts* [PowerPoint presentation].

Mind Tools Content Team. (n.d.). *SMART goals*. https://www.mindtools.com/pages/article/smart-goals.htm

Pett, M., & Rubinstein, G. (2011). *The girl who never made mistakes*. Sourcebooks Jabberwocky.

Swanson, J. D., Russell, L. W., & Anderson, L. (2019). A model for growing teacher talent scouts: Decreasing underrepresentation of gifted students. In S. R. Smith (Ed.), *Handbook of giftedness and talent development in the Asia-Pacific* (pp. 1–20). Springer. https://doi.org/10.1007/978-981-13-3021-6_55-1

Part V

Building and Assessing the Model in Your School or District

12

Assessing the Impact of Teacher Learning

Cara L. Kelly and Laura L. Brock

Quality, constructive professional learning is imperative for inservice teachers, especially given "the revolving door" phenomenon of qualified teachers, which posits that 40%–50% of teachers leave the profession within 5 years due to disempowerment and low pay (Riggs, 2013). However, evidence suggests that one-day-a-year teacher professional development is ineffective and fails to shift teachers' beliefs or in-class behaviors (Corcoran, 1995; Garet et al., 2001). Although previous studies have identified the features of effective professional learning models affecting teacher change (Darling-Hammond et al., 2017), there is little supporting evidence of such effective models being used in schools today (LoCasale-Crouch et al., 2015). Previous research does not effectively demonstrate how to organize professional learning in such a way that it directly influences teachers' classroom practice in a scalable manner (Day, 1999).

Time is perhaps the most valuable, and limited, resource available to teachers, coaches, and administrators. Diverting time and effort toward professional learning requires educators to reprioritize their resources. Creating maximally effective professional learning honors the commitment required to learn new skills. This chapter describes how sustained professional learning can improve classroom practices, how to effectively measure changes in teacher practice, and finally what patterns of teacher engagement are most likely to lead to improvements in classroom practice.

Changes in Classroom Practices

Affecting change at the individual and group levels entails understanding and utilizing models of professional learning for teacher growth shown to be effective. Providing substantive support and development are especially important given the research suggesting that teachers may leave preservice training equipped to try new models of instruction, but teachers will revert back to the teacher-centered approach with which they are familiar when faced with the stresses of the classroom (Robinson et al., 2007). According to a 2017 meta-analysis of 35 peer-reviewed research studies (Darling-Hammond et al., 2017), professional learning that works focuses on content, active engagement, collaboration, coaching, and expert support. Effective professional learning is also sustained in duration. In order to promote change within the classroom, these factors must be taken into consideration when designing professional learning interventions.

Research suggests that coaching is an effective mode of changing teachers' practice within the classroom. Coaching results in significant changes in daily practice, even when used alone rather than paired with typical professional learning interventions (Neuman & Cunningham, 2009). These findings suggest that teachers may benefit more from quality, constructive, individualized feedback versus lecture-style professional learning. Furthermore, coaching empowers teachers by increasing their autonomy and self-efficacy; coaches focus on positive components of teachers' classroom practices and provide constructive feedback meant to emphasize the positive (Reinke et al., 2012). Coaching allows teachers to become more autonomous over time, because teachers are receiving valid, constructive feedback from a professional within their field (Neuman & Cunningham, 2009). Thus, professional learning interventions must incorporate individualized feedback to create change within the classroom.

Effective coaching and support, however, cannot take place without a deep understanding of teachers' individual characteristics, those interpersonal attributes that promote or hinder incorporation and implementation of new skills. If professional learning providers seek to change classroom practices and change teachers' attitudes and beliefs, the providers must take into consideration teachers' existing characteristics and belief systems (Guskey, 2002). As stated previously, without support, teachers will revert back to teacher-centered approaches. Teachers need support, from multiple levels, in order to shed their impractical ideas and practices and try something new and innovative within their classroom practice (Brighton, 2003).

Assessing the Effects of Professional Learning

Enhancing instructional strategies known to improve student learning is an important component of effective professional learning. The primary goal of most teacher-focused professional learning is to impact a specific aspect of teacher behavior or instructional practice anticipated to bolster student outcomes. Assessing the effects of professional learning is a crucial, yet often overlooked, component of professional learning interventions. This section discusses the ways in which structured classroom observations can be used to assess the effects of professional learning . We will present a case study to highlight the usefulness of this professional learning assessment. Specifically, results from the Talent Development Academies (TDA; Swanson et al., 2020) study will be shown to demonstrate the usefulness of assessing professional learning interventions using the William & Mary Classroom Observation Scale-Revised. We chose this scale because it is free to the public, it assesses instructional strategies that align with a talent development model, and research confirms that the instructional strategies assessed are associated with enhanced student learning outcomes.

William & Mary Classroom Observation Scale-Revised (COS-R)

The William & Mary Classroom Observation Scale-Revised (COS-R; VanTassel-Baska et al., 2007) is a 25-item instrument that allows observers to assess classroom teaching to gauge effectiveness of general and differentiated teaching behaviors. This instrument was developed for use in kindergarten through fifth-grade classrooms, so it is particularly useful for elementary educators and administrators. Using the COS-R, observers can examine teaching across two main domains, each comprised of categories with items describing observable instructional strategies and student responses: general teaching behaviors (i.e., curriculum planning and delivery) and differentiated teaching

Table 12.1
Student Responses to Differentiated Teaching Behaviors

Accommodations for Individual Differences	Engaged in Diverse Self-Selected or Self-Paced Activities
The teacher . . .	**Students . . .**
Provided opportunities for independent or group learning to promote depth in understanding content.	Worked on projects individually or in pairs/groups.
Accommodated individual or subgroup differences (e.g., through individual conferencing, student or teacher choice in material selection, and task assignments).	Worked on tiered assignments or tasks of choice.
Encouraged multiple interpretations of events and situations.	Explored multiple interpretations.
Allowed students to discover key ideas individually through structured activities and/or questions.	Discovered central ideas through structured activities and/or questions asked.

behaviors (i.e., accommodations for individual differences, problem solving, critical thinking strategies, creative thinking strategies, and research strategies). The COS-R provides evidence of the degree of differentiated strategies teachers employ and helps project staff see where growth in desired teacher behaviors is occurring.

The COS-R is beneficial for administrators and educators because it allows both groups to determine the effectiveness of specific teaching practices that promote higher order thinking strategies and connect the use of a talent development model of instruction. Teaching requires educators to split their attention and think in a complex manner; the COS-R effectively assesses these extensive and in-depth teaching behaviors. For example, a teacher must follow a lesson plan, pace the lesson to match the needs of all of their students, and promote positive student-teacher interactions. Teachers with gifted and talented students in the classroom need to differentiate instruction to match the needs of all students in their classroom. One example of a need to differentiate is teachers designing structured activities and questions that allow students to discover ideas individually. The COS-R is an effective tool to rate these differentiated teaching behaviors. As shown in Table 12.1, the COS-R assesses the teacher's behavior as well as the students' responses to teaching behaviors. Teachers must continuously engage in these complex behaviors in order to promote effective teaching practices.

Table 12.2
COS-R Rating Scale

Effective	The teacher evidenced careful planning and classroom flexibility in implementation of the behavior, eliciting many appropriate student responses. The teacher was clear and sustained focus on the purposes of learning.
Somewhat Effective	The teacher evidenced some planning and/or classroom flexibility in implementation of the behavior, eliciting some appropriate student responses. The teacher was sometimes clear and focused on the purposes of learning.
Ineffective	The teacher evidenced little or no planning and/or classroom flexibility in implementation of the behavior, eliciting minimal appropriate student responses. The teacher was unclear and unfocused regarding the purpose of learning.
N/O (Not Observed)	The listed behavior was not demonstrated during the time of the observation.

COS-R observations generally last between 30 and 50 minutes. During this time, the observer takes copious notes about the instruction occurring in the classroom. The observer focuses on both the teacher's behavior and the students' responses to the teacher during the observation window. Students' responses provide a window into the degree to which the observed instructional strategies are authentic and familiar to students. The observer takes notes on instructional behaviors during the observation, such as a description of the teacher's actions, time spent on activities and transitions between activities, and a record of teachers' questions and student responses as well as the pattern of the interaction. After the observation period ends, the observer begins the coding process; coding should never occur during the observation as key teachable moments may be missed. First, the observer must determine whether the behavior was observed or not observed. If the behavior was not observed during the observation window, the "N/O" column should be checked on the COS-R protocol. If the behavior was observed, the observer must determine the effectiveness of the behavior. The observer chooses between three ratings: effective (3), somewhat effective (2), and ineffective (1). See Table 12.2 for a description of the rating scale.

Case Study: The Teacher-Focused Intervention

In a study examining implementation of a talent development model (Swanson et al., 2020), four schools were selected as part of TDA, a multiyear project focused on teacher learning. The intervention focused on learning designed to impact teachers' classroom practice and beliefs about student academic potential and talent. Starting with a 2-day summer immersion, followed by in-school coaching and demonstration, small-group focused learning, and whole-group sessions, teachers learned how to use innovative curriculum and higher level instructional strategies in combination with strategies focused to strengthen knowledge and application of noncognitive aspects surrounding learning (e.g., motivation, persistence, goal setting) and culturally responsive practice.

The COS-R observational measure was used in the TDA study (Swanson et al., 2020) to examine the effects of the intervention. Each spring, observers conducted classroom observations to assess the effectiveness of the Talent Development Instructional Model (TDIM) intervention. For the TDA study, observations lasted between 30–45 minutes, and teachers were asked to implement a TDIM lesson during the observation window. Observers did not know which teachers had participated in professional learning to reduce any potential bias and provide an objective assessment of teacher instructional strategies and students' reactions to instruction. The COS-R was chosen for this study because the professional learning intervention focused on impacting teachers' classroom practice that promotes student academic potential and talent. The COS-R comprehensively assessed these behaviors and provided useful results to the research team.

The COS-R was used across all 3 years of the study to detect change across time. As is displayed in the following section, the number of teachers fluctuated each year due to the design of the professional learning intervention. During the TDA study, the first year was considered a baseline year in which teachers were observed implementing a lesson of their choice prior to any professional learning participation; data were collected this year to understand how teachers' behaviors and instruction changed after participating in the professional learning intervention. Second-year observations occurred after the teachers had attended the professional learning training and had received coaching from mentors. In the third-year observations, teachers were still being mentored by coaches; however, they were not required to implement a TDIM-specific lesson plan.

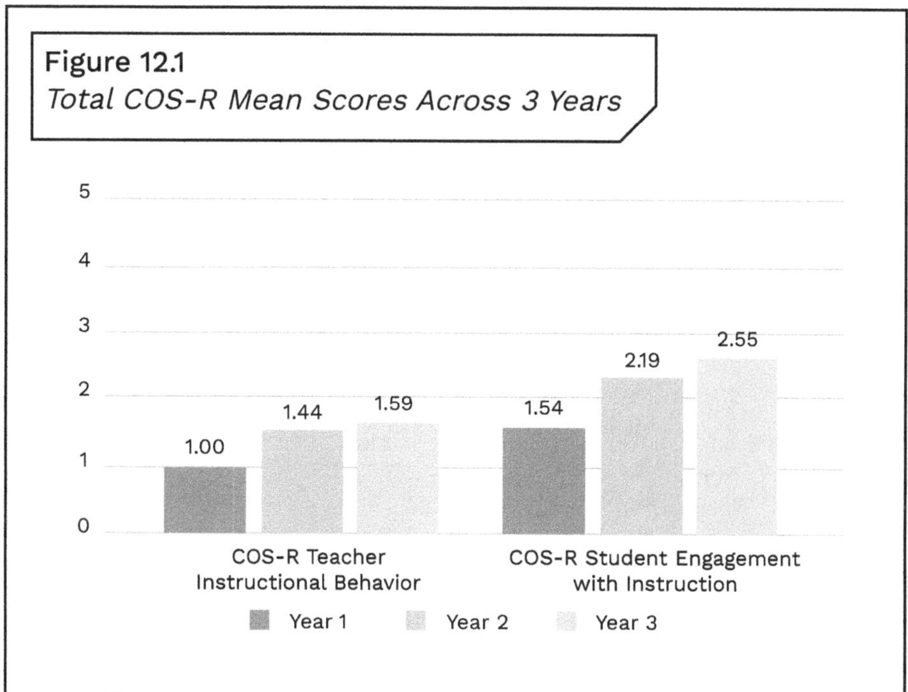

Figure 12.1
Total COS-R Mean Scores Across 3 Years

Note. This figure depicts total average COS-R scores across all 3 years of the study. (Teacher totals by year: Year 1 = 70, Year 2 = 60, Year 3 = 61.) In both categories, scores increased over the 3 years, which indicates that the intervention may have impacted differentiated teaching strategies that teachers used in their classrooms.

Results of COS-R Observations

This section reviews the results of the TDA study (Swanson et al., 2020). Each figure displays the change in COS-R scores over time. Figure 12.1 depicts total average COS-R scores across all 3 years of the study. In both categories, scores increased over the 3 years, which indicates that the intervention may have impacted differentiated teaching strategies that teachers used in their classrooms. The next group of figures, Figures 12.2–12.7, depicts COS-R mean scores broken down by grade level because the intervention may have had differential impacts based on grade level. As you will see, there was a general trend of improvement for each grade level across the 3 years.

Figure 12.2
Kindergarten COS-R Scores Across 3 Years

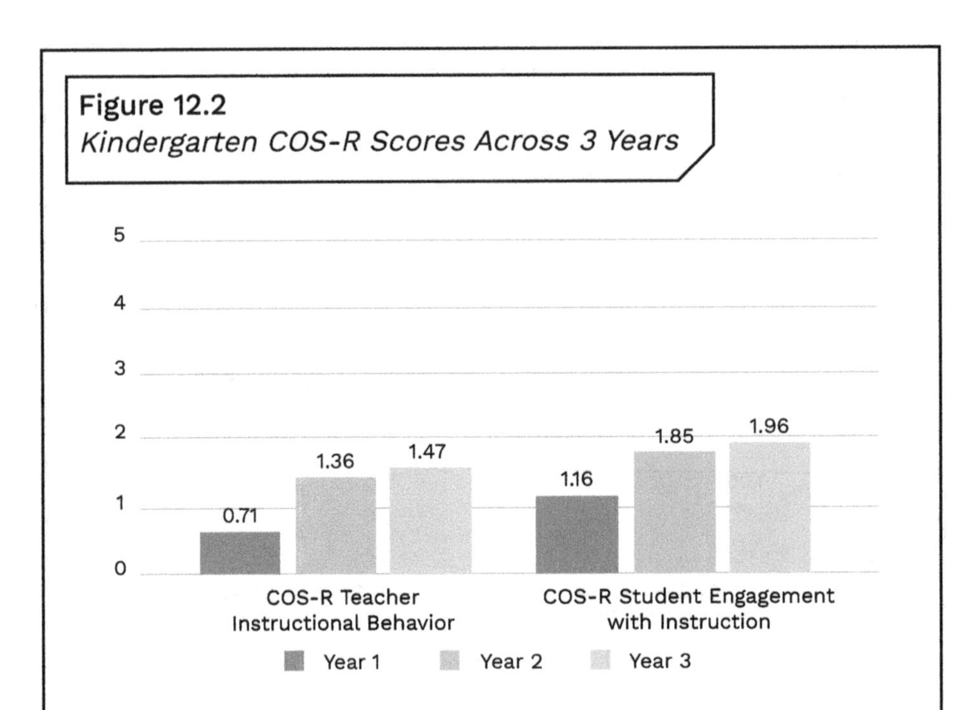

Note. This figure depicts COS-R mean scores for kindergarten. This figure shows a general trend of improvement for kindergarten across the 3 years.

Figure 12.3
First-Grade COS-R Scores Across 3 Years

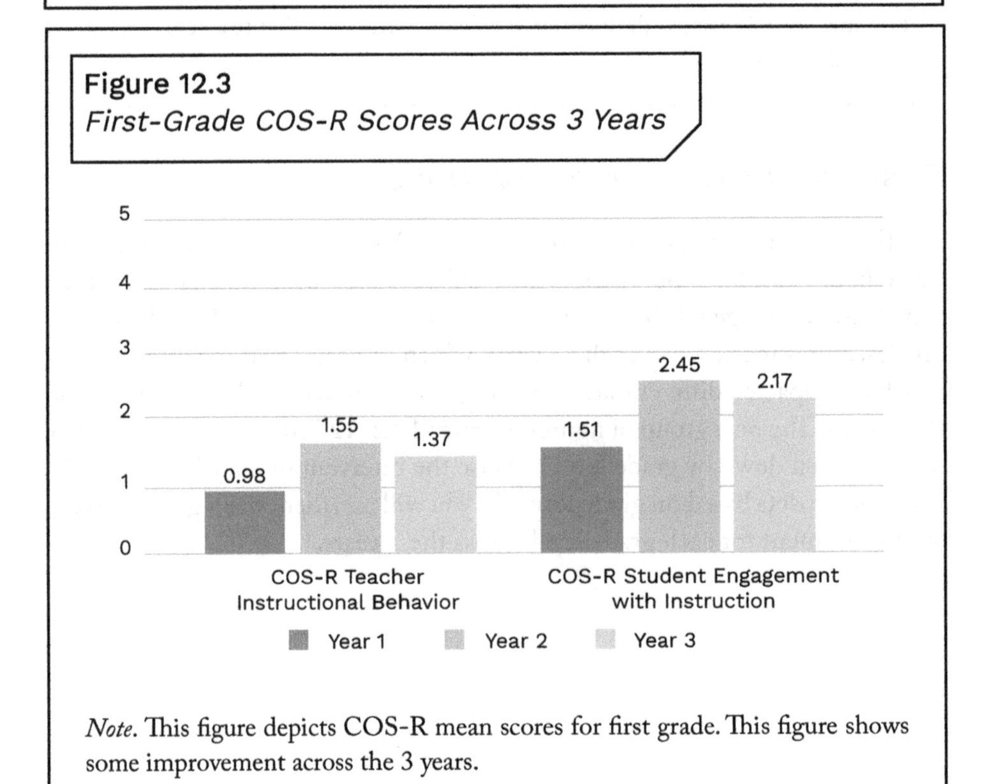

Note. This figure depicts COS-R mean scores for first grade. This figure shows some improvement across the 3 years.

Figure 12.4
Second-Grade COS-R Scores Across 3 Years

5
4
3
2
1
0
1.03
1.35
1.71
1.56
2.12
2.81
COS-R Teacher Instructional Behavior
COS-R Student Engagement with Instruction
Year 1
Year 2
Year 3

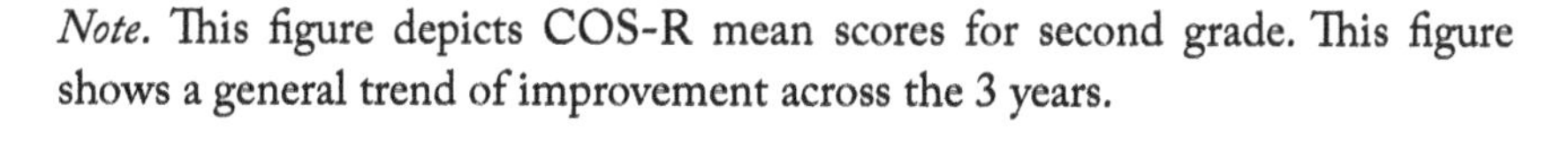

Note. This figure depicts COS-R mean scores for second grade. This figure shows a general trend of improvement across the 3 years.

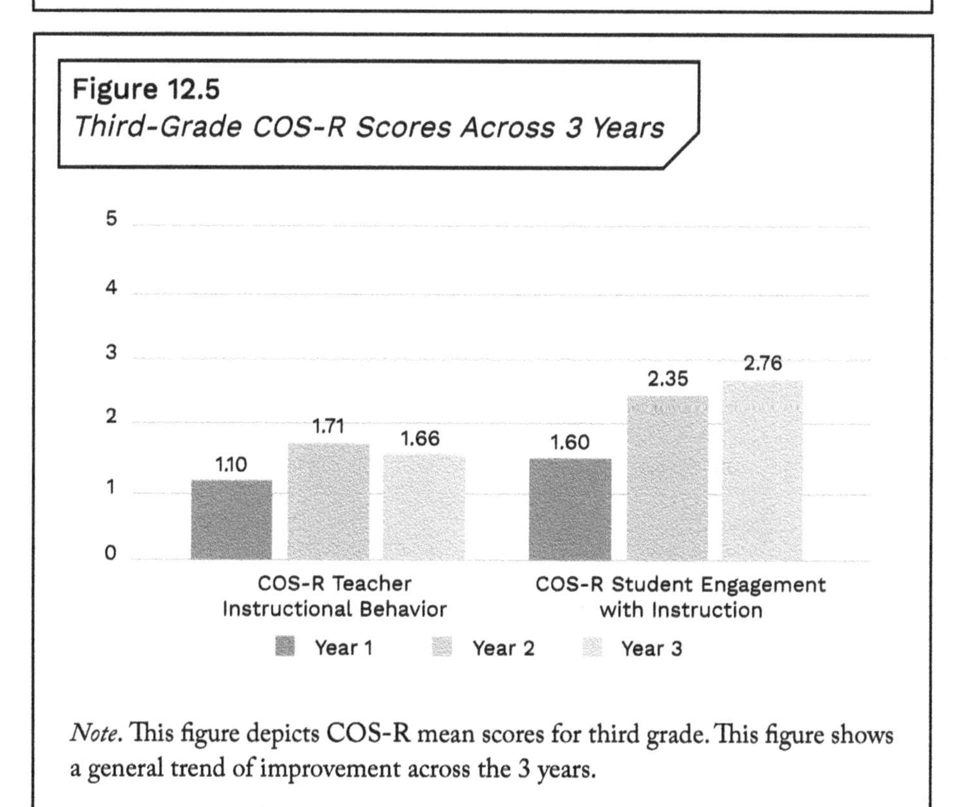

Figure 12.5
Third-Grade COS-R Scores Across 3 Years

Note. This figure depicts COS-R mean scores for third grade. This figure shows a general trend of improvement across the 3 years.

Figure 12.6
Fourth-Grade COS-R Scores Across 3 Years

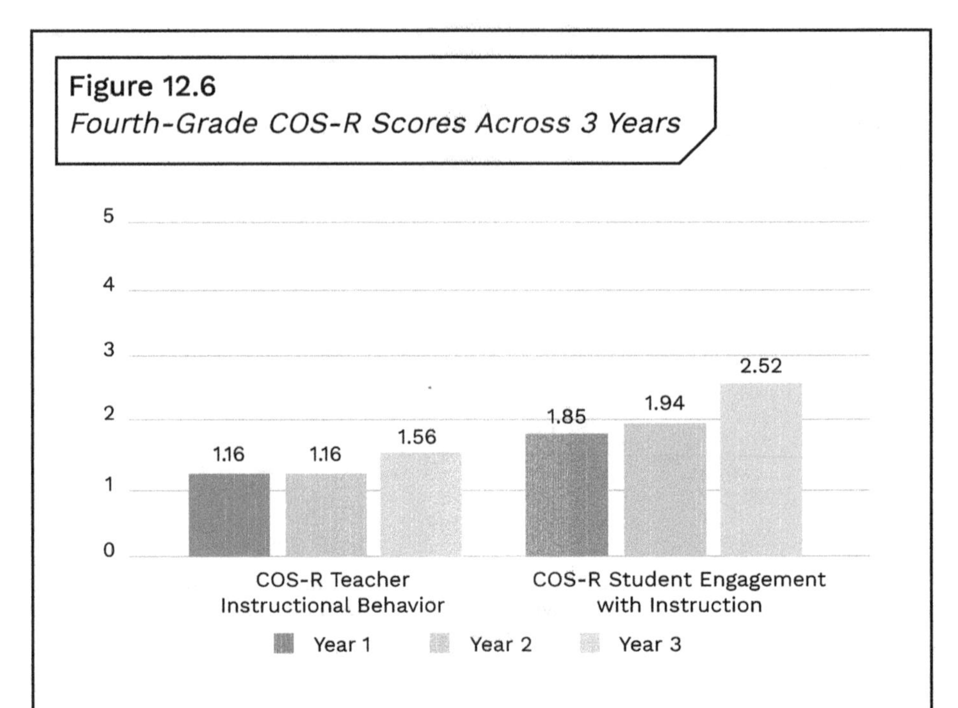

Note. This figure depicts COS-R mean scores for fourth grade. This figure shows a general trend of improvement across the 3 years.

Figure 12.7
Fifth-Grade COS-R Scores Across 3 Years

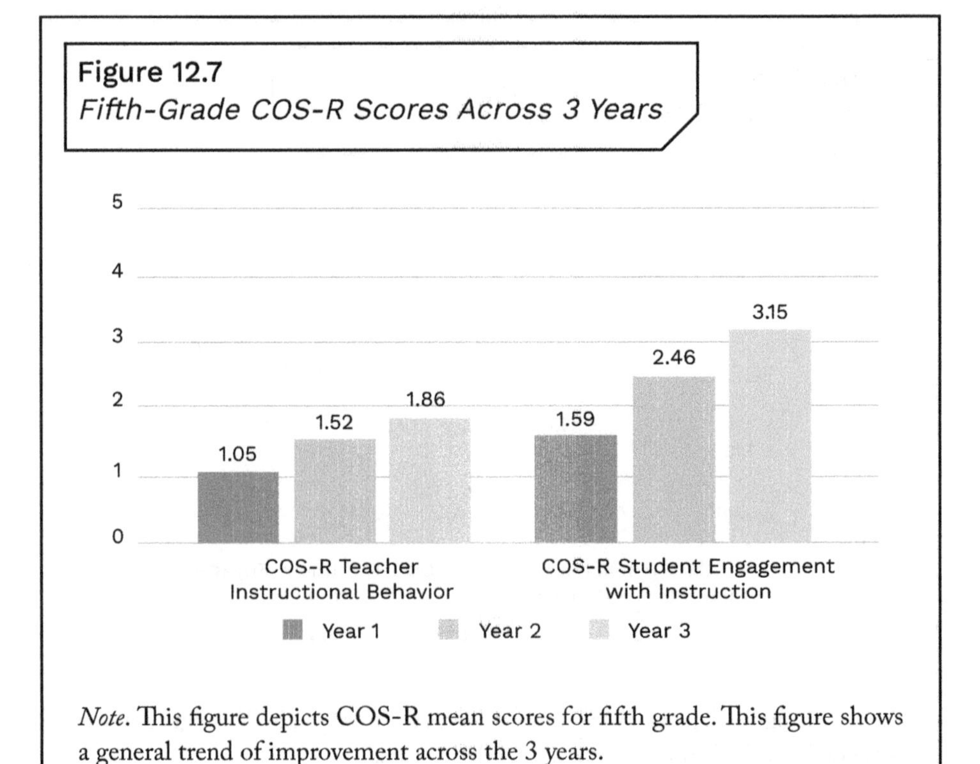

Note. This figure depicts COS-R mean scores for fifth grade. This figure shows a general trend of improvement across the 3 years.

Explanation of COS-R Results

During the intervention, baseline data were collected during the first year. In the second year, the intervention was implemented at each of the schools. The strongest gains would be expected during the second year because the intervention was actively occurring. In this year, the intervention was intensive, with teachers receiving focused, on-site support. During the third year, the coaches were available to assist teachers at their request, but the intervention was less structured. During this year, participation was voluntary. Thus, a dip in scores during the third year is normal due to the nature of competing demands and priorities for teachers.

Administrator and teacher buy-in greatly impacted overall scores. Schools with high administrator and teacher buy-in experienced greater gains on the COS-R during the intervention. Teachers who were excited to implement the curriculum were more likely to be open to changing their daily practice in their classroom. As noted previously, some differences were observed at individual grade levels due to grade-level buy-in, cross-curricular planning, and collaboration. When entire grade levels planned and coordinated lessons together, overall quality was higher during the observation periods. Another important note about these results is the number of teachers included in each graph. The more teachers that were included in each year, the more students would be exposed to enhanced instructional strategies. Therefore, large schools that report gains on the COS-R experienced meaningful change as a result of the intervention.

These results suggest that teacher buy-in and collaboration is highly important when implementing a professional learning intervention. Teachers need to feel supported by their administrators in order for real change in teaching practices to occur. Educators also need to feel as though they have a choice in participating in either an intervention or an observation. Teachers who had a choice about their observation schedule were much more willing to host observers in their classrooms, and the observers were more likely to experience high-quality teaching practices as a result of the teachers' autonomy in scheduling an observation period. Our findings hold implications for administrators as well. Ensuring that teachers feel as if they have a choice and a voice in decisions that affect them will promote change in teachers' instructional practices. The following section describes teacher engagement in professional learning for administrators and coaches to help understand where teacher buy-in is successful and where opportunities for further engagement and buy-in exist.

Guiding Questions for Administrators and Coaches Seeking to Implement a Sustained Professional Learning Model

Following several years of sustained professional developing implementation at TDA schools embracing the Talent Development Instructional Model, we noted patterns of teacher engagement that tended to predict whether or not teachers embraced new pedagogy that translated into more effective classroom instruction (as measured by the COS-R). Eight guiding questions emerged for coaches and administrators to ponder that we think matter for successful implementation. Indeed, research suggests that the extent to which teachers demonstrate professional learning engagement across these eight guiding questions is associated with improvement in COS-R scores one year following professional learning (Swanson et al., 2020). Coaches and administrators may choose to reflect on guiding questions elucidated in the following sections in efforts to increase teacher buy-in and strive for continuous improvement of professional learning delivery. Following each question, we describe three tiers of engagement: Tier 1 predicts minimal teacher engagement, Tier 2 predicts improvement in effective teaching practices, and Tier 3 predicts the greatest improvement in classroom instruction leading to student academic success.

Question 1: How Purposeful Was Teacher Communication With Professional Learning Coaches?

At the first tier of engagement, teacher communication can be described as perfunctory. Teachers may request materials or ask for help with standards alignment, but they shy away from coaching questions related to instructional practice. Teachers in the first tier attend mandatory meetings with limited verbal participation; however, they do not initiate additional contact, nor do they engage in self-reflection. Teachers in the second tier can be described as enabling. Teachers may initiate communication and seek coaching but generally to ask for help without first attempting a lesson or asking the coach to conduct the lesson on their behalf. Teachers in this category are modestly reflective but often report confusion. The third tier of purposeful communication describes teachers who are genuine and vulnerable in their descriptions of successes and failures. Teachers in Tier 3 ask for specific feedback or advice after applying a new skill. They tend to be openly reflective and willing to fail forward in order to meet student needs. Teachers in this category tend to initiate further opportunities for development.

Question 2: How Comfortable Was the Teacher as a Learner?

Teachers in Tier 1 are characterized by a fear of losing control or doing something wrong. They may feel uncomfortable with open-ended questioning and demonstrate a lack of confidence: "I'm not good at this." They may be resistant to alter their current routines and approaches, whereas teachers at the second tier of engagement with learning are willing to try new approaches that feel within their comfort zone. A teacher in Tier 2 takes small steps forward, incorporating chunks of new instructional strategies within an existing framework. They may express some trepidation about the risk of trying new approaches but proceed nonetheless. Teachers in Tier 3 are willing to step outside their comfort zone, take risks, and embrace new approaches. Teachers in the third tier are moderately comfortable with the idea of failing forward and growing skills as a dynamic process.

Question 3: To What Degree Was the Teacher Self-Reliant?

Teachers in Tier 1 can be described as dependent. For example, teachers may ask: "How do I manage this logistically/instructionally?" or "Can you do this for me?" Teachers in Tier 1 may expect instructional coaches to do the work for them. Teachers in the second tier have some barriers to independence. They may understand that the work of learning a new instructional practice lies with them but rely on the coach to scaffold the experience. They may ask coaches to find, prepare, or organize lessons and materials for them, or ask the coach for help with differentiating instruction. Teachers in the third tier of self-reliance autonomously implement lessons and interactions with the coach involve brainstorming, reflecting, and information sharing as equal partners.

Question 4: To What Degree Did the Teacher Demonstrate Flexible Thinking?

Teachers in Tier 1 appear unable to apply new concepts to existing teaching frameworks. They may feel stuck inside current routines and structures and not immediately see a way to change. They may ask "How does this fit with the reading workshop model?" because it has not occurred to them that change is possible. Teachers in Tier 2 can see some opportunities for improvement in their instructional delivery methods, but their insights can be described as thinking inside the box. Tier 2 teachers will more easily see how they can apply new strategies or concepts within a familiar instructional approach or content area. For example, Tier 2 teachers may say: "This model would work well with our current curriculum; when I use Talk Moves, first I ask students what they heard. Then I ask, 'Do you agree or disagree?'" suggesting new strategies can be accommodated within existing frameworks. Teachers at the third tier of flexible thinking can more readily see the big picture. They understand how models and strategies apply across contexts and use models strategically as a means of better understanding and developing student talent. They can engage in a holistic approach to planning and as a consequence reinvent the existing framework.

Question 5: How Did the Teacher View Students as Learners?

Teachers in the first tier see students as doers and focus on discrete skills or factual knowledge. Teachers in Tier 1 are typically deficit-oriented, focusing on students' struggles rather than strengths as learners. They may wonder "What standards should be accomplished? Where are my students the weakest?" to know where to focus their efforts. Teachers in the second tier may see students as individuals on different points along the same path. Although all children receive the same instruction, pacing is individualized. Teachers in Tier 2 may think in terms of grade- or standard-level norms and see challenging students' thinking and learning beyond those boundaries as developmentally inappropriate. Teachers in Tier 3 see students as creators. They focus on understanding, application, synthesis, concept development, and what students can do as opposed to what they cannot. Teachers in the third tier offer opportunities that reflect students' individual talents or gifts in a given area. They wonder "What can students accomplish?" without any boundaries on what students can achieve in mind.

Question 6: To What Degree Did Teachers' Views of Rules, Authority, and Group Membership Affect Their Development?

Teachers in Tier 1 do not like to rock the boat and adopt the team mindset regardless of their individual opinion. These teachers tend to be bound by the norms of the school, grade level, or team; are confined by or dependent upon authority; and have an external locus of control (e.g., professional learning is happening to them and there is nothing they can or should do). Teachers in the first tier may feign responsiveness to appear compliant or shirk stepping up to appear part of the team, whereas teachers in the second tier may be cognizant of and perhaps overwhelmed by competing demands. They can see what is best for students but express trepidation. Teachers in Tier 2 may be willing to challenge existing definitions of appropriate instructional methods and team norms. Teachers in the third tier tend to have an internal locus of control. They are responsive and rely on their own judgment and expertise within parameters. These teachers are unafraid of bending rules when they believe students will benefit.

Question 7: How Did the Teacher View Themselves as a Professional?

Teachers in the first tier are more likely to see teaching as a "job" where work parameters are defined by school hours. Teachers in the second tier are proud to define themselves as a teacher and see the profession as part of their identity. Yet, most learning around the art and science of the teaching profession occurred during teacher preparation, and teachers in Tier 2 are not likely to seek continuous improvement beyond administrative and credentialing mandates. Finally, teachers in the third tier see teaching as a vocation or calling. They view continuous improvement as a personal and professional responsibility. Teachers in the third tier might be described as lifelong learners who are excited to develop and refine their skills.

Question 8: To What Degree Did the Teacher Assume a Leadership Role?

Leadership comes in many forms, from a formal title and responsibility, to informally supporting and answering questions for a junior colleague, to being a model for what's possible in one's own classroom. It is possible to land in any of the three tiers by engaging in observable behaviors that demonstrate either formal or informal leadership. Teachers in the first tier are generally uncomfortable or uninterested in collaborating or sharing with colleagues. Although they are physically present in professional learning workshops, they tend to be hesitant to share their own experiences. Teachers in the second tier agree to participate in demonstrations when asked and are available to share their materials, plans, and experiences with colleagues during scheduled team meetings or professional learning workshops, whereas teachers in the third tier actively seek out opportunities to model and coach. They are seen by colleagues as a valued resource, and they tend to enjoy mentoring junior colleagues or new team members.

Moving to the Next Tier of Engagement

Figure 12.8 is a simple checklist that teachers, coaches, or administrators may use to evaluate the level of engagement with a sustained professional learning model.

Taken together, the eight guiding questions can help educators and administrators identify early on whether professional learning is helping teachers to reach optimal potential. Responses tend to cluster around a specific tier within a given timeframe, but responses can change over the course of professional learning in either direction depending on how approaches to and communication about professional learning evolve. It is rare to achieve the third tier of engagement without some amount of struggle. Teachers and administrators may openly question, challenge, or wonder as they assimilate new concepts. Another simple way to check the level of engagement is to ask oneself or others if the task feels hard. If the consensus is that the task is challenging, then one can rest assured they are doing good work. If it all feels easy and fleeting, then one might be in the first tier of engagement. Alongside awareness comes opportunity to move into the next tier once the obstacle is identified and addressed.

Often, teachers may be struggling to see how they can prioritize new learning in the context of many competing demands. Occasionally, teachers may worry they are not "doing it right" or professional learning is interpreted as a criticism of current practices. These concerns can be effectively addressed through open communication between administrators and educators. Principals can alleviate apprehension and increase buy-in by asking teachers what challenges and obstacles they anticipate and by helping teachers see how professional learning fits in with larger goals shared by all faculty. In turn, administrators

Figure 12.8
Level of Engagement Checklist

Guiding Question	Tier 1	Tier 2	Tier 3
How purposeful is teacher communication with professional learning coaches?			
How comfortable is the teacher as a learner?			
To what degree is the teacher self-reliant?			
To what degree does the teacher demonstrate flexible thinking?			
How does the teacher view students as learners?			
Do rules, authority, and group membership affect professional learning?			
How does the teacher view themselves as a professional?			
To what degree does the teacher assume a leadership role?			

may find ways to foster teacher engagement by creating an environment (e.g., time, space, resources) where teachers are able to collaborate, coplan, coteach, and embrace mistakes as a natural part of the learning process. When teachers are able to be vulnerable and feel supported, professional learning buy-in is greatly enhanced. The role of administrators and coaches is to provide the right level of support.

Conclusion

This chapter provides a framework for understanding how professional learning can improve classroom practices, how to measure changes in teacher practice, and how to promote teacher engagement to improve classroom practices. Sustained, effective professional learning can increase effective instructional practices within the classroom setting; however, many skills and resources are necessary for implementing and sustaining long-term solutions. The skills that teachers gain during professional learning affect the manner in which they interact with their students. Sustained professional learning in talent development models can promote higher order thinking skills with students and encourage teachers to rely less on rote instruction. Measuring changes in teacher practice is imperative to understanding how teacher instructional strategies change as a result of professional learning. By measuring and self-reflecting on engagement with professional learning, administrators can better understand how to support teachers to reach their optimal potential.

End-of-Chapter Discussion/ Reflection Questions

1. Teacher learning is a key to talent development. What are the three most significant ideas about professional learning you gleaned from this chapter? Why are they most significant?
2. Why is assessment important in understanding the impact of teacher learning?
3. How might you use the Classroom Observation Scale-Revised (COS-R) in your efforts to move toward a talent-focused classroom or school?
4. Review the guiding questions regarding sustained professional learning. In what ways might these questions guide your professional learning plans?

References

Brighton, C. M. (2003). The effects of middle school teachers' beliefs on classroom practices. *Journal for the Education of the Gifted, 27*(2–3), 177–206. https://doi.org/10.1177/016235320302700205

Corcoran, T. B. (1995). *Helping teachers teach well: Transforming professional development*. CPRE Policy Briefs.

Darling-Hammond, L., Hyler, M. E., & Gardner, M. (2017). *Effective teacher professional development*. Learning Policy Institute.

Day, C. (1999). *Developing teachers: The challenges of lifelong learning*. Falmer Press.

Garet, M. S., Porter, A. C., Desimone, L., Birman, B. F., & Yoon, K. S. (2001). What makes professional development effective? Results from a national sample of teachers. *American Educational Research Journal, 38*(4), 915–945. https://doi.org/10.3102/00028312038004915

Guskey, T. R. (2002). Professional development and teacher change. *Teachers and Teaching: Theory and Practice, 8*(3/4), 381–391. https://doi.org/10.1080/135406002100000512

LoCasale-Crouch, J., DeCoster, J., Cabell, S. Q., Pianta, R. C., Hamre, B. K., Downer, J. T., Hatfield, B. E., Larsen, R., Burchinal, M., Howes, C., LaParo, K., Scott-Little, C., & Roberts, A. (2015). Unpacking intervention effects: Teacher responsiveness as a mediator of perceived intervention quality and change in teaching practice. *Early Childhood Research Quarterly, 36*(3), 201–209. https://doi.org/10.1016/j.ecresq.2015.12.022

Neuman, S. B., & Cunningham, L. (2009). The impact of professional development and coaching on early language and literacy instructional practices. *American Educational Research Journal, 46*(2), 532–566. https://doi.org/10.3102/0002831208328088

Reinke, W. M., Stormont, M., Webster-Stratton, C., Newcomer, L. L., & Herman, K. C. (2012). The incredible years teacher classroom management program: Using coaching to support generalization to real-world classroom settings. *Psychology in the Schools, 49*(5), 416–428. https://doi.org/10.1002/pits.21608

Riggs, L. (2013). *Why do teachers quit? And why do they stay?* The Atlantic. https://www.theatlantic.com/education/archive/2013/10/why-do-teachers-quit/280699

Robinson, A., Shore, B. M., & Enerson, D. L. (2007). *Best practices in gifted education: An evidence-based guide.* Prufrock Press.

Swanson, J. D., Brock, L., Van Sickle, M., Gutshall, C. A., Russell, L., & Anderson, L. (2020). A basis for talent development: The integrated curriculum model and evidence-based strategies. *Roeper Review, 42*(3), 165–178. https://doi.org/10.1080/02783193.2020.1765920

VanTassel-Baska, J., Quek, C., & Feng, A. X. (2007). The development and use of a structured teacher observation scale to assess differentiated best practice. *Roeper Review, 29*(2), 84–92. https://doi.org/10.1080/02783190709554391

13

Adding Talent Development to School and District Services

Julie Dingle Swanson

Are you and your school ready for the challenge of shifting to a talent-focused philosophy? The purpose of this book is to provide educators in the field the foundational knowledge that both persuades and enables you to incorporate talent development as an essential philosophy in your school or your district. The knowledge that we, the authors and editors, share was drawn from experiences with talent development, specifically work in the Talent Development Academies (TDA) project (Swanson et al., 2019, 2020), as well as from some of the best thinkers in the field on talent development (e.g., Coleman et al., 2010; Horn, 2015; Little et al., 2018; Robinson et al., 2018; Stambaugh, 2018; Subotnik et al., 2018). We advocate for equitable opportunities for all students, an openness in teachers to see and build upon student strengths, and educators' engagement with learning to grow talent-focused teaching.

Much of what we have learned from the TDA project is reported in this book. This chapter revisits themes from previous chapters and the "why" behind talent development, and reiterates big ideas and guiding propositions for consideration. The chapter concludes with discussion of lessons learned from our own research and that of others, and offers recommendations for schools and districts interested in adding talent development to their continuum of services.

Recurring Themes

Several themes resonate throughout the book, including the importance of a guiding framework, powerful curriculum, and teachers.

A Guiding Framework

A major recurring notion is the importance of a guiding framework and an instructional model that allows implementation. The Talent Development Megamodel (Subotnik et al., 2011, 2018) is a foundation to guide understanding of talent development across the life span. Familiarize yourself with the megamodel, and use it to develop the rationale for a talent-focused philosophy in your school or district. As a guiding framework, the megamodel is easily understood—it is both straightforward and comprehensive at the same time. What are connections of the Talent Development Megamodel (Subotnik et al., 2011) to the Talent Development Instructional Model (TDIM), a model of practice? One connection is the importance of enrichment early for all students in order to grow emergent talent. Opportunities for talent must be made available to all. The megamodel ensures we understand that student abilities are domain-specific and malleable, that mental and social skills are important in talent development. The TDIM offers educators a framework to plan for and put the megamodel's principles into practice. By attending to the megamodel's features, schools and districts can implement the TDIM, a powerful instructional model for practice built from the megamodel. In this book, we describe the TDIM and explicate three pillars for teacher-focused learning (i.e., advanced curriculum, culturally responsive practices, and neuroscience and psychology of learning) for talent development at the early childhood and elementary levels. The megamodel as a guiding conceptual framework translates into classroom practices across the TDIM's instructional pillars.

Powerful Curriculum

Over and over in this book, we include descriptions of powerful and interesting curriculum and ways in which students respond when challenged. Integrated and advanced curriculum is so much stronger and more engaging for students than cookie-cutter curriculum that is often used. Teachers in TDA incorporated rigor and challenge in student learning, as they knew the importance of those elements in talent development. The examples of evidence-based powerful curriculum and instructional strategies that promoted advanced thinking and inquiry drew upon work done by scholars at the Center for Gifted Education at William & Mary, the University of Connecticut, and the Frank Porter Graham Early Childhood Center. All curricula reported in this book have a strong evidence base supporting student learning, which illustrated that rich and interesting learning fueled passions and underlined curricula's significance in talent development. Teachers in TDA shared the impact of student learning that was relevant, authentic, and promoted real-world applications. Clearly, a well-designed and rigorous curriculum is a foundation upon which to cultivate talents and leads students to discover their passions and interests, and ultimately, develop expertise.

Teachers, Teachers, Teachers

Teachers are the keystone of influence. Throughout this book and throughout what we learned in the TDA project, it is clear that teachers matter the most when it comes to talent development—what they know, how they view the world, their understanding of self, and their knowledge of students. Culturally responsive educators who work to know themselves and understand their biases, slow down their thinking and assumptions, and take time to see and know students are essential. Use of Teacher's Observation of Potential in Students (TOPS; Coleman et al., 2010) is described by several authors as a tool employing an assets-based lens in student talent spotting. Do not underestimate the importance of teacher buy-in and teacher willingness to learn, and be vulnerable as you transition to a talent development approach to learning.

Supporting teachers in their learning is essential. Whether that involves helping teachers learn how to purposefully weave in neuroscience and noncognitive influences (Gutshall, 2020) or how to use engaged dialogue in mathematical reasoning (Chapin et al., 2009), or how to teach conceptually using Taba's (1962) model, teachers need the time, space, and support to grow their talent and practices. In TDA, teachers learned by doing, by taking a leap of faith, as many of them believed that the work was too hard for their students. Talent development instructional coaches showed teachers "how to" in their classrooms with their students. Coaches scaffolded learning for teachers, breaking complex and layered instruction into smaller parts that were more easily digested. Coaches responded to where teachers were and provided constructive feedback as teachers tested out talent development strategies. Effective supports positively influenced teacher learning and growth.

One teacher in the TDA project described her lack of confidence in her ability to use Taba's (1962) model with her students. She was not only uncertain that she would be able to teach the model, but also uncertain that her students would be able to think conceptually, make generalizations about the big idea, and extend their understanding of the generalizations out to other content areas. She took a risk and made herself vulnerable when she applied Taba's model with her students in their study of *Autobiographies and Memoirs* (Center for Gifted Education, 2011). During the unit study, the teacher had students develop generalizations about autobiographies. Students were successful in the work, and their teacher built on that success and continued to adapt and use Taba's (1962) model.

A cross-cutting theme that runs deep in three pillars of the TDIM (i.e., advanced curriculum, culturally responsive practices, and neuroscience and the psychology of learning) is an ethic of care. In an ethic of care, one can care for self, other humans, other living things, nonliving things, and ideas (Noddings, 2005). First, teachers in TDA needed to learn to care for themselves and then their students as they learned to care about ideas. When teachers developed or used an ethic of care, they understood the need for and desired to enhance the educational opportunities for their students. To do so, they also needed to care for the concepts the students deserved to learn across the content areas. Once this level of care developed, the teachers were able to address student needs more thoroughly and through examples the students understood and wanted to study. This is the point at which the classroom became an opportunity for joy and passion.

A Rationale for Talent Development

When considering the arts or sports, one can see a very different approach to growing abilities. In both the arts and sports, individuals seeking to excel participate in regular practice and rely on teachers and coaches for skill development, feedback, and guidance. Artists and athletes know that to get better, to stand out, and to be competitive, time and effort must be invested. Accomplished artists and athletes see their work as developmental and focus on growing their skills and knowledge to move closer to expertise. Exposure to mentors and experts is a part of how artists and athletes challenge themselves to improve. These approaches seen in the arts and in sports (e.g., skills development, practice and effort, and coaching that provides specific, feedback focused on growth) are systematic and develop over time. In many successful and highly accomplished artists and sports figures, it is evident that persistence, grit, and a growth orientation are part of their process. These approaches grow abilities and must be included as tools to grow academic talent. Consider how to harness them in academic talent development.

Strengths, Passions, Interests

We suggest that schooling, too, can be talent focused, more like what is seen in the arts and sports. Educators can build on strengths and grow academic aptitudes through successively developmental work. Students can learn to persist, to put in effort and time to improve, and to persist despite obstacles. What are strengths, weaknesses, opportunities, and threats in becoming a talent-focused school or district? Strengths of the approach were evident in student learning impacts seen in other programs, such as Young Scholars (Horn, 2015), STEM Starters + (Robinson et al., 2018), and Project SPARK (Little et al., 2018). Teacher-focused learning that responds to where teachers are and grows teacher talent was a strength.

In TDA, using teacher talents in their chosen academic areas of interest was a doorway into gaining teacher engagement and buy-in. Choice was empowering. Teachers being able to choose academic domains as the starting point for their students' talent development resulted in teachers gaining expertise in their strength area, then moving on to a new academic area. For example, one teacher waited until the third TDA professional learning course to "do math" because she "did not like math" and was not "good at math." In the math teacher development session, she became so inspired and interested in the conceptual, inquiry-driven math that, after the session ended and she went home, she worked for hours on a problem until she figured it out. She communicated later with the session leader, excited to share the answer she finally reached. This story of a teacher who was "not good" at math engaging with passion and interest in math learning exemplifies what is possible with students when using talent-focused learning.

Seeing Students, Opening Opportunities

The talent development focus on strengths, passions, and interests of learners means that as learner potential grows, students become accomplished and expert as they grow into adults. Throughout this book, strengths are evident in the verbs used to describe talent development: build, grow, nurture. Educators underestimate what children and youth are capable of—talent development presents an opportunity for opening and broadening learning. Biases and stereotypical thinking complicate which students get the rich and interesting opportunities. Accessibility of advanced, rich, challenging, and interesting curriculum for all students can create opportunities for more just and equitable schooling. Really seeing students—who they are and what they bring—and deeply knowing students can be the impetus for teachers to design learning opportunities that are strength-based. Opportunities for teachers and students to engage in rich learning that broadens horizons are strengths of a talent-focused school.

Weaknesses and possible pitfalls in regard to talent development are that there are no recipes to follow, no one way to do "it," and no step-by-step instructions to get you there. Commitment, careful attention, and a learning attitude are necessary. There is no "magic bullet" or singular program that answers the question: "How do we maximally develop talent in each student who sits in our presence?" There is an art and a science to teaching for talent development. The science is in the study of the curricula chosen—the art is in each teacher making it their own for the students for which it is intended. Schools undertaking this philosophical shift must be prepared to show constant attention to and continuous monitoring of results. Schools must be ready to examine compatibility of the endless parade of trends and new approaches that come down the pike. Before jumping on the bandwagon, educators should ask, "What is the value added of this innovation? Is it worth the effort and time?"

Value Added

What is the value added in a talent development philosophy? What is known about talent development and why it is important at this particular time in schooling is related to access, opportunity, and social justice. As a strength-based approach, talent development requires shedding dated practices of grouping, labeling, and observing students. Educators recognizing and dismantling their own hidden biases and the structural obstacles to equity (O'Connell-Ross, 1993) is a part of the shift necessary in implementing a talent development philosophy in your school. So much lost potential—students not growing into the accomplished individuals of society—is a strong reason for talent development.

Further, talent development gives educators a more understandable direction of how to support and nurture students with academic talent. Schools employing a talent development lens utilize all students' strengths as the starting point for learning. As stated earlier in the book, talent development can serve as an umbrella over gifted programs and support a philosophical orientation that encourages the search for strengths, abilities, and potential in all students.

Challenges to Expect

Challenges and obstacles of a talent development focused school or district are often found in faltering leadership. Changes in leadership are a constant in schools and districts, and new leaders bring their own vision of what needs to be done. They often have specific ideas of how they want to make changes. In schools where talent development has not yet taken root and become foundational to the work of the faculty, a new leader who lacks understanding may stall or circumvent progress in talent development schools gaining learning outcomes. Developing a multiyear plan that builds in how to navigate the pitfalls, such as a leadership change, will help.

Thus, building structures for sustained development over time is essential to a successful talent development plan. In the TDA project, we found that building understanding was best accomplished over multiple years, with a minimum of 2 years to fully implement. Teacher learning started with the whole group during a summer conference, followed by small-group learning and then individualized learning.

Teacher content knowledge is important in schools using a talent development lens. In the TDA project, the lack of deep content knowledge was an issue in some schools with some teachers. A way we combatted the issue was to have teachers become the students and experience the lessons as students would. In these learning sessions, teachers had to struggle, grapple, and experience the struggle. This strategy was employed not only to strengthen teacher content knowledge, but also to develop a growth mindset orientation (Dweck, 2006/2016) to learning so that teachers could model for students the grit (Duckworth, 2016) and persistence key to growing talent. In addition, teacher learning sessions on planning, analyzing, studying, and thinking through what comes before, after, and during lessons were held specifically for teachers with weak content knowledge. In those sessions, teachers learned how to make implicit lesson objectives explicit by exploration of questions to consider during the lesson analysis. This structured learning helped to reveal and address teacher misconceptions and gaps in content knowledge.

Overstressing fidelity of specific curricula (e.g., William & Mary units, Project Clarion units, etc.) endangers teacher buy-in. We suggest, based on our experiences, that teachers need a degree of freedom to adapt and make curricula and instructional strategies their own. Otherwise, teachers will not innovate. In schools adopting a talent development focus, you may lose teacher support if you do not allow them flexibility to modify and adapt. Similarly, allowing for and supporting leeway to for teachers to blend talent development with other initiatives, such as arts-infused learning or personalized learning, strengthens the results with students. Meeting teachers where they are—and differentiating learning opportunities to match where teachers are—means that a responsive and supportive approach drives professional learning. Teacher readiness level, teacher interest, and teacher learning modality are vehicles for teacher development. Responsiveness, not a recipe, is the driving principle of teacher learning.

Conclusion

Creating a school based on a talent development philosophy or shifting your school's current philosophy to one using a talent development lens requires clear, purposeful decision making, effort, and planning. To conclude, I suggest a metaphor to revisit the TDIM—building a structure. Lasting structures need a strong foundation. Consider the guiding principles of TDIM as the bricks in the foundation. The first brick is schoolwide buy-in to using a talent development approach with all students. The commitment to looking for and building upon all students' assets is basic. The second brick in the talent development school's foundation is that necessary human and material resources must be available, as the shift to talent-focused learning takes time, effort, and growth. The third brick is leadership that shares and shepherds the vision of a talent-focused school. The final brick in the metaphorical foundation is compatible innovations that will enhance and support talent development. Schools need to stick to innovations that blend together, not splinter, effort and resources.

Rising up from the brick foundation are pillars to support the roof. The first pillar is powerful curriculum as instructional practice with all learners. Students grow passions when engaged in interesting, authentic, relevant curriculum that challenges them to think, do, and grow. Malleability of the brain means that challenge and rigor promote growth. Careful attention to what and how students learn is one of the key pillars in talent development.

The second pillar of a talent development school is where teachers tap into and think about their own backgrounds, the set of biases and assumptions they each bring to the classroom through who they are. This pillar of talent development pushes teachers to think about their own stories—as well as the stories of their colleagues, their students, and students' parents—to become more responsive to students. Instead of being known as the gatekeeper who lets some students in and keeps some students out, these culturally responsive teachers open up access and opportunities for their students because they see students' potential and assets.

The final support, the third pillar is neuroscience and the psychology of learning, including noncognitive influences on learning. Understanding the brain, how it works, and how it affects student learning, engagement, and motivation is essential to talent development. Application of what is known about the brain to teaching and learning in the classroom strengthens teaching and learning. This pillar of becoming talent development focused is teachers understanding and using strategies that are brain-based and grounded in the psychology of learning.

The roof over the metaphorical talent development academy is teacher learning. Providing an ongoing, sustained, responsive environment for professional learning develops teacher talents. As stated many times, teachers are key to the success of talent development. They create the learning environment, provide the psychosocial learning students need, and guide students on their pathway to accomplishment.

End-of-Chapter Discussion/ Reflection Questions

1. Assess your readiness to implement the Talent Development Instructional Model (TDIM) in your classroom, school, or district using SWOT: strengths that will support the efforts, weaknesses that might undermine the work, opportunities that make the time right, and threats to success.
2. Three themes across the book are described in this chapter: the importance of a guiding framework, powerful curriculum, and teachers. Rank these themes in order of importance in your school or district, and explain the ranking. How do the themes inform educators moving toward talent development?
3. Develop your own persuasive rationale for talent development in your school or district. What is it? How will you accomplish your goals? Why does talent development matter?

References

Center for Gifted Education. (2011). *Autobiographies and memoirs* (2nd ed.). Kendall Hunt.

Chapin, S. H., O'Connor, C., & Anderson, N. C. (2009). *Classroom discussions: Using math talk to help students learn, grades 1–6* (2nd ed.). Math Solutions.

Coleman, M. R., Shah-Coltrane, S., & Harrison, A. (2010). *U-STARS~PLUS: Teacher's observation of potential in students (TOPS): Individual student observation form*. Council for Exceptional Children.

Duckworth, A. (2016). *Grit: The power and passion of perseverance*. Scribner.

Dweck, C. S. (2016). *Mindset: The new psychology of success*. Ballantine Books. (Original work published 2006)

Gutshall, C. A. (2020). When teachers become students: Impacts of neuroscience learning on elementary teachers' mindset beliefs, approach to learning, teaching efficacy, and grit. *European Journal of Psychology and Educational Research, 3*(1), 39-48. https://doi.org/10.12973/ejper.3.1.39

Horn, C. V. (2015). Young Scholars: A talent development model for finding and nurturing potential in underserved populations. *Gifted Child Today, 38*(1), 19–31. https://doi.org/10.1177/1076217514556532

Little, C. A., Adelson, J. L., Kearney, K. L., Cash, K., & O'Brien, R. L. (2018). Early opportunities to strengthen academic readiness: Effects of summer learning on mathematics achievement. *Gifted Child Quarterly, 62*(1), 83–95. https://doi.org/10.1177/0016986217738052

Noddings, N. (2005). *The challenge to care in schools: an alternative approach to education* (2nd ed.). Teachers College Press.

O'Connell-Ross, P. (1993). *National excellence: A case for developing America's talent*. Office of Educational Research and Improvement.

Robinson, A., Adelson, J. L., Kidd, K. A., & Cunningham, C. M. (2018). A talent for tinkering: Developing talents in children from low-income households through engineering curriculum. *Gifted Child Quarterly, 62*(1), 130–144. https://doi.org/10.1177/0016986217738049

Stambaugh, T. (2018). Curriculum and instruction within a talent development framework. In P. Olszewski-Kubilius, R. F. Subotnik, & F. C. Worrell (Eds.), *Talent development as a framework for gifted education: Implications for best practices and applications in schools* (pp. 95–128). Prufrock Press.

Subotnik, R. F., Olszewski-Kubilius, P., & Worrell, F. C. (2011). Rethinking giftedness and gifted education: A proposed direction forward based on psychological science. *Psychological Science in the Public Interest, 12*(1), 3–54. https://doi.org/10.1177/1529100611418056

Subotnik, R. F., Olszewski-Kubilius, P., & Worrell, F. C. (2018). The talent development framework: Overview of components and implications for policy and practice. In P. Olszewski-Kubilius, R. F. Subotnik, & F. C. Worrell (Eds.), *Talent development as a framework for gifted education: Implications for best practices and applications in schools* (pp. 7–24). Prufrock Press.

Swanson, J. D., Brock, L., Van Sickle, M., Gutshall, C. A., Russell, L., & Anderson, L. (2020). A basis for talent development: The integrated curriculum model and evidence-based strategies. *Roeper Review, 42*(3), 165–178. https://doi.org/10.1080/02783193.2020.1765920

Swanson, J. D., Russell, L. W., & Anderson, L. (2019). A model for growing teacher talent scouts: Decreasing underrepresentation of gifted students. In S. R. Smith (Ed.), *Handbook of giftedness and talent development in the Asia-Pacific* (pp. 1–20). Springer. https://doi.org/10.1007/978-981-13-3021-6_55-1

Taba, H. (1962). *Curriculum development: Theory and practice.* Harcourt, Brace & World.

About the Editors

Julie Dingle Swanson, Ed.D., has taught in and coordinated K–12 gifted education programs and directed federal projects for underrepresented gifted students. She is a professor emerita at the College of Charleston, directed the College's Gifted and Talented Education Certificate Program, and taught graduate courses in gifted education. Julie has published articles, chapters, and books on culturally diverse gifted learners, talent development, teacher development, and policy. She is recipient of the Richard W. Riley Award for service to gifted children of South Carolina. Swanson serves on the Center for Gifted Education Advisory Board and as well on the SC Consortium for Gifted Education Board of Directors as a past president.

Meta Van Sickle, Ph.D., is a professor at the College of Charleston. Meta graduated from the University of South Florida with a Ph.D. in 1992. She has several research interests, most prominently studying the ethics of care in science education and science for all, including the linguistically diverse. Most recently, she coedited *Identifying, Describing, and Developing Teachers Who Are Gifted and Talented.*

About the Authors

Samantha E. Blake is an instructional coach and former elementary educator with 15 years of experience in grades 3–5 across two states, North and South Carolina. She began her career as a North Carolina Teaching Fellow at East Carolina University, where she earned a bachelor's degree in elementary education and a master's degree in instructional technology. Samantha is also National Board Certified in the area of literacy and was awarded Teacher of the Year honors by Sadie Saulter Elementary in North Carolina and E. B. Ellington Elementary in South Carolina. She continues to share her expertise with colleagues through curriculum writing for her school district and frequent conference presentations across the district, state, and region.

Laura L. Brock has had the great opportunity to teach at a juvenile detention center, a residential facility, and a struggling public high school. She became fascinated by her encounters with untapped potential. She earned her Ph.D. in applied developmental psychology from the University of Virginia as an Institute of Educational Sciences Research Fellow. As a professor at the College of Charleston, Laura spent several years conducting research on ways in which social environments can promote executive function, theory of mind, and socioemotional skills for children living in underresourced communities. More recently, she has turned her efforts toward exploring the intersections among neuroscience, problem-based learning, and systems thinking.

Sarah DeLisle Fecht, Ed.D., is the director of programs and operations at Vanderbilt Programs for Talented Youth (PTY). Sarah has presented at national and state conferences and served as an adjunct professor for Vanderbilt's Peabody College of Education. Prior to joining PTY in 2012, Sarah taught elementary school students. She holds an undergraduate degree in education from Vanderbilt University, with a double major in early childhood education and child studies. Her master's degree is in learning and instruction from Vanderbilt, and she holds a doctorate in learning organizations and strategic change from Lipscomb University. Sarah enjoys working with educators to support gifted students.

C. Anne Gutshall is an associate professor and department chair of the Teacher Education Department, School of Education, Health, and Human Performance at the College of Charleston in Charleston, SC. Prior to joining the College, Anne was a school psychologist for 13 years. In addition to leading faculty in the Teacher Education Department, she also teaches educational psychology courses to future and current teachers. Anne enjoys supporting students to grow and develop into successful and compassionate classroom educators by bringing her real-life experiences and research interests to the college classroom. Her research focuses on teaching educators, parents, and students basic educational neuroscience concepts to improve teacher efficacy and student motivation by understanding how the brain learns. In addition to her work with Talent Development Academies, she also works with teachers, administrators, parents, and students via a project entitled BrainBuilders in a variety of schools across South Carolina.

Cara L. Kelly is a doctoral student at the University of Delaware in the Human Development and Family Sciences Department. She attended the College of Charleston for both her undergraduate and graduate degrees. She has her Bachelor of Science in Psychology, and she received her Master of Education in Teaching, Learning, and Advocacy. Cara's research interests focus on quality in early childhood education and the nonacademic skills necessary for a successful transition to kindergarten.

Margaret M. Lee, Ed.D., is an assistant professor of education and Director of Gifted Education at Converse College in Spartanburg, SC. Before joining Converse, Dr. Lee taught gifted students in public schools for 18 years. In addition to serving as gifted program director and teaching graduate courses in gifted education, she is the director of the Athena Summer Academy for gifted students. Dr. Lee currently serves as a mentor and district coordinator for Citizen Scholars, a mentoring and scholarship program that seeks to guide and support high-potential students from lower income backgrounds on their academic journey beginning in their fifth-grade year through their college graduation.

Melanie J. Lichtenstein, Ph.D., is the Talent Development Specialist for Albemarle County Public School, VA. Her areas of research are culturally responsive teaching practices, educational advocacy, college bridge programs, systems and policy change for equity and access, asset-based thinking, middle grades curriculum, and talent development practices. She has presented nationally and regionally on culturally responsive teaching, underrepresentation, and curriculum design for culturally responsive teaching in gifted education. She serves on the Virginia Advisory Committee for the Education of the Gifted. She was a teacher of the gifted in South Carolina prior to getting her Ph.D. in Educational Planning, Policy, and Leadership with an emphasis in Gifted Education Administration from William & Mary.

Jessica Ross is a licensed early childhood teacher currently living in Charleston, DV. Jessica received her Bachelor of Science in Public Relations from West Virginia University in 2012 and her Master's in Early Childhood Education from The Graduate School at the College of Charleston in 2015. She is currently in her sixth year of teaching and teaches Advanced Studies Kindergarten at E. B. Ellington Elementary in Ravenel, SC. Jessica was named the Charleston County Early Childhood Rookie Teacher of the Year in 2016 and the E. B. Ellington Teacher of the Year in 2018.

Tamra Stambaugh, Ph.D., is an associate research professor in special education and executive director of Programs for Talented Youth at Vanderbilt University. Her research interests focus on students living in rural settings, students of poverty, and curriculum and instructional interventions that promote gifted student learning and talent development. She is a frequent keynote speaker at national and international conferences and the coauthor/editor of several books, curriculum units, and book chapters. She is the recipient of several curriculum and coedited book awards, the National Association for Gifted Children's Early Leader Award, distinguished Peabody faculty recognition for service to field, and the Margaret the Lady Thatcher Award from the William & Mary School of Education.

Emma Tartt, a native of Charleston, SC, received her Bachelor of Science in Elementary Education from South Carolina State University, a Master's in Education Administration from The Citadel Military College, and her Ed.S. from The Citadel Military College. She has worked for Charleston County School District for 25 years as an instructional reading teacher, instructional developmental teacher, and reading coach. Emma is currently a fifth-grade teacher, the Project Lead the Way Lead Teacher, STEM enrichment teacher, and the grade-level chairperson at Springfield Elementary School.

Denise E. Zacherl, retired, began teaching in 1988. She served as a gifted and talented coordinator for 10 years and was honored for her service as National Association for Gifted Children Coordinator of the Year. Denise has a deep passion for working to address the students most neglected for opportunities of realizing gifted potential, particularly gifted in schools of poverty. She worked with teachers, administrators, and coaches in improving their instructional competency. She has authored two Center for Gifted Education English language arts units for primary grades. She was instrumental in involving schools in the primary and elementary gifted mathematics field-testing and implementation through Project M^2: Mentoring Young Mathematicians (grades K–2) and Project M^3: Mentoring Mathematical Minds (grades 3–5).